Green Economics in Iı

Photo: Amandeep Gill and Kanupriya Bhagat at the Oxford Union

Edited by Professor, Dr Natalie West Kharkongor (India), Associate Professor, Dr Indira Dutta (India), Kanupriya Bhagat (India), Odeta Grabauskaitė (Lithuania) & Miriam Kennet (UK)

The Green Economics Institute (GEI)

Green Economics in India © September 2014 Published by The Green Economics Institute
Registered Office: 6 Strachey Close, Tidmarsh, Reading RG8 8EP greeneconomicsinstitute@yahoo.com

Edited by Professor, Dr Natalie West Kharkongor (India), Associate Professor, Dr Indira Dutta (India), Kanupriya Bhagat (India), Odeta Grabauskaitė (Lithuania) & Miriam Kennet (UK)

Typeset by Miriam Kennet
Printed on FSC approved stock by Marston Book Services Ltd.

This book should be cited as " West Kharkongor N., Dutta I., Bhagat K., Grabauskaitė O & Kennet M. (2014) **Green Economics in India** The Green Economics Institute UK.

www.greeneconomics.org.uk
greeneconomicsinstitute@yahoo.com
A catalogue record for this book is available from the British Library

Contents

6.3 Gandhian Green Paradigm: A new vision for sustainable development
By Dr. Indira Dutta

The Green Economics Institute Publications

Leading thinkers now publish with The Green Economics Institute with over 50 titles.

Titles available from The Green Economics Institute ©:

Economics Books

Handbook of Green Economics: A Practitioner's Guide (2012). Edited By Miriam Kennet, Eleni Courea, Alan Bouquet and Ieva Pepinyte, ISBN 9781907543036

Green Economics Methodology: An Introduction (2012). Edited By Tone Berg (Norway), Aase Seeberg (Norway) and Miriam Kennet, ISBN 978190754357

The Green Economics Reader (2012). Edited By Miriam Kennet ISBN 9781907543265

Rebalancing the Economy (2014). Edited By Christopher Brook & Miriam Kennet, ISBN 9781907543845

An Alternative History of Economics and Economists for students (2015). Edited by Miriam Kennet

Finance Books

The Greening of Global Finance: Reforming Global Finance c (2013). Edited By Professor Graciela Chichilnisky (USA and Argentina), Michelle S. Gale de Oliveira (USA and Brazil), Miriam Kennet, Professor Maria Madi (Brazil) and Professor Chow Fah Yee (Malaysia),ISBN 9781907543401

The Reform and Greening of Global Banking (2014). Edited by Miriam Kennet, Professor Maria Madi and Stephen Mandel, ISBN 9781907543203

Islamic Banking from our team in Bangladesh (2015)

Geographies of Green Economics

Greening the Global Economy (2013). Edited by Sofia Amaral (Portugal) and Miriam Kennet , ISBN 9781907543944

Green Economics: The Greening of Asia and China (2012). Edited by Miriam Kennet (UK) and Norfayanti Kamaruddin (Malaysia), ISBN 9781907543234

Green Economics: Voices of Africa (2012). Edited By Miriam Kennet, Amana Winchester, Mahelet Mekonnen and Chidi Magnus Onuoha, ISBN 9781907543098

Green Economics: The Greening of Indonesia (2013). Edited By Dr Dessy Irwati and Dr Stephan Onggo (Indonesia), ISBN 9781907543821

The Indigenous Women of Bangladesh: Shifting Livelihoods and Gender in the Matrilineal Garo Community of Madhupur (2014) Dr. Soma Dey, ISBN 9781907543807

The Greening of Latin America (2013). Edited By Michelle S. Gale de Oliveira (USA and Brazil), Maria Fernanda Caporale Madi (Brazil), Carlos Francisco Restituyo Vassallo (Dominican Republic) and Miriam Kennet , ISBN 9781907543876

Africa: Transition to a Green Economy (2013). Edited By Dr Chidi Magnus (Nigeria), ISBN 9781907543364

The Greening of the Indian Economy: The Economic Miracle (2014). Edited by Associate Professor, Dr Natalie West Kharkongor (India), Dr Indira Dutta (India), Kanupriya Bhagat (India), Odeta Grabauskaitė (Lithuania), Miriam Kennet (UK) & Professor Graciela Chichilnisky (Argentine, USA), ISBN 9781907543500

European Books
The Greening of Europe (2014). Edited by Miriam Kennet, ISBN 9781907543463

The Greening of Eastern Europe (2013). Edited by Miriam Kennet and Dr Sandra Gusta (Latvia), ISBN 9781907543418

Green Economics: Policy and Practise in Eatern Europe (July 2014). Edited by Professor Dr Dzintra Astaja (Latvia), Miriam Kennet and Odeta Grabauskaitė (Lithuania), ISBN 9781907543814

Greening of the Mediterranean Economy (2013). Edited by Miriam Kennet, Dr Michael Briguglio and Dr Enrico Tezza, ISBN 9781907543906

Green Economics: Potential for the Italian Recovery: The Greening of Italy. Edited by Alberto Truccolo and Miriam Kennet, ISBN 9781907543920

The Greening of Norway and the future economy. Edited by Miriam Kennet (2014)

Europe, an analysis for the future of its economy. Edited by Martin Koehring Senior Editor of the Economist Magazine, Miriam Kennet, Volker Heinemann (2015)

Social Policy Books
The Greening of Health and Wellbeing (2013). Edited by Michelle S. Gale de Oliveira, Miriam Kennet and Dr Katherine Kennet, ISBN 9781907543760

The Vintage Generation, the Rocking Chair Revolution (2014). Edited by Miriam Kennet and Birgit Meinhard – Siebel (Austria), ISBN 9781907543517

Citizen's Income and Green Economics (2012) By Clive Lord, edited by Judith Felton and Miriam Kennet, ISBN 9781907543074

Green Economics: Women's Unequal Pay and Poverty (2012). Edited by Miriam Kennet, Michelle S Gale de Oliveira, Judith Felton and Amana Winchester, ISBN 9781907543081

Young People: Green Jobs, Employment and Education (2012). Edited by Miriam Kennet and Juliane Goeke (Germany), ISBN 9781907543258

Garment workers in Bangladesh (2014). Soma Dey (Bangladesh) and others

The Philosophy of Social Justice (2015). Edited by Miriam Kennet and others

Ending the War against women (2015). Edited by Miriam Kennet, Michelle S Gale de Oliveira, Professor Graciela Chichilnisky and Professor Maria Madi

Memories of India by Lynden Moore (2015). Edited by Odeta Grabauskaitė

Migration, Refugees and Population (2015). Edited by Miriam Kennet and others

Mental Health (2015). Edited by Miriam Kennet and Dr Katherine Kennet

Energy and Climate Policy
Green Economics and Climate Change (2012). Edited by Miriam Kennet and Winston Ka-Ming Mak, ISBN 978190754310

Green Economics: The Greening of Energy Policies (2012). Edited By Ryota Koike (Japan) and Miriam Kennet, ISBN 9781907543326

Renewable Energy (2014). Edited by Miriam Kennet and a team of writers, ISBN 9781907543784 . Forthcoming in 2014

Fracking, Black Swan Events and Risk (2014). Edited by Miriam Kennet and Paul Mobbes, ISBN 9781907543791. Forthcoming in 2014

Food, Farming and Agriculture
Green Economics & Food, Farming and Agriculture (2013). Edited by Michelle S. Gale de Oliveira and Rose Blackett-Ord and Miriam Kennet, ISBN 9781907543449

Green Economics & Food, Farming and Agriculture: Greening the food on your plate c (2013). Edited by Michelle S. Gale de Oliveira, Rose Blackett-Ord and Miriam Kennet, ISBN 9781907543654

Towards Sustainable Regional Food Systems: The Langenburg Forum c (2013). Edited By Miriam Kennet, by kind permission of Joschka Fischer and HRH Prince Charles Prince of Wales Forthcoming in 2015

Organic Food (2015)

Biodiversity, conservation and animal protection Books
Biodiversity, Animal Welfare and Protection (2014). Edited by Anna Wainer, Compassion in World Farming and others, ISBN 9781907543227

Forests and Trees (2015) Edited by Miriam Kennet and others

Lifestyle Books
The Green Transport Revolution (2013). Edited By Richard Holcroft and Miriam Kennet, ISBN 9781907543968

Green Poetry, Art and Photography (2013). Edited by Dr Matt Rinaldi, Rose Blackett-Ord, Friedericke Oeser Prasse and Miriam Kennet, ISBN 9781907543784

The Green Built Environment: A Handbook (2012). Edited By Miriam Kennet and Judith Felton, ISBN 9781907543067

Fairtrade in Europe (2014) Jessica Boisseau. Edited by Christopher Brook

Philosophy Books
Integrating Ethics, Social Responsibility and Governance (2013). Edited by Tore Audin Hedin (Norway), Michelle Gale de Oliveira and Miriam Kennet, ISBN 9781907543395

The Philosophical Basis of the Green Movement (2013). Edited by Professor Michael Benfield, Miriam Kennet and Michelle Gale de Oliveira (Brazil), ISBN 9781907543548

Books about Resources and Basic Needs
Water, Flooding and sea level rise (2014)

Technology and Technical Books

The Greening of IT (2014). Forthcoming

Engineering and Technological Solutions to current problems (2015)

Foreword

By Dr Natalie West Kharkongor, IIM Shillong, India

I am also glad that the Green Economics Institute, UK is publishing a Book on **"Green Economics in India"** following the International Seminar on Green Economics: The Road to a Balanced and Healthy Economy on the 7th and 8th August 2014 at State Convention Center, Shillong, Meghalaya, India. The Seminar was inaugurated by Dr. K. K. Paul, the Honorable Governor of Meghalaya. The event was also attended by renowned academicians, politicians, government officials, industrialists, civil society representatives, and students.

The book talks about Green Economics in India. The event is organised by the Meghalaya Economic Association and Indian Institute of Management Shillong. The International Seminar on Green Economics: discusses The Road to a Balanced and Healthy Economy. The main objective of the Seminar is to enrich biodiversity, and to maintaining ecological balance. Hence, a number of sub – themes have been incorporated, and some of these are: Environmental Degradation; Educational Transformation and Gender Issues; Health in the Green Economy; Sustainable Banking and Finance; Healthy Governance for Sustainable Development Agriculture and allied activities; Renewable Energy and its Challenges Mining and Ecological Degradation Communication; Land Use and Environment Uniting Conservation; Communities and Sustainable Tourism.

I believe that the Book will mark the beginning of the role of Green Economics in India, and in particular the North Eastern Region in bringing about an inclusive growth in a healthier and happier economy. This Book has been edited by the team of Miriam Kennet, and the Green Economics Institute, UK, and by Professor Dr Natalie West Kharkongor, IIM Shillong, India, and also by Indira Dutta, India and the Project is supported by Prof. Graciela Chichilnisky, Columbia University, with the editorial team including Don O Neal, Alberto Truccolo and Christopher Brook in the UK.
The book has been created by Odeta Grabauskaitė and particular thanks go to her.

Photo Graciela Chichilnisky: At the Green Economics Conference in Shillong, India

Editors

Professor, Dr Natalie West Kharkongor
Photo: Professor, Dr Natalie West Kharkongor

Dr Natalie West Kharkongor currently is an Associate Professor of Economics and Head, Center for Development of North Eastern Region (CEDNER) at IIM Shillong. Dr. Natalie was earlier with Shillong College in the Arts, Commerce and Management Streams. She was also a Visiting Faculty in the Regional Training Institute, Shillong, Meghalaya Administrative Training Institute, and Meghalaya Khadi and Village Industries.

Graduated in Economics, Dr. Natalie holds a Doctorate Degree in "Development of Banking and Financial Institutions in Meghalaya since 1972". In addition, she completed two Research Projects sponsored by UGC, North Eastern Region. She has twenty one years of teaching experience and eighteen years of research experience.

Photo: Professor, Dr Natalie West Kharkongor

Dr. Natalie received the Broad Outlook Learner Teacher Award from the Prime Minister, Dr. Manmohan Singh on 24th Nov 2004, the Rashtriya Gaurav Award with Certificate of Excellence on the 16th July 2011 in New Delhi. She also received the Innovative New Member Award from the Lions Club 322D in 2011. She has presented and published a number of papers related to Banking and Finance, Entrepreneurship, Agriculture, Industry, Higher Education, Water Management, Women Empowerment, Health Sector, Green Economics and others. She has attended seminars, workshops and conferences at the local, regional, national, and international levels. Currently, Dr. Natalie is the President of Meghalaya Economic Association. She is also a Member, and was the Joint Secretary of the North Eastern Economic Association. Dr. Natalie is a Life Member of the Indian Economic Association, and a Member of Green Economics Institute, UK.

Associate Professor, Dr Indira Dutta

Dr Indira Dutta works at Centre for Studies in Economics and Planning School of Social Sciences at the Central University of Gujarat, Gandhinaga. She has published two books entitled "Poverty to Empowerment" and "Contemporary Issues of Indian Economy", and successfully completed two projects, one funded by UNDP and the other by ICSSR(Indian Council of Social Science and Research). As a Chairperson of (Gender Sensitization Committee against Sexual Harassment) of Central University of Gujarat, she has proven her worth by handling several complicated cases. Recently, her work on "Gandhian Green Paradigm: A New Vision for Sustainable Development" was awarded a certificate at the 9th Annual Green Economics Institute, Green Economics Conference held at Oxford University on July 10,2014.   She is proudly associated with International Journal of Green Economics on its Editorial Board. She is also a member of prestigious institute named Green Economics Institute, U.K. and a life member of Indian Society of Labour Economics, India. Her areas of interest include Environmental Economics, Regional Economics, Microeconomics, Development Economics.

Photo: Associate Professor, Dr Indira Dutta

Kanupriya Bhagat

Kanupriya Bhagat, is currently pursuing Sustainable Development at the University of St Andrews. Originally, from Agra, India, she has been involved with organizations such as CRY (Child Rights and You), New Delhi, where she was part of the Digital Fundraising Department, and has a strong interest in publishing. She works with the Green Economics Institute in developing Green Economics into a global initiative.

Photo: Kanupriya Bhagat

Odeta Grabauskaitė

Odeta Grabauskaitė is a specialist in Public administration in Vytautas Magnus University (VMU). Her main fields of interest are European Union institutions, personnel management, social issues and social psychology. She has been social affairs coordinator of the VMU Student Representative Council for 2 years. She is a member of the Vytautas Magnus University Senate and a member of Political Science and Diplomacy Faculty Council. During her studies in Vytautas Magnus University she studied in Turkey, in Gazi university, as an Erasmus student. Odeta Grabauskaitė is a member of Green Economics Institute.

Photo: Odeta Grabauskaitė

She attended in the 9th Annual Green Economics Institute conference at Oxford University in July 2014 as a member of the management team. She created and edited the academic proceedings of the conference. Odeta was also the editor of "Green Economics: Policy and Practice in Eastern Europe" with Professor Dzintra Atstaja from Latvia. She is also the lead editor for this current volume "Green Economics in India". Odeta Grabauskaitė is a reviewer for the "International Journal of Green Economics", an academic double blind peer reviewed journal, published by Inderscience.

Miriam Kennet

Miriam Kennet, is a specialist in Green Economics, she is the Co-Founder and is CEO of the Green Economics Institute. She also founded and edits the first Green Economics academic journal in the world, the International Journal of Green Economics, and she has been credited with creating the academic discipline of Green Economics. Green Economics has been recently described by the Bank of England as one of the most vibrant and healthy areas of economics at the moment. Miriam has travelled extensively in India from the North to the South overland mainly by train and bus.

Photo: Miriam Kennet

Having researched at Oxford University, Oxford Brookes and South Bank University, she is a member of the Environmental Change Institute, Oxford University. She has taught, lectured and spoken at Universities and events all over Europe, from Alicante to Oxford and Bolzano, and to government officials from Montenegro and Kosovo to The UK Cabinet Office, Transport Department, National Government School and Treasury and spoken in Parliaments from Scotland to Austria and The French Senat and Estonia. She is also a regular and frequently speaks at public events of all kinds, and after dinner speaker, this week advising in the Uk Parliament and the Bank of England and in Brussels on the Eurozone crisis, the high speed rail and the general economic situation. She is also very active in spreading Green Economics in Asia, China, and all round Africa where people find it may be one of the beacons of hope at the moment in an age of Austerity and Cuts as it provides a completely new way of looking at the world. Her work is very practical and she worked in factories and engineering for many years in the past. She is on the Assembly of the Green European Foundation and also on the steering group of the European Network of Political Foundations. She has a delegation to the UNFCC COP Kyoto Climate Change Conferences and headed up a delegation to RIO + 20 Earth Summit: Greening the Economy in RIO Brazil.

INTERNATIONAL SEMINAR ON GREEN ECONOMICS: THE ROAD TO A BALANCED AND HEALTHY ECONOMY

7ᵗʰ & 8ᵗʰ August, 2014

Organized by

Meghalaya Economic Association Shillong, Meghalayain
collaboration with Rajiv Gandhi Indian Institute of Management Shillong

Invitation

We have the pleasure to inform you that Meghalaya Economic Association, Shillong in collaboration with IIM, Shillong is organizing a two-day International Seminar at the Pinewood Hotel, Shillong. Academicians, researchers and scholars from various parts of the world will participate in this two day program. We extend our heartiest invitation to all those who are interested to participate in the seminar.

Theme of the Seminar

Countries have developed during the past 20 years, but questions have remained unanswered: What kind of development have we had? What has really happened in past 20 years? Have things got better or worse for most people and most things on the planet and its systems? What kind of growth we have had? Does the sustainable development concept make societies from developed, developing and undeveloped countries wealthier, happier or healthier? The gap between richer and poorer sections of society has increased. World economies have grown and developed in terms of and in relation to their GDP. On the one side, there is poverty (deficit) and on the other side, there is wastage (excess). The global economy witnessed a high degree of imbalance in terms of extraction and usage of resources. The state of nature and its natural resources like the quality of water and air are on a downward spiral and have reached an alarming point.

The Green Economics Institute

Photo: Bogusia Igielska (Poland)

Green Economics has become very relevant as a means of providing the solutions to some of the challenges of India today. The global social, economic and environmental crisis in all its forms is starting to really impact the life of its citizens but also its economy in various subtle and not so subtle ways. Conflicts and stresses are errupting as a result of the pressure for resources. New efforts are being made, the world over, to try to become self sufficient in energy, and many are moving to renewables, decarbonising and generally trying to limit pollution and create a Green Economy as a way of staying in the global economy or maintaining their own regional or local economy. An economy seemingly unendingly diverted from its aim of provisioning for everyone and generally keeping healthy, beneficial for all and uncorrupted. Green Economics has things to say in all these areas and is being used as one of the beacons of hope around the world and in almost every economy to a greater or lesser extent.

The rapid rise of Nationalism   even in the seat of the origins of democracy- Athens, is truly breath taking but was predicted as people become more alarmed at how the world is changing and worrying about their economy and the future for their children. Sea level is predicted to rise and indeed Venice is flooding, part of Eastern Europe and also the Uk have all experienced catastrophic flooding recently, whilst other areas known for their important precipitation such as snow in Norway, are now experiencing drought in winter. These changes, which have occured within a generation are affecting the economy, for example the wine growing Alpine areas of northern Italy have suffered changes or reduction in precipitation which have changed or limited the HEP energy hitherto taken for granted.

So everything is changing especially in the natural world and climate and this is affecting the economy. The economic crisis itself seems to be never ending and although some areas are experiencing GDP growth, this is now very much more unevenly distributed and society is much more unequal, foodbanks and homelessness are common place right across the area. All these factors   lead to geo political instability both within countries and between countries and leads to rioting and general unrest which affects the economy. Big business is pushing for trade treaties which might well roll back many of the environmental and social gains Europe and the EU have made over the last few years.

The Green Economics Institute has been working to create and establish a discipline or school of Economics called "Green Economics" and seeks to reform mainstream economics itself into a well-defined goals-based discipline which provides practical answers to existing and future problems by incorporating all relevant aspects, knowledge and complex interactions into a truly holistic understanding of the relevant issues. It uses complexity, holism, pluralism and interdisciplinary working in order to widen the scope of economics, adding the science from the green aspects, and the social ideas from economics discourses. This new scope for the first time avoids partial explanations or solutions and also biased and partial perspectives of power elites.

The Institute has begun to influence the methodology of mainstream economics, according to Professor Tony Lawson of Cambridge University's Economics Department (2007). It uses trans-disciplinary and interdisciplinary methods so that it can factor in the complexity of nature into economics. It seeks to provide all people everywhere, non human species, the planet and earth systems with a decent level of well-being based on practical and theoretical approaches targeting both methodology and knowledge and based a comprehensive reform of the current economic mainstream. It can, for example, comfortably incorporate glacial issues, climate change and volcanic, seismic and earth sciences into its explanations and thus in this, and many other ways, it is far more complete and reflects reality much more closely than its predecessors on which it builds. The current narrow conventional economic approach using purposely designed methods, is challenged to bring areas and concepts into its scope which have been until now neglected. Existing outdated or inappropriate propositions and solutions are examined and revised to provide a realistic and more comprehensive understanding of the subject.

The Green Economics Institute argues for economic development based on economic access and decision making for all, including respect for cultural diversity and normative freedom. It does this by bringing together all the interested parties, who want to help in developing this progressive discipline, by inviting them to its events, and conferences and by means of such activities as writing books and publications and using its research, its campaigns and its lobbying and its speeches and lecturing all over the world.

The Green Economics Institute created the first green academic journal *International Journal of Green Economics* with publishers Inderscience.

The Green Economics Institute has its own delegation to the Kyoto Protocol, and is a recommended UK government reviewer on the Intergovernmental Panel on Climate Change (IPCC). Members of the Green Economics Institute have lectured or worked in governments and Universities around the world, for example receiving invitations from Surrey University, the Schumacher College, The University of Bolzano, the Tyrollean Cabinet, via Skype in Thessaloniki, FYRO Macedonia, Turkey, the National Government School in the UK with top Cabinet Officials, at University in Cambridge and Oxford, Transition Towns, Oslo, Norway, Liverpool University, Lancaster University, Abuja, Nigeria and Gondar, Ethiopia, Shillong, and Gujerat, in India and attended conferences in many places including Cancun, Mexico and Riga, Latvia and appeared on TV and radio in Italy and Tallin in Estonia and the UK and Bangladesh amongst many others and received invitations the President of Russia and from the governments and several universities in China and from several governments and Princes in several Gulf States as well as several parts of the United Nations and the International Labour Organisation!

This year we are delighted to be working in India and to try to make a real difference with our policy innovations.

The spread of Green Economics is accelerating and hence The Green Economics Institute is pleased to bring these ideas to a broader group of readers, students, policy makers, academics and campaigners in this ground breaking volume and to begin to offer its Green Economics Solutions to the extremely important country of India and to prepare to help with their implementation there as a really useful tool in bringing in sustainability and survivability and more equality. Development in a Green Economics way is a real help in establishing a more beneficial economy and bringing millions more people out of poverty!

Directors
Miriam Kennet, UK,
Volker Heinemann UK, Germany,
Michelle S. Gale de Oliveira UK, USA, Brazil

List of Contributors

Ben Armstrong–Haworth, a researcher in Management at Cass Business School, City University of London. Originally preferring the natural and physical sciences at school and sixth form, his undergraduate studies at Birkbeck College, University of London, moved into the social sciences and gained first class BA (Hons) Management in 2005. This has followed by an MSc Innovation Management & Technology Policies, gained with distinction in 2008, also from Birkbeck College. Ben was a student of Miriam Kennet.

Ranjit Barthakur in 2002 founded Globally Managed Services, an Operational Consulting Incubator where he is the Director. Ranjit has also set up other entrepreneurial ventures such as Agil, Advent Healthcare, Med-Ind Healthcare (and Green Ecological Managed Services. Prior to becoming an entrepreneur, Ranjit was CEO of Hutchison Max-Touch Telecom (Vodafone) in India, Chairman of Marconi in the Indian Sub-continent. Ranjit strongly believes in 'Social Entrepreneurship towards Betterment of Human Health, Education, Environment and Skills Development' and is consistently driving these initiatives and projects.

Abhijit Kumar Bezbarua is a Guwahati based management consultant with a total working experience of over 28 years. After completing his education, he had worked in a variety of capacities before commencing his career as a consultant. His assignments have taken him to all states of the North Eastern region of India, where he has interacted with people at the village level, besides meeting different agencies of the Government of India and State Governments. During the period from 2003 to 2007, he worked as an evaluator for the National Afforestation & Eco-development Board of the Ministry of Environment & Forests, Government of India. He had an opportunity to visit many field level reforestation works being undertaken in the hill areas of North Eastern India by district level agencies in collaboration with village level bodies. This paper is based on his experiences of work being undertaken for resurrecting the region's depleting forest cover.

Christopher Brook studies Economics at the University of Cambridge. His interests lie in sustainable development and poverty alleviation. He spent 10 weeks in Nicaragua on a sustainable watershed management project where he began to understand the needs and challenges that those in poverty face. He hopes to use this gained knowledge in the future to help relieve poverty sustainably all over the world. He currently works for the Green Economics Institute.

Persis Farooqy has a Masters from Tata Institute of Social Sciences, Guwahati, Assam, in Ecology, Environment and Sustainable Development, and is a specialist in 'Conservation Challenges and Prospects through Community Based Tourism (CBT)- A Comparative Case chapter of Laokhuwa-Burachapori Wildlife Sanctuaries, Assam'.

Manan Jain, an economist from India, specialising in the Gift Economy. Manan addressed the Green Economics Institute's Conference at Oxford University in 2012 (India)

Dr J. Cyril Kanmony is an associate professor of Economics at the Scott Christian College in Kanyakumari District, Tamil Nadu. He is author of a book entitled Child Labour Rights and Violations

Dr Katherine Kennet Medical Practitioner and Global Health Specialist trained at Imperial College, London.

Professor Dr Maria Alejandra Madi, holds a PhD in Economics. She works at the intersection between macroeconomics, finance and socio-economic development. Former Professor at the State University of Campinas, Brazil, she is currenty Director of the Ordem dos Economistas do Brasil and Counselor at the Conselho Regional de Economia–SP. Besides her participation as co-author in chapter books edited by the Global Labor University, she is a regular author with the Green Economics Institute.

Ashok Kumar Maurya, is researching at the Centre for Studies in Economics and Planning, School of Social Sciences, Central University of Gujarat, Gandhinagar under Dr. Indira Dutta (Associate Professor) into "The Externalities of Groundwater Exploitation in Agriculture: A Case chapter of

North Gujarat". He completed M. Phil in Economics at Centre for Studies in Economics and Planning, School of Social Science, Central University of Gujarat, Gandhinagar under Dr. Indira Dutta (Associate Professor). His interest is in "Fluoride Menace in Groundwater: A chapter of North Gujarat".

Vinodh K Natarajan is a lecturer at Narayanaguru College of Engineering. He received his Phd in Economics from Manonmaniam Sundaranar University. His current areas of Expertise are : International aspect of global value chains and production networks; emergence of local clusters and their impact on innovation and knowledge transfer; global concerns and issues related to international public goods in the sphere, environment and financial stabilisation.

Michelle S. Gale de Oliveira, is a director of the Green Economics Institute, UK. She is a member of the Law School of the University of London School of Oriental and African Studies (SOAS), holding an MA in Human Rights Law with a focus on Islamic Law, Peace-Building, and Developing Countries. Founder of the Gender Progress Consortium, she holds degrees in Political Science and International Relations from Richmond, the American International University in London (RAIUL), and is currently deputy editor of the International Journal of Green Economics. Her writing has been featured in Europe's World, one of the foremost European policy magazines. She lectures and speaks on Human Rights, Environmental and Social Justice, Gender Equity, International Development and Green Economics internationally. Recently she ran a conference on women's unequal pay and poverty in Reading, UK, lectured at the Oxford University Club on the human rights of land reform, lectured on green economics in Berlin, at retreats in Glastonbury, UK, and is a regular speaker at international conferences. She has appeared in the media in Africa, Europe, and Latin America. Michelle is a member of the Human Rights Lawyers Association, the Law Society of England and Wales Human Rights Lawyers Group, the London Middle East Institute. In 2010/2011, she was a delegate to Conference of Parties (COP15/16) in Copenhagen and Cancun, and in 2012 led our Green Economics Institute delegation to RIO+20, where she ran three side events on green economics.

Don O'Neal has a BSc(Hons) in Mathematics and an MA in Environmentalism and Society. He has been the Oxfordshire Greens Treasurer since September

2000 and is a political columnist for The News and The Vincentian, national newspapers in St. Vincent and the Grenadines. He is a co-founder of the St Vincent Greens.

Mirza Zulfiqur Rahman is a Researcher at the Department of Humanities and Social Sciences, Indian Institute of Technology, Guwahati, Assam, and he is a specialist in "A 'clean' view through the 'clouds'? : Challenges to community participation and impact of tourism and development in Cherrapunjee and Mawlynnong in Meghalaya".

Jiya Shahani is pursing Ph.D (Economics) at CSEP/SSS/CUG, Gandhinagar. She has been part of the Shipping Industry for more than two decades, wherein she is associated with healthcare department. Her broad areas of work include Environment and Health economy. Currently, focus of her research work is on the Sustainability studies. Her research interests include consumerism, green infrastructure and finance, coastal and trans-boundary waters, governance issues, and green economy transitions. She has presented influential research Chapters at national and international conferences and authored a few Chapters for edited books as well as the Journal of Economic and Social Development. Her research work titled 'Green Federalism: A historic leap towards Sustainable Human Development' was awarded scholarship at HDCA 2012 conference organized at Jakarta, Indonesia. The same has been published by Springer, Germany in October 2013 as a chapter in an edited book titled "Environment and Sustainable Development". As an ardent admirer of environment, she aspires to work in collaboration, on green reforms in economic and financial systems; social and educational systems; and political and legal systems.

Dr Seema Singh is Associate Professor in Economics and Head of the Department of Humanities, Delhi Technological University, Delhi, India since 2006. Largely, interested in higher education and skill formation, she has published number of Chapters in referred journals and presented Chapters in national and international seminars and conferences. She has also completed successfully several research projects sponsored by national and international agencies. She received All India Council for Technical Education (AICTE) Career Award for Young Teacher in 2000. She is Joint Secretary of the Indian Society of Labour Economics since 2006 and Vice-President of the WISE-India since 2011. More recently, she has been awarded, "Outstanding Track Chair

Award" at the 4th Conference of Industrial Engineering and Operations Management", held at Bali, Indonesia between January 07-09' 2014.

Dr Enrico Tezza is a senior training specialist and has a background in social research and evaluation studies. After a career in the Italian Ministry of Labour and local public institutions, he joined the International Labour Organisation in Turin in 1992. He is labour market advisor for the Green Economics Institute. Subjects covered vary from training policy to employment and active labour market measures. His current focus interest is on social dialogue for green jobs. His main publication was Evaluating Social Programmes: the relevance of relationships and his latest publications include Dialogue for Responsible Restructuring and Green Labour Market for Transitions.

Alberto Truccolo is keen on macro-economy, political economics and corporate social responsibility. He runs conferences in his institute and in his city discussing themes like the inefficiency of the current capitalism, the potential of renewable energies and the consequences of automation on the socio-economic paradigm. He also manages a blog in order to raise awareness about issues like environmental sustainability, inequality and the development of a more efficient economic system. Recently, he took part in some sessions of the "Youth European Parliament", also being awarded as "Best Delegate". He is starting up a his own green-business, creating a network for the collection and the recycling of plastic wastes in his area.

Dr Jeffrey Turk PhD, holds a doctorate in particle physics from Yale University and after working as a physicist at the European Laboratory for Particle Physics (CERN) he earned an MA in transition economics at the Central European University in Budapest and then a DPhil in contemporary European Studies from the University of Sussex and a research fellow at the Scientific Research Centre of the Slovenian Academy of Sciences and Arts, where he researches realist biography and European Policy. He ran a research conference at the University of Halloween on critical realist narrative biographical methods. He has produced many articles on Green Economics and methodological innovation.(Slovenia and Belgium).

Speech in Shillong Pinewood Hotel India

7thand 8thAugust 2014

By Miriam Kennet

I am most Honoured to be invited to address the conference and to discuss my ideas and work with you.

I have been extremely fortunate to be able to work with some of you in preparing this book about India and its economic miracle which has taken India from a really challenged environment to one of the worlds very biggest- the third biggest economy in one generation- quite a miracle. As an economist I find this incredibly exciting and also a beacon country which I want to know much more about.

Initially as a specialist in archeology, this helped me understand the longer term perspectives which are now challenging us in regard to resource use and climate change. It helped me to see, that it is only when we consider the effect of our lives and activities, not just on next weeks bottom line for a company, and annual results reporting, but actually in 5, 10, 100 years and also not just our children and their childrens' children but also – the 7th and even the 700th generation of people- that we can fully understand our role in the world and our mission to ensure we change the way we humans operate our economy.

It is only by understanding our effects on each other that we can grow together and our economy can flourish. I created the academic discipline of Green Economics, thinking of how earth sciences and earth systems can be described with social science systems so its truly looking at both together and also truly multidisciplinary at its core. I also wanted to think about how we could create an economy which benefits all people everywhere including women and minorities of all kinds, and which looked after nature, other species, the planet and its systems for their own sake and also for people. This approach makes economics much broader than it has been certainly for 200 years. The original concept of Economics, from the Greek word "oikonomia" was about management of the household, our home, -perhaps today that "home" is the earth as

there is certainly no economy today outside the earth. So all economics depends on the natural world for its resources and
we all depend on each other – trading involves other people. The original word for company- com pane meant to break bread with people- a much more human occupation than todays big multinationals which seem to consider people's needs last. So the work of Green Economics is I think to keep these ideas at the forefront of everything we do when we venture into more complex areas and ideas.

The Green Economy is therefore as broad as it is long term. This means that decisions affecting distribution and equality need to consider how they will play out in future generations. Energy decisions are not just about making a quick profit now but rather the question to ask is- how will this impact other people today- or other people and other species tomorrow and the day after. Finance is no longer about how to get the biggest bonus but rather how to finance a transition to a more fair and sustainable economy as soon as possible. Energy in this scenario favours renewables. An Holistic approach to decision making means that economists favourite certeris paribus no longer applies- as the broadest possible considerations need to be made using as much of a realist prospect as possible. Models, mathematics and formulae are servants in this process- not the masters. I foresaw the mathematics and quantitative information as vital in the struggle to conserve biodiversity for us to know how we are doing. Understanding the rate of decline of a rainforest or an endangered species is important. Making up lovely graphs to prove a question not related to reality is less useful so there needs to be shift to more use of mathematics and scientific language where its needed and less where in the past it has been used to baffle people and keep people from asking too many awkward questions.

I am pleased to say that many countries in the world- in fact nearly all of them are starting to implement a Green Economy, and in many cases this presents a real opportunity to meet the pressing challenges of today headlong. For example a greener economy is much better equiped to address climate change, climate instability and extreme events than a mainstream economy. Firstly it aims to predict what is coming and accepts and relies on science – not denial.It can predict for sea level rise, CO_2 and methane increases and temperature increase and precipitation changes and allows for them. It seeks to reverse micro climate changes or to try to halt them or mitigate for their effects. Above all it seeks alternative to business as usual to get a more beneficial outcome for everyone in the community.

India in particular a country endowed with the most charming and stunning of any natural beauty, and indeed it was a visit to India in my youth which really got me thinking that I could try and make real change in the world and its economy, to make a real difference. I had a sort of epiphany I think its called -a light bulb moment -where I knew that I wanted to create a completely new way of thinking about the world and its economy, and to create a complete revision of the economics system, which would include everyone and that moment happened to me in India when I was a young woman, about 26 years old. I was exploring the wonders of India- the gorgeous smell of jasmine- (I still have a jasmine bush outside my own front door today)-and the site, sounds and incredible smells and views of huge high mountains, pure air, fabulous food and wonderful people. It has truly abundant resources and many mouths to feed can therefore profit exceptionally from the implementation of a green economy. It was indeed in India that the Green Economy was born and it is indeed in India where I believe it can thrive and do wonderful good for humanity!

Its myriad of businesses can thrive more with more equality and more future thinking. It can avoid the mistakes- and they are serious mistakes of the west – in depleting reserves and in forgetting about equality, fairness and inclusion. India is home to some of the worlds most beacon species, and also to a lively climate- hot and with monsoons. This dependence of the worlds civilisations and economies on the climate as it has largely been for 10,000 years for this current interglacial period is not necessarily going to remain like this and we need to do everything possible not to aggravate the natural systems -so that we dont end up creating a hostile natural environment.

India also in addition to being the worlds third largest economy is also a place where many of the important rivers of Asia rise and provide drinking water for millions of people and has also some of the worlds greatest mega cities and natural landscapes and habitats. Therefore India has a unique role to play in conservation and in forward thinking development. India's businesses are some of the most important on the planet, many of the worlds millionaires are Indian, the largest film industry on earth -Bollywood is Indian, many of the worlds largest corporations are Indian. It is imperative that we find a modus vivendi for Indian business which is comfortable developing along Greener and more futuristic lines. For make no mistake -greener is also high tech, greener is the future and

greener is about all our futures. And this is where – in the largest democracy in the world- it is absolutely vital that India gets on board to the green economy steam ship. Without India participating it is meaningless, China has many green 5 year plans, many other countries are starting to take part -from Malaysia to Brazil to South Africa. Many are beginning to understand their role and also the impact from climate change as the world heats up. Additionally many lands will become uninhabitable and so we are starting to see mass migration of people and geo political instability. We need India on board to ensure that this change scenario does not create more chaos or resource depletion. We need India's businesses to compete with green as a centre of excellence and Indias vibrant democracy to truly represent all its people including women.

31

There are still some areas of the population who are not quite as well represented and we know that countries who do not educate their women or give them equal opportunities do less well than those that harness the efforts of all their citizens and educate everyone in the same way. A green way is the economics of caring, sharing and supporting each other – equally and for the good of the whole.

So we need a shift in some areas in India but also above all to avoid the nonsensical over consumption we see in the west.

Which brings me to the obsession with GDP Growth in the mainsteam economy that we must all consume more and more and faster and faster! As the distiguished career of your host Dr Natalie West shows, its the networking, the long hours in a variety of areas of activity, the caring, sharing and supporting each other in the community-which actually makes a green economist and which enables others to come together to make a real change. It is not about bonuses or greed. In the Uk it is becoming hugely more fashionable to own a bicycle than to own a gass guzzling Rolls Royce Car. It is becoming hugely more fashionable to do charity work than to be seen to be conspicuously consuming expensive commodities, clothes etc even the Royalty dont throw their money around -they reuse clothes, the new Princes buys her clothes mostly from high street shops. The Queen is becoming known for her Tuperware Suppers. The world is changing and people respect people who respect for others and who share. In the tense and difficult geo political times in which we live

Green Economics can go a long way to easing some of those tensions and mitigating some of the worst effects of global environmental change. Building a Green Economy for India based on social and environmental justice for all its citizens, its nature, its other species and also keeping its natural systems in a benevolent mode will help absolutely everyone in India and also quite possibly right around the planet.

So finally I would like to say that the passage of a Green Economy in India – is really exciting and I cant wait to be able to come out and meet all of you in person. I hugely admire the work you are all doing and doing the India book, hopefully the first of many about India and its opportunities, will really change the face of India in the 21st century. This book was one of the most pleasant we have ever put together. Its emphasis on tourism and the magical places in the district simply have made me and the team want to rush straight over to see them for ourselves. My only regret is that this time I really cant be with you in person but I have thought about nothing else for several weeks and the same is true for our team.

We have been working on our academic double blind peer reviewed academic journal this week International Journal of Green Economics and I am pleased to say that a hugely increased number of papers are now coming out of India – almost every second paper which we receive. This issue -particularly renewables, green energy, wind and solar and also the green built environment and many other aspects- so the Green Economy is now starting to thrive in India which is very pleasing. We are working to convince governments, policy makers and businesses that this is the easiest way to ensure that everyone has a future.

With enormous thanks to Professor, Dr. Natalie West and her collegues, a wonderful event -and we wish you every success in the world.

Kindest regards
Miriam Kennet
The Green Economics Institute

Photo Professor, Dr Natalie West Kharkongor: International Seminar on Green Economics in Shillong, India

Part 1: Introduction - Setting the Scene

1.1 The Greening of India, the Economic Miracle

By Christopher Brook

With a population of 1.252 billion people India currently has the second largest population globally and is projected to overtake China in the middle of this century. It is the 10th largest economy with a nominal GDP of $1.877 trillion and 3rd largest economy, when measured using PPP. India's development will have large repercussions for the entire world, economically, socially and environmentally.

Its growth since independence in 1947 has been a remarkable achievement. Growth has been strong especially since liberalisation in 1991. Between 2003 and 2007 real GDP growth was 8.7%.

The agricultural revolution transformed India from a country with a chronic dependence on imports to a country where over 10% of its exports are food. Life expectancy has doubled to 66. Literacy rates have almost quadrupled to 62% in 2006, although gender inequalities still exist (75% to 50%) and only 10% currently finish secondary school. Poverty rates have fallen over half from around 50% to closer to 20%. It has a middle class comprising more than 250 million people, about 20% of the population. By 2025, 500 million are predicted to be middle class (Times of India). It is a country with great potential. London-based independent think-tank Legatum Institute in its report concluded that India's economy is growing rapidly and the country is likely to leapfrog into the league of economic superpowers by 2030. In the Grant Thornton Global Dynamism Index, India is the fifth best country in the world for dynamic growing businesses. The index is a reflection of the feasible environment it offers for expansion of businesses. According to the World Bank, India's industrial manufacturing GDP output in 2012 was 10th largest in the world on current US dollar basis ($ 239.5 billion). India's services sector has the largest share in the GDP, accounting for 57% in 2012, up from 15% in 1950 It is the 12th largest in the world by nominal GDP, and fourth largest when purchasing power is taken into account. The services sector provides employment to 27% of the work force. Information technology and business process outsourcing are among the fastest growing sectors, having a cumulative growth rate of revenue 33.6% between 1997 and 1998 and 2002–03 and contributing to 25% of the country's total exports in 2007–08. The growth in the IT sector is attributed to increased specialisation, and an availability of a large pool of low cost, highly skilled, educated and fluent English-speaking workers, on the supply side, matched on the demand side by increased demand from foreign consumers interested in India's service exports, or those looking to outsource their operations. The share of the Indian IT industry in the country's GDP increased from 4.8% in 2005–06 to 7% in 2008. In 2009, seven Indian firms were listed among the top 15 technology outsourcing companies in the world. (Indian Government Statistics). India has some of the largest corporations in the world. Well known companies such as Tata Motors, Tata Oil and the largest Indian company is Reliance Industries which is the 135th largest company on Forbes Global 2000 list. Natalie West documents many scenarios of modern firms who are starting to adopt green technologies such as the automobile industry which is developing alternative fuel cars to use electricity and biofuels. India now has 65 billionaires, the richest being Mukesh Ambani who is worth 21 billion. Bollywood is the world's biggest cinema according to the International Business Times, producing 1000 films a year, which is twice as much as Hollywood. It currently has revenue of about $3 billion in 2011with projections $4.5 billion in 2016 (DIBD) In 2013 Indian space research organisation (ISRO) launched space craft to mars. If successful, India will join the USA, the EU and Russia in an elite group.

Although India has experienced a meteoric rise in the future it has also had a large influence in the past. Ghandi was a large inspiration to Nelson Mandela in his anti-discrimination campaign in South Africa and his future Campaigns in India. Although not completely against violence Nelson Mandela saw non-violence as key part of the movement and learnt the essential values of compassion and forgiveness, which served him and his country well when he came to power. Ghandi's influence was so great the South African Ambassador to India said that 'while Nelson Mandela is the father of South Africa, Mahatma Gandhi is our Grandfather'. India set an example for the rest of the colonised world of successful independence. If Indian independence had been a failure how many countries would have followed? Ghandi was also an environmentalist stating 'A civilisation built on renewable resources such as products of forestry and agriculture, is by fact alone superior to one built on non-renewable resources, such as coal, oil etc. This is because the former can last, while the latter cannot last'. According to Indira Dutta Gandhi's two cardinal principles truth and non-violence are green in nature. He wrote 'Nature has enough for everyone's need, but not to satisfy everybody's greed'. His legacy can be seen today in environmental movements such as Silent Valley

Movement. However despite all of the success challenges are starting to mount. In the last few years the economy has stumbled and under 5% a year for the last 2 years, although this is still impressive by Western standards, the new Prime Minister, Narendra Modi, aims to achieve a sustainable growth level of 7-8% within 3 years. India is also suffering from high levels of inflation around 10%(CPI) This has led to high levels of interest rates to counter the issue, rising to 8% in January 2014. This high interest rate has then caused the manufacturing sector to suffer as borrowing costs have increased. This inflation has partly been caused by a depreciation of the currency which has led to higher import prices of vital resources.

Poor governance is also hindering the economy. Decision making is slow, the bureaucracy is extremely cumbersome. But it's difficult to change it as it has been the legacy of the last 60 years.(Kaushik Basu).Poor government policies are also causing poor performance and a rising government deficit, the most prime and controversial policy being the oil subsidy. Regulation also needs to be cut. India ranks 134 out of 185 nations in the World Bank's Ease of Doing Business Survey. The country needs strong reform to help improve its performance again.

The new government however has brought optimism that the situation will soon reverse with ACCA finding that now 67% of finance professionals have confidence in the economy, up from 46% 6 months ago. In addition the FDI crunch that has plagued the economy for the last year seems to be coming to an end. Many people predict Mr Modi to be a serious reformer and to get the economy back on track. He has already announced an investment of over $10 billion in the railway system which currently transports over 27 million a day.

Healthcare in India is also improving. Polio has finally been eradicated in India through vaccination programs and health indicators are improving rapidly such as life expectancy. However there is still high child and maternal mortality rates, perhaps partly due to the gender bias introduced by religion. Maternal mortality is 6 times higher than in Sri Lanka. For every 100 male Indian children under 5 that die, 131 females do — victims of neglect, poorer nutrition and second-rate medical care(NY Times).In some states these figures are comparable to the world's poorest countries. Nutrition is a grave concern with 40% of the world's malnourished children living in India. If India wants to benefit from the demographic dividend created by its fast population growth they need to solve these problems.

Large improvements have been made in water and sanitation access and are set to continue. 251 million in India have gained access to improved sanitation since 1990. (WHO) and 522 million people have improved water facilities. However still only one third of people in India have access to sanitation (Wateraid) and 92 million people do not have access to safe drinking water. Nearly half abillion Indians or 48% of the population lack access to basic sanitation and defecate in the open. The situation is worse in villages where, according to the WHO and Unicef, some 65% defecate in the open. 80% of sewage in India is untreated and is flowing straight into the nation's rivers (Centre for Science and Environment). The report concludes that this is leading to a ticking health bomb in India. Weak or non-existent enforcement of environmental laws, rapid urban development and a lack of awareness about the dangers of sewage are all blamed for water pollution. A 2011 survey by the Central Pollution Control Board revealed only 160 out of nearly 8,000 towns had both sewerage systems and a sewage treatment plant.

India's growth has been very impressive, and India has often been quoted as a development success story since liberalisation, and although it has brought millions out of poverty it has not been wholly inclusive. Inequality affects India in all dimensions, including religion, caste, gender and wealth and needs to be addressed. Income inequality is relatively low compared to other countries with a Gini coefficient in India of 33.9 compared to 41 in the USA and 45 in China. Still despite massive reductions 21.9% of the population live below the poverty line, although this figure itself varies massively by state. Poorer states in India have poverty rates of 3-4 times that of more developed states. GDP per Capita averages at around $1500 although in Uttar radish it is around $450 and in Bihar around only $300

Gender discrimination continues to be an enormous problem within Indian society. Traditional patriarchal norms have relegated women to secondary status within the household and workplace. This drastically affects women's health, financial status, education, and political involvement. Women are commonly married young, quickly become mothers, and are then burdened by stringent domestic and financial responsibilities. They are frequently malnourished since women typically are the last member of a household to eat and the last to receive medical attention. Women receive little schooling, and suffer from unfair and biased inheritance and divorce laws. These laws prevent women from accumulating substantial financial assets, making it difficult for women to establish their own security and autonomy. Gender inequality is one of the largest issues currently in India hindering it becoming a green economy. A UNDP report in 2012 found that when the HDI is adjusted for gender inequality is becomes the lowest in South Asia, even lower than Afghanistan. A 2012 report on Gender

Equality by the World Bank found Indian women earn $0.64 for every $1 earned by their male counterparts. As stated above, young women die at very high rates due to gender preferences. Another issue in India is FGM. Another issue in India is missing women. Infanticide and abortions occur due to gender bias to sons. This bias occurs for several reasons ranging from son prestige, sons are more economically useful and due to dowries. In 2001, for every 1,000 males living in Rajasthan there were only 922 women (Marthur et. al., 2004). Estimates by the World Bank report writers based on Demographic and Health Surveys suggest 15% of Indian women think it is acceptable for a husband to beat his wife if she refuses to have sex with him, 20% if she burns food and 30% if she argues with him. Gender equality is recognised as key to sustainable development. Female education and empowerment can reduce fertility rates bringing the Indian population down to a more sustainable level. In addition empowered females are more able to work and to demand paid work and so this can reduce poverty levels. It will also reduce malnourishment as sons are better fed than girls meaning many young women die from malnourishment. However in a more equal society both boys and girls ill have value to the family.

These issues can be seen in a low HDI index of 0.554 which is 136th. Using the new Multi-dimensional Poverty Index India's poverty rate is 54%, higher than in Bangladesh.

A massive wage of urbanisation is surging across India as about 10 million a year are moving to urban areas every year. Massive investments will be needed to create the jobs, housing and infrastructure to meet the soaring aspirations and make towns and cities and liveable and green. These investments also need to take place to develop infrastructure to develop a green future. One in 3 rural people lack access to an all-weather road. Ports and airports have inadequate capacity and trains move slowly and are oversubscribed. An estimated 300 million people are not connected to the national grid. Currently only 5% of electricity is created using renewable energy (excluding hydroelectric) and 12% from hydroelectric whereas 79% comes from oil, coal and gas. Currently there is a chronic lack of energy leading to shortages. However India has huge potential for developing sustainable energy. It is blessed with 5000 TWh of solar insolation every year. (Darshan Goswami). Solar energy is even more relevant for rural areas where there are still 289 million without access to reliable energy. A partnership with the UK is on the cards to help India realise India's potential. India is aiming to massively expand its nuclear power capacities. There are currently twenty one operational nuclear power reactors in India, across six states. They contribute less than three per cent of the country's total energy generation, but 7 are more are currently under construction (Greenpeace India). It aims to supply 25% of electricity from nuclear power by 2050. Although many see nuclear as a clean source of power there are issues that India need to address. There is currently no radioactive waste disposal treatment in India and with the huge expansion planned this could lead to serious environmental issues if not addressed.

These massive investments could be provided by finance form the New Development Bank. This new bank was set up by the BRICS in 2014 to counter the influence of Western multilateral development organisations such as the World Bank and the IMF. The bank will be able to lend up to $34 billion annually and the primary focus of this will be infrastructure projects. Another source of optimism for these investments is the Wold Bank. They have offered an $18 billion dollar loan to India over the next 3 years. The World Bank Group's Country Partnership Strategy (2013-17) focuses on three areas key to India's goal of faster, sustainable and more inclusive growth: economic integration, rural-urban transformation, and inclusion. Increasingly, The World Bank Group focus is on engagement in India's low-income states, where income per capita is low, poverty is widespread, and development indicators are comparable to those in the least-developed countries in the world.

The incredible growth over the last 6 decades has not come without its costs. Environmental issues are still a big threat to the sustainability of the Indian Economy. CO_2 emissions (metric tons per capita) is 1.666. Although this figure is low compared to America (around 20) and the UK (around 10) there is a risk that as India develops this number will increase dramatically. Therefore it is important that India develops sustainably. A World Bank report in 2013 found that the annual cost of environmental degradation in India amounts to about 5.7% of Indian GDP. In particular the burning of fossil fuels has negative consequences of up to 3% of GDP for health problems alone never mind issues due to lack of access to clean water supply, sanitation and hygiene and natural resources depletion. About 23% of child mortality can be attributed to environmental degradation according to the report. However a 30% reduction in particulate emissions will cost $97 billion whereas the benefits could be as high as $105 billion.

In addition although the Green Revolution was an economic success and has resulted in far fewer famines its environmental impacts have been quite negative. The increasing use of agrochemical-based pest and weed control in some crops has affected the surrounding environment as well as human health. Many pesticides used in India have been banned elsewhere in the world. Increase in the area under irrigation has led to rise in the salinity of the land. Although the many benefits of GM crops it also led to a large reduction to genetic diversity. Ground water levels in various parts of India are declining as the country cannot adequately recharge aquifers in deficit areas where it has been used for irrigation, industries and drinking water needs of the growing population over the years. The Central Ground Water Board found that around 56% of the wells, which are analysed to keep a tab on ground water level, showed decline in its level in 2013. These issues mean that the Green Revolution is not 'green' at all and is in fact very damaging to the environment.

Home to 89,000 species of animals, 46,000 species of plants and nearly half the world's aquatic plants, India's management of its natural resources has regional and global significance. However with half of country's land already under cultivation, rising population and the threat of climate change, protection of diverse habitats poses a formidable challenge. However the UNDP have set up several projects to hep India protect its natural ecosystem.

Climate change will have a huge effect on India. After Bangladesh, India is the most distressed country in the world accounting for 1/5 of global deaths. 40 million hectares of India is vulnerable to flooding. Global warming is leading to wetter wet seasons and dryer dry seasons leading to oscillations between flooding and droughts in the country. Of the total agricultural land in India, about 68% is prone to drought of which 33% is chronically drought prone, receiving rainfall of less than 750mm per year. This is particularly in the states of Maharashtra, Gujarat, Rajasthan, Karnataka, Andhra Pradesh and Orissa.(Climate Emergency Institute) . As a result of global warming, the average number of Category 4 and 5 hurricanes per year has increased over the past 30 years. India has an 800 km coastline, and is therefore very susceptible to cyclonic activity. This is a serious threat as the long coast line of India is very densely populated. A one meter sea level rise is projected to displace approximately 7.1 million people in India and about 5,764 Km2 of land area will be lost, along with 4200 Km of road. Around seven million people are projected to be displaced due to submersion of parts of Mumbai and Chennai if global temperatures were to rise by a mere 2 °C.

India along with the other BRIC economies have been the economic successes of the 21st century. However in India this growth has to become much more inclusive so that it benefits those at the very bottom of society. India is now at a juncture in its development. Although it still faces many challenges it has a potential to become one of the economic superpowers in the world. It has a large supply of skilled labour and the capacity for renewable energy to dominate the energy sector. If India can continue to grow and share the benefits it will change the lives of millions for the better and have a worldwide impact. However if India does not face and overcome the challenges it currently faces than this could have repercussions globally. As the economy grows and people get richer there demand for energy will increase. If this is not met by renewable sources then the potential damages to the climate will be huge. Similarly India has to reduce its environmental degradation if it wants to achieve growth in the long run. Otherwise the even larger generations in the future will struggle to achieve an acceptable standard of living and India may again be faced with famines like the Bengal famine of 1943.

Let us all work together to make changes and to help direct India onto a sustainable development path that will lead to inclusive growth to bring millions out of poverty without damaging the environment for future generations of Indians.

Bibliography

- World Bank Data http://data.worldbank.org/country/india

- I.Dutta Gandhian 'Green Paradigm: A New Vision for Sustainable Development' The Greening of the Indian Subcontinent (2014)

- N.West 'Application of Green Economics in Business and Rural India: methods and tools' The Greening of the India Subcontinent
- Grant Thornton Dynamism Index 2014 https://www.globaldynamismindex.com/gdi.html

- Unicef 'The Infant and Child Mortality India Report' 2012 http://www.unicef.org/india/Report.pdf

- Editorial team 'Child Mortality in India' New York Times (2013)

- Wateraid India http://www.wateraid.org/uk/where-we-work/page/india

- Kaushik Basu Interview with BBC (2014) http://www.bbc.co.uk/news/world-asia-india-25742983

- WHO/UNICEF joint monitoring report 2012 'Progress on Drinking Water and Sanitation' http://www.unicef.org/media/files/JMPreport2012.pdf

- Centre for Science and Environment 'Excreta Matters' (2012)

- Central Pollution Control Board 'Status of Water Quality in India' (2011) http://cpcb.nic.in/upload/NewItems/NewItem_193_WaterQuality2011.pdf

- Climate Emergency Institute (2012) 'Global Warming and its Impact of Climate on   India http://www.climateemergencyinstitute.com/uploads/GLOBAL_WARMING_AND_ITS_IMPACTS_ON_CLIMATE_OF_INDIA.pdf

- Indian   Ministry   of   Statistics http://mospi.nic.in/mospi_new/site/India_Statistics.aspx

- Forbes List of Billionaires (2014)http://www.forbes.com/billionaires/

- Forbes Global 2000 list (2014) http://www.forbes.com/global2000/list/

Part 2: Economics and Finance in India

2.1 Ecology Pricing & Ecology Cess

By Dr. Natalie West Kharkongor, IIM Shillong, India

Introduction

In a world where money talks, it would follow that putting a monetary value on environmental impacts (externalities) would rule the day. This would apply even to land conservation, water use and not only to carbon emission. The main factor behind the pile of junk in the roadside is: it has no assigned monetary value, and hence carries no price. Mawlynnong (cleanest village in Asia) has no monetary value in spite of its high ecological utility, and hence has no price. Apparently, the damage caused to the ecology, and the value added to the ecology is not compensated due to the non – measurability of the ecological value eroded and the ecological value added. Intuitively, pricing of an ecological activity is the need of the hour.

Greenhouse gas emission has no tangible value but companies today are trying to fix a price on carbon for accounting purpose as well as for sustainability reporting. A 2013 Report by CDP reveals that around 29 companies have fixed an internal price on their carbon pollution1. Most companies use internal carbon pricing to fund energy efficiency, water conservation and other investments in sustainable resource management. Carbon emission is not the only activity which pollutes the air; there are a number, like coal and limestone mining, stone and sand quarry, deforestation, buildings and construction, industrial activity, and the like. Hence, a price has to be fixed on any ecological devaluation caused by these activities: the accumulated amount can be utilized as incentives and remuneration for any value added to the ecology.

Ecology Pricing

To correct the imbalance ecological system, the intervention of the Government is of utmost importance. The Government can come up with a concept of Ecology Pricing to reward the ones who add utility to the ecology; and impose a fee on those who devalue the ecology. The ecology pricing is in itself an ecological balancing tool. A policy incorporating ecological pricing needs to be set in place. It is one of the ways to correct the present imbalanced ecology, and if the government realizes its importance, it can work with specialized institutes for its implementation. A time will come that we will have a price tag for the clean air we breathe (an estimated 7 million people died due to air pollution globally in 2012.

Valuation of Ecosystems

Valuation of ecosystem had been done by orthodox environmental economists based on ecological value equivalent to ecological yield. Hence, exchange value or price associated with ecosystems depends on the ability of a system to produce yields that are exchangeable in markets. Robert Costanza in the 1990s, has claimed that the combined value of the ecosystems of the Earth was worth more (US\$33T) each year; more than the whole human exchange economy (US\$25T) at that time (1995), which is rather strange for an exchange value. Other studies have focused on the marginal value of ecosystem changes, as advocated in orthodox economic cost-benefit analysis. In Natural Capitalism, 1999, Paul Hawken, Amory Lovins and Hunter Lovins also advanced an argument to assign a value to the planet Earth in current currency3. Ecocide is thought by some green economists to be accelerated by debt instruments which demand a yield greater than the ecological capacity to renew4. The term ecocide refers to any extensive damage or destruction of the natural landscape and disruption or loss of ecosystem(s) of a given territory to such an extent that the survival of the inhabitants of that territory is endangered. Ecocide can be irreversible when an ecosystem suffers beyond repair.

Ecosystem Valuation Methods

Ecological valuation which been considered as an ignored part of economics currently appears to be significant as dependence of humankind on nature increases day by day. In the article on Economic and ecological concepts for valuing ecosystem services, the three authors, Stephen C. Farber, Robert Constanza and Matthew A. Wilson6 mentioned about six major ecosystem service economic valuation techniques viz. Avoided Cost, Replacement Cost, Factor Income, Travel cost, Hedonic Pricing, and Contingent Value. Yung En Chee in his article An ecological perspective on the valuation of ecosystem services mentioned three methods of economic valuation, viz. Production Function Analysis, Travel Cost Method, and Contingent Valuation7. The Dollar – based Ecosystem Valuation Method8 describe methods to estimate dollar measures of economic values associated with ecosystems. The methods are: Market Price Method, Productivity Method, Hedonic Pricing Method, Travel Cost Method, Damage Cost Avoided, Replacement Cost and Substitute Cost Methods, Contingent Valuation Method, Contingent choice Method, and Benefit Transfer Method.

Limitations of Ecosystem Valuation Methods

Ecosystem is a complex system. Hence, it is difficult to measure the ecosystem and to assign a specific monetary value to ecology. First, many ecosystem services are not feasible to valuation by the available techniques mainly because the value of the services is highly volatile in nature. Secondly, most of the ecosystem valuation methods are profit – driven. Thirdly, most of the results of ecological valuation can be interpreted only by experts. Last, but not the least, traditional techniques tend to ignore certain important socio – economic factors. Taking these limitations into consideration, economic valuation of the ecology should go beyond the domain of economics and to incorporate other fields of chapter.

Ecology Cess

In the absence of a precise and accurate ecology valuation tool, Ecology Cess can act as the best method to compensate the damage caused to the ecology. Ecology Cess of 1% can be imposed on all goods and services as consumers (individuals) directly or indirectly devalues the ecology. The main objective behind is to raise revenue for the government to compensate the loss caused to the ecology, and to pay incentives to all those who add value to the ecology. Exemption to the Cess can be set in place as deemed fit. Ecology Cess is similar to Education Cess imposed in India. The difference is: the former will be imposed on goods and services, whereas the latter is imposed both on income and excisable goods The governments can enforce it by enacting a specific legislation for the implementation of the same after taking into consideration the inputs of all the stakeholders. Important point to be noted here is: the purpose of the cess has to be served (ecological enrichment and ecological balancing)

References:

1. http://www.ghgprotocol.org/files/ghgp/CDP%20Press%20coverage%20Price%20on%20Carbon%20Report.pdf
2. http://www.who.int/mediacentre/news/releases/2014/air-pollution/en/
3. http://en.wikipedia.org/wiki/Ecosystem_valuation
4. http://en.wikipedia.org/wiki/Ecological_yield
5. http://en.wikipedia.org/wiki/Ecocide
6. http://www.pdx.edu/sites/www.pdx.edu.sustainability/files/Farber_et_al.pdf
7. http://www.epa.gov/nheerl/arm/streameco/docs/Chee2004.pdf
8. http://www.ecosystemvaluation.org/dollar_based.htm

Photos: Dr. Natalie West Kharkongor

2.2 Mawlynnong, the cleanest village in Asia

By Prof. Dr Natalie West Kharkongor and Bremley Wanbantei Lyngdoh

In the land of the abode of clouds, in a silent and peaceful corner of the earth, Mawlynnong has emerged as a model of a perfect village and has earned the reputation and a unique distinction of cleanest village in Asia. The accreditation has been given by the travel experts of Discovery India. Mawlynnong is in the state of Meghalaya, along the Indo – Bangladesh border. It is ninety kilometers from Shillong; the capital of the State. The Village has been there for hundred years. It has been a combined effort of the people of this village to make Mawlynnong a sustainable place to live in.

The inhabitants have cherishly and voluntarily enrolled themselves as key players in cleaning and performing civic duties. They regularly perform activities like sweeping the roads and lanes, watering the plants in public area and cleaning the drains. Rains do not deter the inhabitants to get up early in the morning in cleaning the Village. It is a process that is repeated several times a day. The villagers have grown flowers and plants which makes Mawlynnong a beautiful place. Every piece of litter and almost every leaf that has fallen from a tree are immediately discarded. Plastic bags are completely banned and all waste disposals are environmentally friendly. The Village use hand – made dustbins made from bamboo canes which is kept at nodal points. Everyone makes it a point that dirt and waste are not thrown anywhere but kept in dustbins. The wastes collected in these bins are then kept in a pit, which people use it as manure. The locals have grown flowers and plants around their houses, which add to the beauty of their tiny cottages. The houses are connected by cemented pathways. Each house has something beautiful to present. Walking through the village is like walking through a park, with beautiful flowers on both sides of the path. The Village offers many interesting sights such as the living Root Bridge and another strange natural phenomenon of a boulder balancing on a rock. Waterfalls and trees with orchids falling out of their branches add to the beauty of the Village.

The Village has a Village Council to supervise the activities of the Village. It hired some cleaners in maintaining the cleanliness of the Village. Yet, the villagers take turns to make sure that the roads are swept several times a day. The Village Council imposed a fine on anybody found dirtying the place and cutting the trees. It is a nominal fine of just rupees fifty. But, due to humiliation and embarrassment, people make sure they follow the rules. The Village Council or Durbar maintains strict discipline. It carries out inspection of the sanitation facilities in each house. Workshops are also recognized from time to time to make people aware of the dangers of global warming.

The Village is popular not just for cleanliness but also for its hundred percent literacy rate. Lessons in hygiene are taught in the early class of schooling, so that children can learn from an early age how to keep their surroundings clean and green. All its residents can read and write. The Village has a computer school with computers, sponsored by Rotary Club and NEC. The villagers spread the message of conservation and protection of forests. The locals plant trees from May to June, to ensure that the virgin forest is kept intact. The inhabitants are also healthy, educated and environment conscious. The traditional khasi food is served in the Village. The Village has plenty of fresh veggies and the food is always cooked and served fresh. The people are warm and welcoming, and the kids greet the tourists with their cutest smile.

The Village has eighty houses with eight members per house on an average. The main occupation of the people is agriculture growing bay leaves, arcenut, oranges, broomstick and others. The entire Village gets employment including fifty years and above. The number of Indian visitors per month stood at around two thousand and the number of foreign visitors at around twenty to twenty five. The net profit collected by the Village comes to about seventy thousand per month during peak season, and thirty to thirty five thousand during off season. At present, Village has two quest rooms accommodating around ten persons, and three houses as paying quests accommodating three persons per house. The Village has two restaurants. The inns are made of bamboos and thatch and are hospitable and restful.

Inspired for the success story of Mawlynnnong Village the Government of Meghalaya launched a 'Clean and Green' Village Award on July 2013 in all 39 blocks in the state to replicate the "Mawlynnong Model" by promoting sanitation and hygiene through community involvement and partly to promote tourism. The Community & Rural Development Department which is responsible for this project had designed the award to trigger a sense of competition and community action towards cleaner and greener villages in the state.

Under this scheme, cash prizes have been awarded to 56 villages which have been judged as the best based on certain criteria in each of the 39 CRD blocks. The communities in turn have to act on parameters such as full recovery of solid and sanitation, maintenance of common areas and forests. The concept behind the awards is mainly to minimize leakages of sewages and effluents to water bodies and catchment areas and also to encourage best practices in the health and sanitation, environment sectors as well as village management. The category of villages was decided on the provincial census 2011 and the 56 selected villages has been asked to submit a felt need project proposal ranging from Rs 5 to 15 lakhs respectively as per the population and project size.

The Project was initiated by the Meghalaya Tourism Development Corporation, the Durbar, the Bethany Society and Mr. D.D. Laloo. Mawlynnong's fame is drawing huge number of domestic as well as foreign tourists. The lifestyle of the people is a source of inspiration and a role model for all those who want to follow responsible living and clean environment. Cities and villages of today should learn a few lessons from this perfect model in spreading the gospel of sustainable environment.

References:

1. Mohit Joshi, Article on "Mawlynnong Village", 02, October, 2009

2. Saidul Khan, Article on " Mawlynnong Village", 05, June, 2008

3. BBC News, 25th, September 2009

4. Community and Rural Development, Govt. of Meghalaya

5. www.google.co.in

Photo Dr Natalie West Kharkongor: Living roots bridge

2.3 Greening of the Economy: The Indian Perspective

By Kanupriya Bhagat

As the world faces grave economic, social and environmental challenges, Green Economy is widely promoted as the solution to such problems. "Green Economics is one of the fastest growing global movements for change, which has been taken up by many governments and NGOs and is having a huge influence on the worldwide social and economic landscape. It seeks to reform the very concept of economics itself by creating an entirely new discipline which is designed to help all people everywhere, prevent poverty as a given assumption, consider other species, nature and the planet and its systems".

Not only does it prove to be beneficial for the environment, but also holds the power to provide businesses with a "win-win" situation, cutting down on the cost, while simultaneously giving them a competitive edge over their competitors. Two major components of Green Economy are resource and energy efficiencies, which to a certain extent forces us to "rethink how we build our communities, move people and goods around, provide energy and use scarce resources" (Weaver& Michael 2011).

The definition of a "Green Economy" is very subjective to ones perspective. For some "green" could mean using more energy efficient technology, while for the other going "green" may simply mean cutting carbon emissions by any means necessary. Every industry has a different outlook towards "going green" and it is simply impossible to pin point exactly what a "Green Economy" comprises of. However, for the sake of this Chapter, I will use the definition developed by UNEP, which states, "Green economy is one that results in improved human well-being and social equity, while significantly reducing environmental risks and ecological scarcities. In its simplest expression, a green economy can be thought of as one which is low carbon, resource efficient and socially inclusive". Moreover, it also suggests "a green economy is one whose growth in income and employment is driven by public and private investments that reduce carbon emissions and pollution, enhance energy and resource efficiency, and prevent the loss of biodiversity and ecosystem services. These investments need to be catalyzed and supported by targeted public expenditure, policy reforms and regulation changes. This development path should maintain, enhance and, where necessary, rebuild natural capital as a critical economic asset and source of public benefits, especially for poor people whose livelihoods and security depend strongly on nature". Another approach towards looking at Green Economics is that of a holistic approach that brings core drivers of economics such as ecology, equity, social and environmental justice together.

In the recent times, India is being looked as a center for research and development due to its innovation in technology, traditional knowledge, cheap manufacturing, labor power and processes. Moreover, after investing over $10 billion to green energy in the year 2011, India has become largest investor towards green technology amongst all major economies. Additionally, with India being the worlds largest democracy and with the growing concerns about the population, poverty, unemployment, waste, pollution, economy and climate change etc. it is highly significant it takes certain steps to ensure a secure future. If India invests now towards the potential of its green economy, not only will it promote a sustainable and clearer environment, but also the economy will see a generation of thousands of jobs. As India already on path of growth, yet to invest in infrastructure and public services, it is a perfect time to change its direction; if they choose to incorporate environmental and social sustainability in their business practices. Even though their initially cost will be higher but they will sustain their business in the long run as it is inevitable giving them a competitive advantage in the short run.

Furthermore, "Climate Disclosure Project says that the business as usual scenario on climate change shows that by 2100 India's GDP growth will be around negative 9-13% due to the impacts of climate change affecting business, livelihood and hence the economy". While, 2100 is very far away and it is highly unlikely that the business practices will remain as usual but this is not the path India should be taking. A change sooner than later will add to the benefits of a Green Economy. Plus, the growing concern about the environment in the media has made consumers more aware about corporates and their purchases reflect their choices. Similarly, investors and venture capitals are also becoming conscious of their future and are avoiding financial and business risks associated with carbon and environmentally unfriendly practices.

Along with the rapidly growing economy, Indian business owners are also getting involved with Multinational Corporation and business beyond borders. In a very short span of time the involvement of business owners in the International market is rapidly increasing, making it absolutely essential for them to abide by the global climate agreement that will put a price on carbon that will effect business worldwide, including India. With international agencies involved such as the World Bank and United Nations, it posses both as a threat and opportunity for the Indian Economy. For business that start accounting for their activities will have a competitive edge and positive recognition in the international market, while businesses that carry forward as usual will eventually loose the battle to the more innovative with their reputation as a price to pay.

On the other hand, to achieve this idea of green economy, India first needs to tackle many issues coming its way. First of which are deprivation levels, that are constantly increasing, raising many questions over the kind of paradigm being followed by the government. UNEP believes the biggest concern amongst that includes food, energy, water and other essential goods and services to its growing population. Besides, the number of people who lacked access to electricity and clean cooking technologies in India was 404 million and 855 million respectively in 2009 (IEA, 2010). Moreover, India still lags behind many other countries in terms of other measures of development. According to UNDP's Multidimensional Poverty Index (MPI), 53.7% of India's population is poor (UNDP, 2011) making it very difficult for India to invest in green technology when the basic needs for human survival is not met.

Furthermore, with the growing manufacturing sector, increasing mining, expanding infrastructure and increasing power production, along with increasing responsibility to be "greener", India is in a very tough spot "where its emissions could explode upwards or it could move heavily down the 'green' route". Sadly, to add to the problem is the fact that this challenges seem to be getting worse everyday as the efforts to "achieve green growth is translating into a green versus growth issue".

Mc Kinsey & Company published a report in 2012 where they suggested India will grow at a vey fast pace for the 20 next years, where it could build 80% of its infrastructure and industrial capacity that will establish the India of 2030. The problem that lies here is the magnitude of development that will lead result in a tremendous increase of carbon emissions. India cannot afford to do that, specially now where there is an enormous amount of pressure for world communities to reduce carbon emissions. Therefore, the question that lies here is; should India give up developing its infrastructure and services for a better tomorrow of the public and compromise the environment or should it concentrate on the environment now and hope to develop the country in the process.

Elaborating on the growth v/s green debate, at the end of last year there was a disagreement between the Ministry of Environment and Forest and several representative form India Inc. as well as many union ministers on the green issues discouraging development in the country. Union ministers have constantly complaining that environmental laws and clearances are becoming an "weakness" and hampering the countries development, whereas, Ministry of Environment & Forest claims that they are just discharging the duty diligently of protecting the environment. Hence, at this crucial time when various ministers need to work together to achieve the bigger goal of nation's development while keeping the environmental concerns in mind, they seem to be going through the debate of growth v/s green which in turn is leading to indecisions and delays in projects. This is gone so far that a popular Indian

Magazine even went to the extent of calling Ms. Jayanthi Natarajan (Environmental Minister of India) a"Green Terrorist", "claiming that the outdated environmental laws and inflexible minister is turning out to be detrimental to the economic growth". On the other hand, Natarajan apparently also gave clearance to few projects, highly opposed by many environmental groups. For instance, the Lower Demwe hydro project in Arunachal Pradesh. That got clearance from the Environmental Minister, even though the construction of dam will involve deforestation of over 50,000 trees along with serious threat to the habitat of wild animals like the dolphin, the wild buffalo and the Bengal Florican.

Thus the pressure on the government to "do the right thing" is constantly building. They not only have the challenge of ensuring that the growing demands of people for commodities and energy are met without compromising the environment but the production to satisfy those demands also cannot be at the cost of the environment, Making it a very difficult task.

In conclusion, one step closer to solving the problem will be the joint effort of the ministry with the environmental groups, with either one or both groups compromising to a certain extent to get the work done. Specially, with over one billion people, four world religions and over 1500 languages across the country, it is a challenge to come to with a decision that satisfies everyone. During the recent turmoil over Uttarakhand disaster, where the death toll is likely to rise over 5000 due to floods and landslide on the River Ganges and her tributaries, "Environmentalists say the disaster in Uttarakhand was inevitable due to rampant construction, felling of trees and building of dams in the name of development". This river holds more than 505 dams that are a part of 244 hydroelectric projects, constant construction on mountain tops, mining and sewage disposal directly in the river has made it a man made disaster. With several lives still at stake and millions of rupees worth infrastructure already destroyed, maybe this will serve as a wake up call for the people and government of India to take actions promoting a greener economy. In the end, Green Economics has also been called "The Economics of Sharing" emphasizing the need of change in behaviour which will help sustain everything and everybody on a long term basis.

Bibliography:

Staff.N. (2013).*Uttarakhand tragedy: Death toll likely to cross 5000, heavy rain hampers rescue ops.*Available: https://www.niticentral.com/2013/06/24/uttarakhand-death-toll-may-cross-5000-heavy-rain-expected-to-hamper-rescue-ops-94248.html. Last accessed 25th June, 2013.

Varma.S. (2013).*Recipe for disaster in Uttarakhand: 1 crore population, 2.5 crore tourists.* Available: http://articles.timesofindia.indiatimes.com/2013-06-23/india/40146281_1_forest-land-land-revenue-land-use. Last accessed 25th June, 2013.

Aggarwal.M. (2013). *Uttarakhand floods: Deconstructing a disaster.*Available: http://www.dnaindia.com/india/1852688/report-uttarakhand-floods-deconstructing-a-disaster. Last accessed 25th June, 2013.

TERI. (2012). *India's Green Economy: Road map to an inclusive and equitable growth.* Available: http://www.teriin.org/upfiles/projects/ES/ES2011EM08.pdf. Last accessed 25th June, 2013.

Gupta. A. (2012). *Why India's green growth dream is turning into a nightmare.* Available: http://www.greeneconomycoalition.org/know-how/why-india%E2%80%99s-green-growth-dream-turning-nightmare. Last accessed 25th June, 2013.

UNEP. Available: http://www.unep.org/greeneconomy/AboutGEI/WhatisGEI/tabid/29784/language/en-US/Default.aspx. Last accessed 25th June, 2013.

Chabba.A. (2012). *"Green Economy" with respect to India.* Available: http://in.reset.org/blog/green-economy-respect-india. Last accessed 25th June, 2013.

UNEP. (2012). *Green Economy, a mantra for the modern world Read more at: http://indiatoday.intoday.in/story/green-economy-a-mantra-for-the-modern-world/1/199136.html.* Available: http://indiatoday.intoday.in/story/green-economy-a-mantra-for-the-modern-world/1/199136.html. Last accessed 25th June, 2013.

BBC. (2012). *India's boom in green technology business.* Available: http://www.bbc.co.uk/news/world-asia-india-18391116. Last accessed 25th June, 2013.

Green Economy India. (2007). *why a Green Economy.* Available: http://www.greeneconomyindia.com/why_green_economy.htm. Last accessed 25th June, 2013.

Weaver.S, Weaver.A. (2011). *Greening the Economy - A Discussion Chapter.* Available: http://www.globe-net.com/articles/2011/january/11/greening-the-economy-a-discussion-Chapter/. Last accessed 25th June, 2013

Green Economics Institute... Available: http://www.greeneconomics.org.uk/page0.html. Last accessed 27th June 2013.

Kennet, M. and Heinemann, V. (2006) 'Green Economics: setting the scene. Aims, context, and philosophical underpinning of the distinctive new solutions offered by Green Economics', Int. J. Green Economics, Vol. 1, Nos. 1/2, pp.68–102.

2.4 Enriching Greens: Unlocking Investment potential for Green Growth in India

By Jiya K. Shahani

1. Introduction

The world is on the threshold of change in nature protection, as impressive economic gains worldwide have been disguisedly accompanied by a decline in the natural capital, unprecedented level of soil erosion, and air and water pollution. They have put the planet on the edge of climate catastrophe. We have already entered the era of dangerous climate change facing environment emergency and there is a very narrow conduit of guiding the planet back to the safe-climate zone. Dealing with such an emergency demands huge investments. Under existing approaches, investment decisions are structured in a way that creates flaws. Global economic and climate crisis mandate the need for new forms of both dynamic and resilient solutions to complex global challenges, through innovative, multi-stakeholder approaches. They present unique opportunities for moving towards a greener future by creating real and durable assets that strengthen national and global economies. Moreover, the lessons learnt from recent crisis emphasize that the world of investment must adapt to the concept of sustainability, involving sustainable production, consumption as well as sustainable financial returns. Given the scarcity of public funds in India, liquidity issues are widespread. Besides, the risk aversion of Indian investors, and relatively small capitalization (compared to the large quantum and long duration funding needs) of various financial intermediaries entails adoption of innovative financial structures and revisiting some of the regulations governing Indian financial system.

A new approach is needed in investment domain, to fulfill the vision of India's potential that investors and multinationals predict, in cultivating the form of green investment that yields multifold benefits sustainably. Involvement of diverse stakeholders - foreign investors, governments, domestic investors and consumers can further catalyze the reforms needed to infuse sustainability in investment decisions. In such a scenario, financing with transparency and accountability may do more for India than would be obvious. Therefore, it is imperative to think multi-level regarding provision of adequate green investments that can guide the way to realize the full potential of the growth impulses surging through the developing economies. The role of investment banks will be crucial in formulating funding guidelines and policies for assessing the short-term and long-term impacts of the proposed projects, and also developing funds that can act as project securitizations of existing and upcoming green projects. In this regard, the chapter intends to provide a common point of reference to guide policy-makers, financial institutions and investors as they seek to better understand, and address, the global gap in green investment. It also aspires to impel planning and policy work to identify the existing green assets and partnership strengths for prioritizing green investments in India.

2. Drivers of Green investments

Environmental remediation requires providing adequate space to ecosystems for maintaining and creating landscape features, which guarantee that ecosystems continue to deliver services such as clean water, breathable air, productive soils and attractive recreational areas. It therefore supports economies and societies, and makes an essential contribution to natural mitigation of, and adaptation to climate change. To find manmade solutions to replace the services that nature offers for free is not only technically challenging, but also very expensive. Hence, it is essential to know what factors will be driving the demand for green infrastructure investment in coming years so that resources can be secured and targeted to their best effect. The drivers are mostly shaped by public policy, nationally and locally, which in turn influence investments by the private and independent sectors. The four key drivers demanding green investments include:

2.1 Greening growth and ecosystem restoration

Estimates of explosive population growth suggest that there will be an unprecedented rise in demand for energy, water, transport, urban development and agricultural infrastructure. Meeting this demand, while combating climate change and respecting planetary boundaries, will be challenging. Greening growth has the potential to alleviate the risks from future climate change and environmental degradation. A number of studies have underscored the larger gains to be made by expanding investments to enhance natural capital (Millennium Ecosystem Assessment 2005; TEEB, 2010). Improving the economic performance of local and regional economies in terms of production, consumption, tourism development, and overall 'place' branding requires attracting greater levels of green investments. In addition, emphasis is being placed on the need to create quality places, improve quality of life, and achieving a step change in business performance, all of which demand ecosystem restoration. Urban extensions promoting eco-living, delivering strategic urban renewal, supporting rural economic renaissance identify investing in green infrastructure as one of their critical success factors. Consequently, strategies pursuing ecosystem balance will claim significant share of future growth-led green infrastructure funding.

2.2 Climate change

Infrastructure connects goods to the markets, workers to industry, people to services, and the poor in rural areas to urban growth centers. Infrastructure lowers costs, enlarges markets, and facilitates trade. Until now, the economic role and significance of infrastructure was accorded precedence over its social, cultural, and environmental performance. Impacts of infrastructure on these aspects of well-being are equally important, and the positive contribution that well-designed infrastructure can make to improve other dimensions of sustainability is also vital. Nevertheless, increased investments must be underpinned by better policies and governance to ensure effectiveness and sustainability (Briceno-Garmendia et. al 2004). Therefore, future development policies are expected to demonstrate their effectiveness in adapting to inevitable changes in climate, which are already underway. Green growth has a particularly important role to play in helping to ameliorate climate extremes through momentous changes in land use practices. In addition, demand for green infrastructure projects to minimize greenhouse gas production, sequester carbon, and provide alternative fuel sources will also increase. It will come from both public agencies and private business entities seeking means of offsetting all or part of their carbon footprint. Such demands will increase substantially, when public policy instruments become more stringent with impacts of climate change becoming more damaging. It can therefore be assumed that green infrastructure interventions that offer direct and local climate change benefits will be targeted for public and private investments.

2.3 Health and well-being

Although life expectancy in the developing countries is improving, other local health indicators and lifestyle diseases like obesity, diabetes and cardiac disorders are alarming. Research identifies that local green spaces contribute positively towards improving physical and mental health as well as social wellbeing by reducing sickness and improving longevity. Other health benefits are also delivered through well planned and designed multi functional green infrastructure provisions. Consequently, global demand for environmental goods and services is rising, both from consumers and large businesses looking at "greening" their supply chains, resulting in growing and vibrant markets for sustainability-focused entrepreneurship. It is quite likely that the demand for green investments will also increase to meet health and well-being objectives, and that greater preventative public health funding will be made available for this purpose.

2.4 Biodiversity

Despite the rise of environmental awareness and popularity of nature conservation programs over past few decades, studies demonstrate the dramatic and worrying loss of biodiversity and deterioration of terrestrial and aquatic ecosystems. Public policy at every level underlines declining biodiversity as a major environmental challenge. There is a growing recognition that the traditional approach to protecting wildlife, through designating sites, is not enough to halt the loss of biodiversity or ensure that existing biodiversity remains viable into the future. Consequently, working at landscape scale by improving functional habitat networks, and enhancing the wider environment of rural and urban areas is essential. Environmental organizations also recommend investing in green transitions to specifically improve biodiversity. Hence, the future demand for green investment to secure biodiversity gain will increase, if new habitat banking or biodiversity offsetting mechanisms are introduced.

Each of these drivers presents increasing challenges that are stimulating the demand for financing arrangements of green transitions. While budget appropriations remain the major source of financing green transitions, drawing on well-functioning capital markets also carries significant potential. If low-cost debt (concessional finance) from Development Finance Institutions can provide debt at lower interest rates over a longer term compared with commercial bank loans, it will play a significant role in distributing long-term green finance, particularly in developing countries (Venugopal et. al 2012). Such a market scenario will provide signals to motivate and reward the sustainable use of capital for properly planned, financed and integrated, green solutions. It will a have implications for the way we pursue development. Since private sector plays a vital role in providing both intellectual and financial capital, active green financing solutions are required with the overall desire for better governance and a more attractive business climate for private investment.

3. Enticing Green Investors

Greening global growth requires investor confidence through strategic allocation of limited public resources. Conventional, business-as-usual investment trends are reducing economic resilience by locking in a carbon-intensive path that leads to costly environmental damage and huge adaptation costs in the long term (Stern 2006). Hence, de-carbonizing existing and planned infrastructure by means of changing future investment priorities and policies is must. It also requires withdrawing harmful government subsidies that induce unsustainable patterns of consumption and production in rich and developing countries alike. If non-green investments continue to grow along with green efforts, it will significantly dampen the benefits of green investments and cost the economy and society dearly, by impairing the ambitious national and global plans of achieving green growth objectives. As a result, governments are under increasing pressure to support growing populations in ways that are fiscally accountable, environmentally responsible, and socially enriching. Green growth offers a way to balance these needs by pursuing economic growth necessary for enhancing quality of life, while simultaneously minimizing pressure on the environment's limited carrying capacity (ESCAP, 2007). It does so, by improving eco-efficiency of infrastructure development. Eco-efficiency is often expressed as the creation of more value with fewer resources and less impact, or doing more with less (WBCSD, 2000). The recent awakening in the form of green infrastructure development demonstrates multiple benefits from deliberate re-planning for restoring and enhancing integrated natural systems. To secure its true benefits, there is a need to make ambitious choices on how best to prioritize investments to shape the health, wealth and identity of our future generations. Past experience of short-sighted financial practices has witnessed drying-up of investments, but what type of investment paradigm should emerge from these ashes? It is advocated that the environmental and social dimensions of investments must take their rightful place alongside financial returns. It is also important to stress that green investments are not anti-development but an efficient approach towards sustainable development. However, this approach requires significant reconfiguration of current and future investment, with further incremental costs. Given the current financial crisis, public resources are limited, and reliance on public-sector investment in the longer term must shrink to ensure sustainable green growth. This places private finance at the core of green transitions. Unlocking private finance can be challenging, since green technologies generally have real or perceived higher risks for a potential investor, when compared with conventional fossil-based investments having a track record of consistent returns. Unfamiliarity with technologies also plays a role, particularly in developing and emerging markets, where green growth needs are high. Green technologies often have higher capital costs and are not commercially viable during the earlier stages of development, which can further deter investors. Institutional inertia, first-mover disadvantages, and resistance to change are other barriers to green investments. Therefore, it is the responsibility of policy makers to justify and fill the incremental cost gap between conventional and green investments. By using a range of proven instruments and mechanisms, and improving the risk-reward calculus, government action can attract adequate private investments. Taxonomy of public mechanisms and instruments, which could entice green investors include:

- *Public Support Mechanisms*
  - Overarching policy support through national legislation e.g. Feed-in tariffs, Tax credits, Quotas, Repealing support from 'brown' sectors
  - Project level assistance e.g. Grants, Subsidies

- *Public Financing Instruments*
  - Lending (debt) e.g. Project lending, Debt funds, Bonds, Concessional/Flexible loan terms
  - Equity Instrument e.g. Direct Capital Investment
  - De-risking Instruments e.g. Loan guarantees, Insurance, Foreign exchange/liquidity facilities

These mechanisms on public policy front, and instruments on public finance front, have the strong potential to reduce risk, lower cost of capital, provide incentives to green investors, and achieve substantial leverage. Global Network on Energy for Sustainable Development suggests that clearly set government targets are fundamental for bolstering confidence among private investors seeking to develop green projects. Thus, we need both green technology and natural solutions along with economic aspirations in our infrastructure toolbox. This makes green infrastructure, an emerging new asset class, which should be music to the ears of global investors.

4. Greening India's Investment potential

Indian market is reshaping the world economy by offering rich business opportunities and strong foundations for growth. It is among the most attractive business destinations with the available large manpower base, diversified natural resources and comparatively strong macroeconomic fundamentals. India has become a trillion dollar economy with a self-sufficient agricultural sector, a varied industrial base and a well-established financial and services sector. There are several sectors that offer lucrative business opportunities in India. Indian markets have significant potential and a favorable regulatory regime for foreign investors, according to a survey titled World Investment Prospects Survey 2012-2014 by UNCTAD. India aspires to shape its economy to the twenty first century needs of its citizens, who rightly demand equal opportunities for development. Delivering such inclusive development in a sustainable way requires improving governance, adopting green growth model to restrict resource exploitation, and re-evaluating investment priorities. Private financing will be critical in the shift towards an economic model that results in greener growth in developing countries (BIAC 2012). However, incentives for this private financing will only emerge if a sound, coherent and predictable investment framework is in place. The Government of India has undertaken several policy initiatives to garner investments in the Indian energy sector. Consequently, the power sector has witnessed a surge of higher investment flows than envisaged. In 2012, India retained its position in top five world wind energy markets. The Ministry of Power has set a target for adding 76,000 MW of electricity capacity in the 12th Plan (2012-17) and 93,000 MW in the 13th Plan (2017-22). Some of the major investments towards greeing the Indian energy sector include:

- National Aluminium Company Ltd (Nalco) has set up its second wind power plant in Jaisalmer, Rajasthan with a capacity of 47.6 MW. The Rs 283 crore wind power project is being executed through Gamesa Wind Turbines Private Ltd
- Jakson Power Solutions is setting up the 80 kilowatt peak (KWp) solar rooftop unit with a facility of battery back-up at Bengaluru. It has also won order for installing solar rooftop systems at Pune
- Vikram Solar plans to put up a 10 MW power plant at Tamil Nadu (TN) under the second phase of the state's solar policy
- Mytrah Energy Ltd plans to acquire 59.75 MW of existing operational wind power assets in Tamil Nadu (TN) and Maharashtra. The company expects to have a capacity of 370 MW against previously anticipated 334 MW

Despite signs of increasing private finance into clean energy and other green investments, there remains a considerable shortfall in investment. Closing this gap is our collective task, where failure is not an option. India, being capital-scarce country, government's contributions to closing the gap will depend on the efficiency of public investments. An investment is efficient in allocating resources if it delivers the highest ratio of benefits to costs compared to other alternatives (Chan et. al 2009).The efficiency is also determined by its effectiveness in mobilizing private finance. Moreover, global economic and climate crisis mandate the need for new forms of both dynamic and resilient solutions to complex global challenges, using innovative, multi-stakeholder approaches. Driving greater investment in green growth by unlocking potential sources of finance is the DNA of such approaches. The thirteenth Finance Commission (FC-XIII) of India adopted one such approach for achieving a greener and more inclusive growth path. The commission recognized the need for a fiscally strong centre, fiscally strong states and fiscally strong local bodies, or the third tier of government. It proposed the strategy of 'expansionary fiscal consolidation', assuming that such a fiscal strategy will provide more encouraging environment for increasing both public and private investments, as well as for better handling of adverse economic shocks. The commission has recommended three grants under Environment category of Rs. 5000crore each, for forest, renewable energy and water sectors. The commission has also recommended grants to incentivize state and local governments to demonstrably improve outcomes, which are vital for achieving the ultimate sustainability goals. The Government has accepted these recommendations, realizing that the incremental costs of greening growth are insignificant compared to the costs of inaction. By investing in green growth measures, it foresees a virtuous cycle of improvements in governance, in every sphere of public activity. Furthermore, Indian governments, led by both major political parties at the federal and state levels, have consistently implemented pro-business reforms in capital-starved sectors. Driven by a historical scarcity of capital, Indian entrepreneurs have learned to be capital efficient, wherein each rupee has to go a long way for its business entity. Thus, Indian companies generate better return-on-equity (ROE) than their international peers, as shown in Table 1:

Table 1: Industry-wise comparison of ROE

INDUSTRY	US	CHINA	INDIA
Basic materials	5.4%	6.0%	16.0%
Healthcare	13.8%	13.3%	11.9%
Information Technology	12.8%	10.5%	22.0%
Industrials	8.7%	8.7%	14.6%
Banking and Financial services	-3.0%	16.3%	14.7%
Telecom	7.5%	6.0%	14.6%
Utilities	10.5%	6.3%	10.7%
Consumer goods	16.0%	11.6%	9.9%

Source: Bessemer venture partners, October 2010

In three out of eight sectors, India has managed to achieve relatively high capital efficiency. However, in consumer goods domain, its performance is inadequate. To improve its performance and address the global issue of ecological starvation, India should also learn to be eco-efficient. For this, eco-efficiency should be the focus of consumption patterns to maintain ecological-economic balance. As India continues on its rapid-growth path, large investment sectors offer significant opportunities for savvy investors, having potential to turbo-charge this growth. Thus, Indian business landscape is ripe for foreign investment with key advantages in terms of large market opportunity, high capital-efficiency, supportive regulatory environment, and entrepreneurial management skills. As it modernizes and deregulates, green infrastructure development, diligent domestic consumption, and financial services emerge as the most attractive sectors for investment in India. Lured by India's fast-growing economy and its improving regulatory environment, private-equity investors are now interested in funding Indian companies. This provides a great opportunity to India for greening of its consumption patterns, so that the mix of average Indian's consumption basket comprises greener products and services obtained through greener retail formats and modified channels. However, green investments are overwhelmingly preferred from a societal perspective, but in the real world, several odds are stacked against them. India's largest companies are mostly run by professional managers with shareholders as their primary stakeholders. Hence, the government is unable to direct its banks to provide loans to strategic industries that are not economically viable. This is distressing, because when all the required measures are in place, financial barriers are apparently limiting the march of green economy. To address that, a performance system akin to stock market system is proposed for corporations, based on their investment in green infrastructure, their carbon footprint or the lack thereof, in addition to their financial performance. The system aims to develop a decisive factor for providing finances to Green Enterprises at different development stages as per their rating. It will also aid policy-makers in building infrastructure projects that are both environmentally sustainable and economically feasible, resulting in low-carbon high quality infrastructure provisions. The system would also provide a focal point for marketing of new and existing green products and services.

5. Enriching Greens – The Proposition

The ecosystem coherence is being increasingly threatened, due to unwisely planned gray infrastructure development. To avoid that, we must concentrate our resources towards greening of ventures. Since resources are limited, targeted sustainable outcomes can be achieved when our efforts are measured, monitored, and appropriately responded. Therefore, it is important to develop a "toolbox" of innovative financing solutions that offer aid to developers adopting green solutions. While performance measurement is important, prevalent practices are inadequate, since aspects of environmental stewardship and sensitivity to long-term project impacts are not included. To fully embrace sustainability, quantitative measures are required to be developed for qualitative aspects of performance. Greening the performance will be neither quick nor smooth, because transitioning existing and new systems to support greener communities will require different policies and financing arrangements for innovative technologies. Although, new technologies most often entail greater upfront costs, sustainability takes a long term and broader view of costs, where higher initial costs are mitigated by reduced maintenance costs. But, current practices reveal that there is inadequate financial support to meet the needs of green enterprises at different development stages. Various financing instruments can support a variety of green transitions, and provide interesting opportunities for investments, but getting the right formulas is a major concern.

To this effect, establishment of Green Stock Exchange (GSE) is proposed to respond to the increasing appetite for direct green investments. The exchange is based on the capital market finance approach to track and compare the non-financial performance of project investments, reduce prohibitive transaction costs for investors, increase efficiency and impact with which investment capital is deployed, and attract more capital to the sector. The intention of the exchange is to increase liquidity in the market for green investment, by opening new avenues for raising capital, through share and bond issues, and for equity investors in social enterprises to disinvest when they need to. In order to raise capital for green projects, governments, multi-national banks or corporations can issue green bonds. These bonds have significant potential as a means to access deep pools of relatively low-cost capital held by institutional and other investors. Project bonds can also be issued to recycle limited quantities of capital through refinancing projects. The exchange will provide real, inexpensive solutions to reducing 'Green Poverty'. It will raise environmental and social standards among listed companies, thus increasing transparency and investor confidence, as well as providing a focal point for the marketing of new and existing ethical products. However, there is an apprehension regarding the right balance between the need for a flexible, genuine exchange and the need to protect the exchange from exploitation for private benefit through speculation. Other issues that could influence its effectiveness include management, oversight, ownership and financing of the exchange, as well as pricing mechanisms.

The rating of companies on the proposed exchange will be influenced by their environmental and social performance beyond economic performance. For banking and financial institutions, extent of financing green projects out of total amount of project finances will be crucial to their rating. Table 2 provides the matrix for collecting data from all the business entities in the form of various efficiency and performance indicators.

Table 2: Performance-Efficiency Matrix

ACTIVITY	INDICATOR	DATA REQUIRED
Operating Revenue Growth	Business Growth	Difference in operating income turnover or revenue this year & last
Procurement Amount	Economic footprint of the company	Amount spent on equipment, material, supplies and other inputs
Additional Finance Mobilized	Leverage generated by initial investment	Amount of additional debt & equity secured by investee, subsequent to the initial investment by the fund
Jobs Created	Social Well-being	Difference in Employment this year & last year
Wage Growth	Benefits passed to community	Difference in Salary/Payroll expenses this year & last year
Carbon Offsets	Carbon footprint of the company	Carbon offsets generated by the investee
Green technology Investment	Reduction in non-renewable energy consumption	Ratio of amounts spent on green energy to the total energy
Eco-friendly product/ service development	Green offers introduced	Revenue generated from green offers

From Table 2, quantities in the last column will be added to arrive at final rating. Also, Green Enterprise rating agencies could be hired and promoted to provide better insights on rating and ranking mechanisms. What makes these stocks different from others is that investors (or fund managers) will pay more attention to quantifiable measures of sustainability and demonstrate, whether the project (or company) meets a series of predetermined environmental standards compatible with SRI (Socially Responsible Investment) guidelines or not. Adopting the proposed method implies that the sponsor of the project is willing to disclose information about factors that would be required to assess rating. This is precisely one of the challenges that asset owners and managers face in emerging markets, where disclosure on environmental, social and governance factors is not common.

The Taylor-Made Financial Support System is also proposed for providing finances at different development stages, based on their Green Enterprise rating. Table 3 shows the structure of the proposed support system and describes the eligibility criteria for obtaining finances based on their rating at GSE:

Table 3: Structure of Financial Support System

Rating	Maximum Volume of Finance (%)	Rate of Interest charged
1 – 20	95% of the project cost	Up to 5%
20 – 50	90% of the project cost	5% - 8%
50 – 100	80% of the project cost	8% - 10%
100 – 200	75% of the project cost	10%-15%
> 200	60% of the project cost	> 15%

Apart from the volume and interest rate incentives, there will be a threshold level of ranking, say 100 to demark the green companies from non-green ones. As an added advantage to green companies, government should provide strong assistance in the form of sufficient tax incentives to them as well as their financers, to motivate them towards green practices. In this way, the proposed system will reduce and possibly avoid financing of the projects that are only profit oriented and not green. It will recreate a system which is robust and self sustaining, by obviating the need for significant spending in human-engineered solutions. It will transform our economic system along ecological design principles, emphasizing nature appreciation and environmental protection, which are important concerns and overwhelming preoccupations of the mainstream environmental movement. To intensify the movement, policymakers could also establish strong focus on:

- Introducing Green Business Certification programs, which are specific to industry, technology, business type and size
- Promoting free trade in green goods and services by coordinating industrial and technical standards, eliminating tariff and non-tariff barriers, and initiating trade liberalization on green products and services
- Accelerating low-carbon innovation by using revenues from carbon pricing measures to increase support for research, development, demonstration and pre-commercial deployment of low-carbon technologies by pooling international efforts. This will underpin innovative resource and energy efficient solutions, increase competitiveness and create business opportunities to drive long-term green economic growth
- Introducing the Environment Relationship Management (ERM) strategy for managing company's interactions with the environment. The strategy will necessitate focus of all business activities directed at nurturing, appreciating, satisfying and protecting environment. To achieve this, there should be mandatory environment-interface department to track the impact of business activities on environment. The dedicated department will maintain the database of environment related activities of the company and provide guidance on related issues. Measuring and valuing environment relationships would be critical to implementing this strategy. Providing green business solutions would be department's commitment at the highest levels of planning commanding entitlement to priority financing. As Customer Relationship Management (CRM) has worked wonders in the marketing field, ERM is bound to do miracles for pursuing green transitions
- Initiating a shift from current Risk Prevention Spending (RPS) based on technological solutions, towards a Risk Prevention Approach (RPA) that includes green investment solutions. The stated shift could be facilitated by setting up adequate administrative structures, developing new and reviewing existing management plans, establishing monitoring systems, and generating required information through targeted studies and public awareness campaigns
- Promoting development of Coherent Ecosystems through cross sectored work including agriculture, forestry, tourism, leisure and energy, leading towards multiple quality of life benefits. Since many activities have both benefits and trade-offs, it is necessary to adopt a holistic approach towards their implementation

With the bundle of additional recommendations mentioned above, the proposal is highly suited for infrastructure-challenged India, in terms of attracting needed financial resources for sustainable development and allows even greater participation in the global economy by increasing cross-border listings. In addition, investment within the region in both corporate bonds and equity issues by local institutional investors will overcome impediments to local capital markets, and may hold significant promise for financing cross-country infrastructure projects. It will act as a multifunctional resource capable of delivering a wide range of economic, social, environmental and quality of life benefits. I believe that the solution would be appreciated, accepted and adopted across the globe, to make a real difference in the lives of billions of people by providing them with access to efficient, affordable, and sustainable services in energy, water, transport, and information and communications technology. Thus, it will showcase ecological living for the ecological age and will prove to be the standard anti-crisis weapon for every government.

6. Conclusion

Green investment has been developed as a concept with many facets through this chapter. It ensures a resource efficient approach addressing many aspects of society entailing integrated multi-win solutions. Since private sector has started applying offsetting measures on development schemes as part of its corporate social responsibility, reinforcing such endeavors is crucial. It is therefore proposed to analyze the current legal framework and include green investments as a distinct funding article in the proposal for future regulations. Importance of investing structural funds in direct measures is also accentuated to create and maintain green infrastructure. This will build connectivity and robustness of natural areas on land, and in water, so that the provision of valuable ecosystem services can be safeguarded. Local governments have begun to experience the benefits of strategic development through green investments. These include, increased property tax revenue, reduced expenditure on government services, improved individual and social health through increased access to green spaces, mitigation of ill-effects of climate change and strengthening of local economies through reduced carbon footprint and increased green-collar jobs. To realize these benefits fully, integrated planning is required, which will bring different sectors together, in order to come up with "win-win" or "small loss, big gain" combinations. The positive sign is that the recent draft statements on significance of maintaining and restoring healthy natural environments have established green infrastructure as a core principle in achieving sustainable development and tackling climate change. Strengthening the sector by investing in, will further help to scale the solutions and construct a new paradigm for both economic growth and sustainable development. I believe that India's future policy will include budget lines well suited for supporting green growth strategies, and overall policy framework consisting of a coherent set of policies, regulations and standards will encourage the transition to a green economy. Proactive engagement of government, industry and consumers would enable India to fully participate in shaping the norms for environmentally-sound goods and services. It will raise national profile as an attractive destination for investments of economic, social and environmental importance. The proposition will <u>induce</u> symbiotic relationship between people and their environment, through innovative financing solutions. It will also contribute to enhancing the returns on green investments, while increasing the total stock (tangible & non-tangible) of green infrastructure assets in the world. This will restore planet health, thereby improving the quality of life of millions of people. I strongly believe that India must pilot-test the GSE model, feed-in results into international processes, and engage in active global debate with its own views, perspectives, lessons learned and experiences. Early implementation of the model implies that the results will be better and costs tolerable. Truly, 'Enriching Greens' proposition .has the potential of putting India on the global map as an Innovation Capital.

References

OECD (2011) "Social Cohesion: Making it happen":
http://oecdinsights.org/2011/11/21/ social-cohesion-making-it-happen
Green Growth Action A (2013) "The Green Investment Report: The ways and means to unlock private finance for green growth" World Economic Forum, Geneva
Venugopal S., Aman Srivastava, Clifford Polycarp, Emily Taylor (2012) "Public Financing Instruments to Leverage Private Capital for Climate-Relevant Investment: Focus on Multilateral Agencies", WRI Working Chapter, World Resources Institute, Washington DC
Bessemer (2010) "Investing in India: The Power, and Potential, of Family-Run Groups":
http://www.bvp.com/sites/default/files/bvp_india_family_Chapter_oct_2010.pdf
ESCAP (2007) "Sustainable Infrastructure in Asia: Overview and Proceedings" UN Publications, Thailand
WBCSD (2000) Eco-efficiency: Creating more with less:
http://www.wbcsd.org/web/ publications/eco_efficiency_creating_more_value.pdf

BIAC (2012) "Green growth and Development"
http://www.biac.org/statements/ greengrowth/FIN12-05_GREEN_GROWTH_DEVELOPMENT.pdf
Chan, C., Forwood, D., Roper, H., and Sayers, C. (2009) "Public Infrastructure Financing — An International Perspective", Productivity Commission Staff Working Chapter, March 2009
TEEB (2010) "The Economics of Ecosystems and Biodiversity Ecological and Economic Foundations" Ed. Pushpam Kumar, Earthscan, London and Washington
Millennium Ecosystem Assessment (2005) "Ecosystems and Human Well-being: Synthesis", Island Press, Washington, DC
Stern N. (2006) "Stern Review: The Economic of Climate Change":
http://mudancasclimaticas.cptec.inpe.br/~rmclima/pdfs/destaques/sternreview_report_complete.pdf
Briceno-Garmendia C., Estache A., Shafik N. (2004) "Infrastructure Services in Developing Countries: Access, Quality, Costs and Policy Reform", World Bank Policy Research Working Chapter 3468. pp.1-33

Photo: Jiya K. Shahani

2.5 Gifting: the New Approach to Economy

By Manan Jain

Introduction: Capitalism and the ideology of overproduction

According to Marx, in capitalism, improvements in technology and rising levels of productivity increase the amount of material wealth. Capitalism, the economic system is based on the principles of maximizing the shareholder's wealth. Thus, it is a system based on the private interests of a few. In capitalism, the motive for producing goods and services is to sell them for a profit, not to satisfy people's needs. Thus, overproduction became one of the ideology of this system and it is believed that the more one produces, more are the profits. Though, economists argue, that overproduction results in lesser profit as greater supply reduces the profitability of the goods. However, with innovative marketing, latent needs are created among the mass, which ensures a good demand for the products. The concept of overproduction makes sense, if it is to satisfy the needs of people, but not, when it is for the profit motive. Man's greed knows no bounds and if not for the physical and capacity constraints, there would have been no ends to the production levels.

Going back to the history, the concept of overproduction started from the agriculture, which brought a revolution in the society. Agriculture satisfied the basic need of hunger of man, who was a hunter. It is to be noted that this overproduction was not for any profit motive. It was just to give food security to man and for the greater good of the community and the society. However, in today's world, agriculture has been restricted as another means of livelihood. Crops are grown and harvested to generate profits by selling it in market. Thus, land is exploited to get as much produce as possible.

Excessive use of pesticides and fertilizers has put a toll on the fertility of the soil. However, it is not the agriculture which is to be blamed for this; it is the present socio-economic system to which the society has evolved to, resulting in the capitalist mindset of the people.. Apart from overproduction, it can further be debated that capitalism also results in increasing the divide between the rich and the poor. Increase in production does generate employment opportunities for the working class, but the value that is generated for the capitalists, far exceeds that for the workers. The gap only

73

widens and at times the worker's farewell is neglected, which only adds to the growing frustration and creates a rift in the society. For instance, the jasmine revolution saw massive protests.

Effect of capitalism on environment

Overproduction of goods has put a lot of toll on the environment and the natural resources. Be it agriculture or manufacturing, each and every industry adds to the consumption of the natural resources, with most of them being non-renewable. As stated above, the quest for producing more and more has resulted in the soil becoming barren and infertile. Excessive use of pesticides and fertilizers has changed the soil chemistry and has made it devoid of minerals and nutrients.

No development can take place without the use of natural resources, and one needs to meet up with the incessant growing energy requirements to keep up the pace of the economic development. Energy is required for exploration and extraction of resources, and also to transform it to the finished goods. Further, energy is required for the transportation of these goods to the end consumers. Thus, every good that is produced has a significant carbon footprint. Though, the models to calculate the precise carbon footprint still needs to be researched upon, but the manpower used in the process also adds to the carbon footprint, which needs to be considered. Thus in nutshell, every good is costly and is of much more ecological value than its economic value as precious natural resources have been used, which are limited in nature.

However, this ecological value is not being realized at all, and one only looks at its economic value. Majority of these goods are not reused or recycled and end up being dumped in the landfills. This waste is only piled up and it takes a lot of time for biodegradation. Additionally, it's not just the resources that are limited, but also the land, which is being used as dumping sites. Besides, without proper disposal techniques harmful and toxic chemicals from the waste find its way into the soil and air, thereby affecting the food-chain and disturbing the natural equilibrium.

The cradle to grave system that is followed is not sustainable unless we return back all the constituents to the nature, in its natural form. The need of the hour is to follow a cradle to cradle approach, wherein we take the responsibility of the consumption of the energy and resources and ensure that we maintain the balance in nature by returning back what we take.

Furthermore, in the pursuit of profits, one seems to flounder all rules and regulations to minimize costs. Illegal mining of minerals, dumping of waste into rivers and seas are to name a few of these practices and form the tip of an iceberg.

The unsustainable consumerist culture

The rise of the capitalism along-with overproduction has been fuelled by a change in the consumer behavior as well. No longer are we satisfied by what we have and it is the human tendency to always aspire for more. This has no end, and is precisely the reason for the thriving consumerist culture.

Food, shelter and clothing form the basic necessities of a man, categorized in the bottom level of Maslow's hierarchy of needs. The basic human requirement is to have clothes to protect the body from the extreme weather. However today, it's more of a fashion statement. One aspires to have clothes as per the latest fashion, which gets outdated with each season. Wardrobes are filled with latest designer clothing, only to be dumped in the next season, to make space for the latest trends. It's an irony, that in-spite of so much of cloth production; so many people in the world still don't have anything to cover their naked bodies. The advances in technology has further proliferated the increasing wants of consumers. Such is the advent that latest gadgets and gizmos, which were being introduced in the market couple of years back, are getting obsolete. The shelf life of these products is decreasing with each passing day. Maybe this is one of the ways of being in the business, by introducing gadgets with fancier features.

But one needs to stop here and ponder, is this what is really needed? For instance, televisions provide a great source of entertainment. With technological advances, LCD televisions are replacing the Cathode Ray Tube models. These are further being replaced by the LED TV's. Though not a basic necessity, but this need is being replaced by want, and marketers are finding innovative ways to tap these latent needs of the consumers. This is also complemented by the increasing purchasing power, but then there would be no end to this madness. Some other technology will further replace this, and the process is endless. What one fails to realize is the ecological consequences of this consumerist culture which is unsustainable at its core.

We need to slow down our rate of consumption. But won't that mean slowing down the development? After all the more the goods and services are produced, the more the employment, and the more the wealth and thus more the prosperity.

Effect of consumerist culture on society

With this consumerist culture, and the capitalist mindset, it can be argued that earth has become a better place to live in, with all the so called development. In comparison to our ancestors, we have a better education system, higher life expectancy, advanced medical facilities, better communication and transport infrastructure. The world has become a place with no boundaries. One knows what is happening in other parts of the world and can travel anywhere in the world. The evolution of mankind to the present day and the growth story has been prolific. However, one needs to look at the complete picture.

The current system has bred an atmosphere of tension and worries. CEO's are worried about the top and the bottom-line, government is worried about managing the growth amongst all the economic turmoil, corporates are worried about hikes and bonuses they will be getting, parents are worried about managing the household with the rising prices and inflation. Everyone is in a rat race to acquire more assets, more wealth and more money, hoping to get a sense of security out of it. But what results is growing discontent, dissatisfaction, disharmony and lack of prosperity. We might become rich, but there is no communal harmony as that wealth is at the expense of others, and only widens the economic gap. This widening of the gap further leads to frustration among the lower halves and creates enormous pressure in the society. This pressure is released in the form of protests, social uprisings and revolutions that have changed the course of the mankind. One does not have to go far in the history for such examples.

Poverty, unemployment and political repression were the reasons which led to the Tunisian revolution of 2010-11 in the Arab country of Tunisia. Again, the world witnessed the Egyptian revolution wherein people frustrated by the rising unemployment, high food inflation, low minimum wages and increasing corruption toppled the government in 2011. 2011 also witnessed Wall Street protests, where people stood against the issues of social and economic inequality, greed, corruption and undue influence of corporates on governments.

Though the technology is bringing people close together, yet there is no closeness within the society. Had it been the case, people would have stood for each other, helping each other out to ensure that people meet at-least their basic needs. This wouldn't bring affluence to lives of poor, but contentment to lead a peaceful life.

Ideologies of Gift Economy

In this context, Gift economy seems to be a very constructive and innovative solution. Gift economy is an economy based on giving in the context of relationship rather than making transactions simply for profit or personal material gain. Valuable goods and services are regularly given without any explicit agreement for immediate or future rewards.

The foundation of a sacred economy, then, is gift consciousness. It is based on the following principles:[1]

1. Over time, giving and receiving must be in balance. The internalization of ecological costs ensures that we will take no more from earth than we can give.

2. The source of a gift is to be acknowledged. The restoration of the commons means that any use of what belongs to all is acknowledged by a payment that goes to all.

3. Gifts circulate rather than accumulate.

4. Gifts flow toward the greatest need. A social dividend ensures that the basic survival needs of every person are met.

Let's discuss these one by one. The first principle tries to bring the human civilization in harmony with nature. All the natural resources are a gift of nature to man. It doesn't differentiates humans based on demography or geography. As put by Mahatma Gandhi, earth has everything to satisfy man's need but not for man's greed. To pay back to the nature, is paying out of gratitude and to ensure that the same gifts are enjoyed by one and all, including the future generations. It also encompasses the cradle to cradle approach of production and ensures that whatever is taken, is given back to the nature, thus ensuring that the system, the growth and the development are sustainable.

Additionally, today, pollution and various other activities that degrade environment are at the expense of society and future generations. Shifting these costs to polluters will guarantee that they pay back entirely for all the pollution caused by them. This further keeps a tab on the pollution levels and ensures it to a level which is under control and has been offsetted.

The second principle acknowledges the source of the gift, be it nature or a fellow human being. The acknowledgement brings closeness in the community and meaningful relationships develop as there is no selfish or profit motives. The receiver overwhelmed with gratitude, in turn strives to pay back to the society and gifts to others in need. One looks towards helping others, and these feelings create close associations.

This further lowers the social and economic disparity. In a capitalistic economy, the goods and services are paid up with money. It leaves no obligation to help the society in return for the goods and services rendered, even though they may be at the expense of society. For instance, production of good, results in pollution which affects the society equally, but the money is paid only to the producer. The second principle helps in ensuring that all the stakeholders are acknowledged and gifted back. Moreover, it eliminates the divisions in the society based on one's wealth and tries to bring in equality, social as well economic.

The third principle is based on the ideology of non-accumulation. One receives gifts, and in turn gives gifts back to the society. This translates to non-hoarding of material. One is well versed with the evils of hoarding in a capitalistic society. Hoarding creates artificial scarcity which causes price rise and inflation, giving profits to the hoarders at the cost of the common man. The continuous flow of gifts ensures that needs of all are met, and a greater circulation of goods gives the sense of security that capitalistic minds seek in accumulation of materialistic wealth. Moreover it gives a peace of mind in not having to indulge in a rat race to acquire these material possessions.

A thing can be want for one and need for other, or in other words, a luxury for someone may be a need for another. For instance, a person might have hundreds of designer labels in his/her wardrobe, while at the same time, clothing is a necessity for someone else and he might not have even a single piece of clothing to cover his body. The fourth principle ensures that the benefits of the gifts are enjoyed by those who need it the most. Furthermore it also tries to bring in economic and social parity by ensuring that basic survival needs of all the persons are met. In this world, in spite of all the growth and developments, millions die of hunger and malnutrition, and millions do not have access to proper clothing and shelter. Wouldn't it be nice if our fellow brothers and sisters are all able to live a better life, satisfying all their basic needs? Imagine, if you yourself was fighting to get two square meals a day, and if someone gifts you enough to eat, how much happiness it would bring to you. Imagine, if there is so much of happiness, contentment, harmony and prosperity within the society, then will there be Wall Street protests or Egyptian or Tunisian revolutions?

Gift Economy initiatives

There are various ways to promote this concept and put these ideologies into practice. A lot of initiatives have already been put into practice and the results are promising.

Seva café, in the city of Ahmedabad in India is one such example. A diner at Seva café is not viewed as a customer, but instead as a treasured guest, as part of a family. When someone dines at Seva Café, the meal is offered as a genuine gift, already paid for in full by previous guests, and one has no obligation to pay. One becomes part of a Circle of Giving, which is modeled more closely to that of a family. Thus there are no bills and the diner is free to pay anything or nothing, without any obligation. the wholesome vegetarian meals are cooked and served with love by volunteers and by a small, modestly paid staff - mostly graduates from Manav Sadhna's Earn N' Learn program.

The menu changes daily and they offer a delicious variety of options, both Indian and continental. They believe that everyone - volunteers, staff, and guests alike - all should leave the space feeling more nourished - body, mind, and spirit - and that together they can help set in motion, a more abundant, more generous mode of interacting that leaves everyone feeling happier and more closely connected. The inequities of the world derive from our own internal walls of separation from one another, and Seva Café strives to leave these walls behind. All their costs and income are made clearly transparent, and 100% of any profits that they take in, are used back in the community through Seva Cafe.[2]

Application of gift economy to solve current socio-economic issues

A probable application of this concept of gift economy could be to have an organization, primary goal of which is to provide a platform for the gifting. A non-profit organization, it would bring together people from all walks of life and apprise them of various gifting opportunities. It would be a medium wherein people can gift goods and services to be used by other in need. Today, the desire is there to donate or give to the society, and there are several NGO's for this as well. For instance, there are toy banks, there are NGO's which collect and distribute old and used clothes and so on.

However, this is limited to the domain in which the organization operates, and the operations are usually localized in nature. These organizations fail to connect the giver and the receiver. Thus we need a medium which connects the giver and the receiver by providing them a common platform.

Moreover, we need to build an organization, which can also further the reuse and recycling of goods. Thus doing a value-add to the good and increasing its shelf life. Very often, a small problem in the working of an electronic gadget, or availability of fancier gizmos forces us to dump these goods into the waste bin. However, with small repairs, these become good enough to be operational for some more time. A person, who can't afford such a good, would be very happy if he gets to have that product in working order. A small personal example, I had an old desktop at my home in a good condition, lying unused. With small repair, it was gifted to a sweeper having a meager monthly salary of $100. His joy knew no bounds as he now had access to a computer, which fulfilled his dreams.

The point to be made is that there is a lot of scope for re-use and recycle of products and goods. Besides, this value addition to the goods has the potential to generate employment opportunities for people as well, and this could be supported by government welfare schemes. Based on a not for profit model, this organization can be run by volunteers, who can gift their time and render their services. For instance, people can gift their fully functional or part-functional devices. These can be further refurbished by people with suitable skills and gifted to the needy people. These skilled persons can be the individuals who have the required technical know-how and have volunteered. Additionally, corporates under their CSR initiatives can impart technical know-how to refurbish the goods and add more value to them. Today, the leaders talk of the need to transfer the technical know-how from the developed nations to the developing ones in order to solve the climate issues. The solution, the vision for an organization that is presented in this chapter can very well be a means to achieve that.

Conclusion

Thus with the participation of corporates, the government and the individuals, one can hope to achieve the desired objectives of the gift economy. This would further help in achieving sustainable consumption by the virtue of sharing of goods, thus reducing demand at-least for the goods which are sparingly used in daily life. Initiatives like Seva café, Karma kitchen[3] have shown to the world that such initiatives are sustainable as well as practical. What is needed in today's world is an understanding of the various issues at hand and a shift in the mindset to achieve a solution for that. Gift economy, with its ideologies offers a practical and sustainable solution, which is for all to uncover.

References and supporting tables are available on request.

2.6 Green Gujarat: a blueprint for sustainable development

By Indira Dutta

Introduction

Gujarat, the growth of engine of India came into existence in 1960 when the bilingual state of Bombay was divided into two parts, Marathi speaking Maharashtra and Gujarati speaking Gujarat. The state has made it long glorious journey right from 1960 to 2012 with full of landmark achievements and spectacular performance. Its dynamic economic growth has made Gujarat more prosperous and more affluent but side by side it has brought huge environmental damage and depletion which has posed a big threat to both human resource and natural resource. Our common future is at stake and sustainable development is a common challenge for all of us. It is a million dollar question that whether today's prosperity will push us towards destruction or bring a promising tomorrow. It is true that Gujarat has become a role model for other states of India but environmental sustainability is the biggest challenge in Gujarat's development path. The population explosion has brought fuel to the fire. The state is facing two types of risks, poverty related risks and growth related risks. The poverty related risks such as lack of sanitation, indoor air pollution and water pollution in rural areas are very damaging and growth related risks are manifested by deteriorating urban environment, industrial wastes and chemical pollution. Both together have put a bar towards sustainable development.

The greatest dilemma of sustainable Gujarat is that in the land of prosperity a big chunk of population remains in the midst of intense economic and social struggle. The reproductive power of nature has been bought by productive power of big industrial tycoons. But not everything is lost. The state is concerned and alarmed to repair the fast altering face of the mother earth. At present the Government of Gujarat is dedicated to create a green Gujarat to bring environment sustainability and social equity. The government has taken some pioneering green initiatives which will enable people to produce, protect and sustain resources in such way that not only the present generation will enjoy better health, education and material comfort but the future generation will also enjoy the same.

Sustainable Development: Past and Present

The root of sustainable development is visible in Marsh's "Man & Nature" in 1864. He observed "Man is everywhere a disturbing agent. Wherever he plants his foot, the harmonies of nature are turned to discords. The proportion and accommodation which ensured the stability of existing management are overthrown." From the 20th Century onwards the term "sustainable development" has become a subject of debate all over the world. In the first half of 20th century, conservation movement was instrumental in preservation and conservation of deteriorating resources. Neo Malthusian arguments were a prominent feature of environmentalism in the 1960's and 1970's. The "Tragedy of Commons" also reflected the neo–classical concern about the exhaustion of living resources, Garret Hardin (1968). Hardin observed that a finite world can support only a finite population and therefore, population growth must eventually go. The publication of Rachel Carson's "Silent Spring" is accepted as a key turning point in the emergence of environmentalism as maintenance of political force. It generated a storm of controversy over the use of chemical pesticides. She questioned humanity's faith in technological progress and helped to set the stage for the environmental movement. The sustainability debate gained momentum with the "Blueprint for Survival" (Goldsmith and Allen 1972). It has been argued that indefinite growth of whatever type cannot be sustained by finite resource.

During the 1980's with the release of World Conservation Strategy (IUCN, UNEP and WWP) the term "sustainable development" became more popular. The strategy encouraged paradigmatic change, a new international economic order and a new environmental ethic. Daly and Townshend (1993) both argue that sustainable development must be "qualitative development" rather than "qualitative growth". Thereafter in Brundtland Report "Our Common Future" (1987) sustainable development was put forward as a major agenda to solve the problem of environmental degradation. Later on, the sustainable development was discussed in three mega conferences at Stockholm (1972), Rio-de-Janerio (1992) and Johannesburg (2002). In Stockholm it was discussed that for the purpose of an aiming freedom in the world of nature, man must use knowledge to build in collaboration with nature for a better environment. To defend and improve human environment for present and future generation has become an imperative goal for mankind, a goal to be pursued together with, and in harmony with the established and fundamental goals of peace, worldwide economic and social development. In 1992 – UNCED held in Rio-de- Janeiro signed up a global partnership for sustainable development articulated in Agenda 21. Though production and consumption pattern of developed countries were acknowledged as the major source of environmental problem but UNCED documents recommended more economic growth in both developed and developing countries. In twenty years from Stockholm to Rio, economic growth once the problem has been recast as a solution. It has been noted that human beings are the centre of concern for sustainable development. In order to achieve sustainable development, environmental protection shall constitute an integral part of the development process and cannot be considered in isolation for it. A decade after Rio in 2002 World Summit on Sustainable Development in Johannesburg made it very clear that they are committed to curb environmental governance. With it we find the dawn of a vibrant global civil society of cooperation, participation, community and innovation. The world commission on Environment and Development mainly referred as Brundtland Commission defined the concept as development "that meets the need of the present without compromising the ability of future generation to meet their own needs". The 21st century will be the century of ecological transition where we will see that sustainable development offers challenges and opportunities for the development of renewable energy, sustainable building, new technology, best quality of life for all people and great security.

Perils of Environmental Crisis

Gujarat has been blessed with highly heterogeneous physiographical conditions and a variety of environmental resources but the greatest mistake is that man has tried to conquer over nature and hence it faces the anger of nature in form of flood, cyclone and earthquake. Because of regular shocks we notice a phenomenon of distress migration. Distress migration creates negative impact on health, nutrition, education, literacy and welfare. Migrating population are not properly absorbed in urban areas and this has given birth to mushrooming of illegal settlements with primitive facilities. This has led to various health problems which finally lead to morbidity and mortality. The glittering industrialization and urbanization in Gujarat has brought no doubt an urban revolution. It has brought dynamic change in social, cultural and economic fabric of the state but under the carpet of dynamism we have pressed the panic button in Gujarat by putting a red signal in ecosystem's overall economic integrity. The environmental decay is noticed in form of water pollution, air pollution, coastal pollution and noise pollution.

Gujarat has more than 90,000 industrial units. Major polluting industries are located in Vadodara Petrochemical Complex, Nandesari, Ankleshwar, Vapi, Vatva and Hazira near Surat. Near 400 km stretch between Vapi in Southern Gujarat and Vatva in Northern Gujarat is known as the golden corridor of India, but the reality is that it is not golden at all. This stretch has become the hot bed of pollution. Another environmental nightmare is Alang, the largest ship breaking yard of the world situated 50 kms from Bhavnagar. The 11 kms coastline of the yard has been severely polluted due to scrapping of hazardous ships. Ship breaking releases a large number of dangerous pollutants, including toxic waste, oil, polychlorinated biphenyls and heavy metals into the water and seabed. High concentration of oil and grease are found in the coastal water chocking marine life. Gujarat's rivers are bearing the brunt of industrial pollution and people who are living on the banks of the rivers remain in a pathetic state. All the major rivers and streams of Gujarat are in a bad state due to effluent discharged by industry, be it Kolak, Mahi, Damanganga, Amlakhadi and Sabarmati. The Supreme Court Monitoring Committee Report has stated "In the case of Vapi, Ankleshwar, Nandesari (Vadodara) and the villages around the Effluent Channel Project, the Committee itself has physically verified that groundwater in all these areas is unfit for drinking, displayed colours of bright red, orange, chocolate and cannot be used for drinking water or even washing clothes as they get stained. Villagers are forced to use the coloured water for agriculture". Water pollution in Gujarat has posed a serious threat to our eco-system. Water is not only the basic need but it is also the core of sustainable development. Unsafe water and inadequate sanitation are two great drivers of poverty and inequality. They claim millions of lives, destroy livelihoods, and diminish the prospects for economic growth. Poor people, especially poor women and children bear the brunt of human cost (HDR 2006). We can get a glimpse of status of water quality of some major rivers of Gujarat:

Status of water quality of major rivers of Gujarat in 2010-11

		Parameters			
Sr.	River	pH	D.O.	B.O.D.	C.O.D.
1	Sabarmati	8.1	7.3	4	19
2	Meshwo	8.0	7.8	3	11
3	Shedhi	7.6	7.7	6	27
4	Mahi	7.9	7.7	2	10
5	Narmada	8.2	7.7	1	4
6	Kaveri	8.2	6.8	2	9
7.	Tapi	8.0	6.9	2	28
8.	Damanganga	7.8	3.7	22	64
9.	Bhadar	8.3	4.6	6	77
10	Kolak	8.0	5.6	9	33

Source: Gujarat Pollution Control Board, Annual Report (2010-11)

The ground water pollution is equally threatening because it causes many life threatening diseases. The following table indicates the status of ground water pollution in Gujarat

Status of Ground Water Quality of bore well /hand pumps in Gujarat

(Yearly average 2010-11)

Sr.	Place/ City	Location	pH	T.D.S.	D.O.	C.O.D.
1	Jamnagar	Shanker Tekri Bore well water	7.8	1129	2.3	6
2	Bhavnagar	Chitra	7.6	747	3.6	9
3	Amreli	Pitan Para	7.6	1002	3.6	9
4	Mahuva	Kuberbaug	7.6	1034	3.6	10
5	Surendranagar	Parmeshwar Tiber Mart	7.6	3921	3.1	12
6	Rajkot	Gurukul Gondal	8.1	644	2.9	10
7.	Junagadh	GIDC	7.3	1660	4.3	10

Except pH all the parameters are expressed as Mg/L

Source: Gujarat Pollution Control Board, Annual Report (2010-11)

Air pollution is another major hindrance in the path of sustainable development. A bunch of causes like vehicular pollution, industrialization, urbanization, domestic activities and natural occurrences together bring air pollution. The status of ambient air quality of major cities in Gujarat is listed in the following table:

Status of Ambient Air Quality of Major Cities

Sr.	Location	pH Mg/Ms	RSPM Mg/M3	SOX Mg/M3	NOX Mg/M3
1	Vapi	187	91	15.67	23.25
2	Surat	202	89	20.00	26.25
3	Ankleshwar	177	85	17.50	24.17
4	Vadodara	309	133	22.83	42.08
5	Ahmedabad	319	134	19.92	29.08
6	Bhavnagar	209	109	10.25	17.83
7.	Bhuj	253	141	12.00	28.00
8.	Sabarkantha	144	552	7.9	24.6
9.	Banaskantha	41	343	12.5	18.2
10	Anand	109	429	0.7	0.9

Source: Gujarat Pollution Control Board, Annual Report (2010-11)

Air pollution causes many health problems like respiratory diseases, bronchitis, burning of eyes and nose, deprives body cells of oxygen, causes unconsciousness, affects central nervous system, respiratory paralysis, lung cancer, brain damage and muscular paralysis.

The state has the longest coastline in the country measuring to 1,650 kms. It harbours right and unique ecosystems including the country's first Marine National Park. Various estuaries, two gulfs and coral islands make the coastal zone of the state as major area of concern. Due to development of port induced industrialization and urbanization there has been tremendous pressure on coastal and marine environment. The quality of coastal outfalls and coastal water is presented in the following table.

Quality of coastal outputs and coastal lakes

(Yearly average 2010-11)

Sr.	Location	Parameters			
	pH	D.O.			
1	Sea water at Dhuvaran, Kheda	7.7	8.1	1	0.98
2	Sea water of Jamnagar	7.8	7.8	1	1.36
3	Estuarine water of river Damanganga	8.2	6.7	4	4.35
4	Estuarine water of river Kolak	7.9	7.0	11	4.2
5	Sea water at Kandla	7.9	5.7	5	0.42
6	Estuarine water of river Narmada of Golden Bridge	8.1	7.2	1	BDL

Except PH all the parameters are expressed as Mg/L

BDL = Below Defection Limit

Source : Gujarat Pollution Control Board, Annual Report (2010-11)

The current Controller & Auditor General (CAG) Report 2011-12 and adresses the impact on its the green image of Gujarat, has highlighted the fact that Gujarat Government has failed to keep pollution under control. The Government has remained unaware of the ecological health of rivers, lakes and groundwater which could lead to destruction of ecosystem beyond redemption and loss of valuable species besides affecting human health. CAG regretted, "Government of Gujarat has not formulated any policy based on local conditions for prevention of pollution of rivers, lakes and groundwater. While treatment of industrial effluent before its discharge is compulsory, no programme has been introduced to prevent such pollution from different sources".

When we look towards environmental sustainability index we notice that Guajrat presents a sorry spectacle. This is clear from the following table which contains the ESI scores and ranks of all the 28 states of India: The rank of Gujarat is 27.

States	ESI Scores	ESI Rank	States	ESI Scores	ESI Rank	
Manipur	100.00	1	Kerala	53.71	15	
Sikkim	90.99	2	Bihar	51.98	16	
Tripura	85.81	3	Jammu & Kashmir	48.73	17	
Nagaland	82.08	4	Goa	45.16	18	
Mizoram	81.58	5	Madhya Pradesh	43.01	19	
Arunachal Pradesh	75.45	6	Maharashtra	37.28	20	
Chhattisgarh	74.09	7	West Bengal	35.72	21	
Orissa	71.88	8	Tamil Nadu	33.75	22	
Uttaranchal	71.18	9	Andhra Pradesh	32.55	23	
Assam	70.15	10	Rajasthan	26.52	24	
Meghalaya	66.79	11	Haryana	25.59	25	
Jharkhand	64.33	12	Uttar Pradesh	21.40	26	
Himachal Pradesh	61.26	13	Gujarat	10.46	27	
Karnataka	55.79	14	Punjab	0.00	28	

Source: Institute for Financial Management and Research, Center for Development Finance (2008).

ESI is a composite index assembled from 15 indicators that are derived from 44 variables or datasets, which cover a wide range of issues such as population, air and water pollution, waste management, land use pattern, forest and other natural resources, air and water quality, environment degradation, impacts on health, energy management, GHG emission, and governance. The following table contains 44 variables, 15 indicators and 5 policy components.

No.	44 Variables	Sl No.	15 Indicators	Sl No.	5Policy Components
1	Population density	1	Population Pressure	1	Population Pressure
2	Population growth				
3	Total fertility rate				
4	% Change in forest area	2	Natural Resource Endowment	2	Environ-mental Stress
5	% of Forest land encroached				
6	Annual ground water draft				
7	NOx emission per capita	3	Air Pollution		
8	SO2 emission per capita				
9	CO2 emission per capita				
10	Number of motorized vehicles				
11	Untreated waste water discharged	4	Water Pollution		
12	Fertilizer consumption				
13	Pesticide consumption				
14	Per capita municipal solid waste	5	Waste Generation		
15	Per capita hazardous waste				
16	% of protected area to forest	6	Land Use	3	Environ mental Systems
17	% of land under grazing to total land				
18	% of land under agriculture to				

	total land				
19	Total replenishable ground water				
20	Average annual rainfall	7	Natural Resource Endowment		
21	% of Wetland area to total land				
22	% of state under forest cover				
23	Annual concentration of SO2 levels	8	Air Quality		
24	Annual concentration of NO2 levels				
25	Annual concentration of SPM levels				
26	Annual concentration of RSPM levels				
27	Biological Oxygen Demand	9	Water Quality		
28	Electrical Conductivity				
29	Total Suspended Solids				
30	% of degraded area	10	Disaster Management	4	Health Vulnerability
31	Area affected by flood and heavy rains				
32	% of total districts affected by drought				
33	Hazard prone area				
34	Incidence of acute respiratory diseases	11	Health Vulnerability		
35	Incidence of acute water diseases				

36	Per capita energy consumed	12	Energy Management	Environmental Governance
37	% of renewable energy in total energy			
38	Energy-GDP ratio			
39	Area under joint forest management	13	People's Initiative	
40	Presence of environmental NGOs			
41	% of defaulting industries	14	Government's Initiative	
42	Fund allocation by Union government			
43	Fund allocation by state government			
44	% Change in total GHG emissions	15	GHG emissions	

Source: Institute for Financial Management and Research, Center for Development Finance (2008).

It is clearly visible that the progressive Gujarat in fact is digging its own grave if environmental degradation is not checked in time. Today the culture of consumerism and urge for materialism has put us in a dilemma. The fundamental solution lies in development strategy which could make Gujarat green and evergreen by combining the three pillars of sustainability - economic, social and ecological.

A Transition: From Crisis to Hope

Gujarat's GDP has grown by 12 percent in the last decade but the success story of two digits growth has been marked by several digits realities of loss of natural resources, livelihood and displacement. Environment is a social justice issue and environment is a peace and security issue and that is why at present Government of Gujarat is dedicated to make Gujarat green to bring environmental sustainability. The concept of green economy has been discovered by UNEP where it has been mentioned that green economy results in improved human well being and social equity while significantly reducing environmental risks and ecological scarcities.

Karl Burkat defines green economy as based on six main actors:-

1.	Renewable Energy	(Solar, wind, geothermal, marine including wave, biogas and fact cell)
2.	Green Building	(Green retrofits for energy and water efficiency, residential and commercial assessment, green products and material and LEED constructions).
3.	Clean Transportation	(Alternative fuels, hybrid and electric vehicles, car sharing and carpooling programmes).
4.	Water Management	Water reclamation, grey water, rain- water, system low water landscaping, water purification and storm water management.
5.	Waste Management	Recycling, Municipal solid waste salvage, brownfield land remediation and sustainable packaging.
6.	Land Management	Organic agriculture, habit conservation and restoration, urban forestry and park).

Gujarat is all set to become one of the greenest states in the country and for that several environmental friendly approaches have been developed in various sectors. In agriculture, Government is seriously thinking to bring sustainable agriculture. The economic cost of agricultural externality is increasing day by day. Policy reforms aiming greening agriculture will offer opportunities to diversify economy and reduce poverty through increased yields. It will create new and more productive green jobs especially in all the rural areas. Side by side it will ensure food security on a sustainable basis and significantly reduce the environmental and economic cost associated with today's scientific farming practices. Green agriculture will pave the way for nutritional security which will finally remove poverty from its very root. With green agriculture Gujarat will increase its agricultural productivity, reduce negative externalities and rebuild ecological resources like soil, water, air, biodiversity and natural capital assets. It will restore and enhance soil productivity and finally reduce soil erosion. With the removal of chemical pesticide agricultural output will be more healthy and with all these there will be low ecological footprint on agricultural sector.

After agriculture, forests play an important role in earth's ecological infrastructure. It is the backbone of Green Gujarat. Forests meet the critical livelihood needs of the local communities in rural Gujarat by providing fuel wood, construction materials, food sources and medicinal plants. The major challenge which Gujarat faces today is loss of forest, compelling land uses, market policy etc. But at present, Gujarat Government is trying its level best to promote green investment by conserving existing areas of primary forest and promoting expansion of forest through regeneration and representation. The remarkable improvement in the forest cover has been observed in the Gir and Girnar, Cantonment area of Sardar Sarover Project and Panchmahal. A Medicinal Plant Development Project has been started with the help of Forest Co-operative Societies. It has tried to benefit the maximum number of villages to promote more medicinal plant cultivation among the forested area of Valsad and Navsari districts. It has been planned in such a way that tribal farmers can get the financial benefit because the products will be purchased by pharmaceutical companies. The site has been developed in such a manner that people would learn about medicinal plants and enjoy ecological benefits. Every year Gujarat celebrates Van Mohotsava (Forest Festival) to motivate people and institution for afforestation. The Government has declared Van Panchamrut Yojana (Forest Five Nectar Plan) which consists of Urja Shakti (Energy Power), Gyan Shakti (Knowledge Power), Raksha Shakti (Security Power), Jan Shakti (Man Power), Jal Shakti (Water Power). The Urja Shakti includes wood, tree harnessing and solar energy. Raksha Shakti comprises bio diversity ecological security, safe environment, check salinity and erosion. Gyan Shakti includes training, research, workshop, chapter tour, extension and expansion of bio-technology. Jan Shakti takes care of nature education, social forestry, Joint forest management, eco-club and green guard. Jal shakti keeps an eye on check dam, forest water body, water and soil conservation. With all these Gujarat is marching towards sustainable forest management for a green tomorrow.

Gujarat is making sincere efforts to bring green industrialization which means that sincere efforts have been made to make a right balance between industrial growth and environment. It has started investment in renewable engineering technologies, more resource and energy efficient production process which could generate multiple benefits not only for the present generation but also for the future generation. It will open up vast new markets such as services in the prevention and management of waste and market created through the application of life cycle approaches. Investment in natural capital and green physical capital are important in moving towards a green economy but side by side Government has tried to create awareness and empowerment of individual and communities. Greening of the industrial belt also holds improvement in the health of the workforce by reducing the occupational diseases and injuries. Recently, Government is also supporting grass-root entrepreneurs to make economy green. Supporting green entrepreneurs can help to tackle energy and food security challenges. Social and environmental enterprises will make contributions in mitigating carbon emissions, facilitating adaptation to climate change and push the economy towards sustainable development.

The Government has chalked out a massive plan to add about 7000 MW of renewable energy in the next three to four years attracting investment to the tune of about Rs.80,000 crore. The state Government has come out with a separate solar power policy under which it proposes to purchase 500 MW of solar power every year. On 19th April, 2012 Gujarat Government has started 600 Mega Watts (MW) on grid solar power plant at Gujarat Solar Park in Charanka village, Patan District. A rooftop solar power policy has also been announced where anyone can put up solar panels on their rooftops and sell power to the state government. With the continuous effort of Gujarat Government the cost of solar power has came down to Rs.8.50 per unit from Rs.15 per unit.

Industries from Gujarat are estimated to collect anywhere from Rs.3000 crore to Rs.3900 crore from carbon credit more than industries from any other states according to data available with National Clean Development Mechanism Authority (NCDMA). The authority has approved 226 projects from Gujarat which make up 11.88 crore capital Emission Reductions (CER). A CER is equivalent to a tonne of carbon and one CER is currently being traded at 4 to 5 crores, according to a Belgium based group called CDM Watch which monitors the carbon trading market or Clean Development Mechanism (CDM) functioning under United Nation Framework Connection on Climate Change (UNFCCC). In 2011 Gujarat Government has passed Green Cess Bill that stipulates levying a cess of Rs. 0.02 per unit of electricity generated by power firm using non-renewable sources.

Gujarat has also developed a concept of green housing. Adani Group, Gokul Group and Tata all have joined hands together to make green housing mission a grand success. The Adani Group has developed Shantigram where investment upto Rs.10,000 crore has been made. The township has been developed in an environment friendly manner.

The green measures are expected to bring down the township temprature by two degree celcius. A "museum of trees" has been planned where 75,000 trees of different varieties will be planted. It will be 80% open area with 100% recycling water facilities with zero discharge. The recycling water will be used for landscaping, air-conditioning and cleaning purpose. The drinking water will come from Narmada Canal. Gokul Group has developed "Canyon Experience". The township near Chandkheda will have a well crafted green canyon spread our an area of around 50,000Sq. yds. The central Canyon will traverse through the entire neighbourhood soar upto 20 ft. at the Shikhar (Pinnacle) and dip down 50 ft. at the Jalkund (Water Reservoir) creating a sense of movement from piety to pleasure. The Tata Housing Ltd. has started a venture with Arvind Limited to develop an integrated mega township spread over 134 acres in Western Ahmedabad. The projects will be developed under the guidelines of Indian Green Building Council (IGBC). Of late, Gujarat has developed green transport where it encourages people in walking and cycling, green vehicles (battery operated) and car sharing. Green transport system will create green urban environment which will make a positive contribution to environmental, social and economic sustainability.

Last but not least; Gujarat has established a separate department of climate change. These initiatives are trend setter not only for India but also for the whole of Asia, as it is the first in Asia and fourth in the World. The green priorities of Department of Climate Change(DCC) are the following:

- Promote Green Technology

- Earn more carbon credit

- Power saving

- Preserve ground water

- Promote CNG Network

- Increase Mangrove cover

- Preparation of comprehensive multi dimensional climate change policy in Gujarat State – Conservation of land, water & air.

- Promote public participation and public awareness.

- Cooperation with National and International Agencies

Apart from DCC, Gujarat Ecological Commission, Gujarat Forest and Environmental Department, Gujarat Pollution Control Board all are engaged in ecological and environmental protection. They are trying to integrate environmental concern with regular economic activities, even to the extent of relating the conservation of biological diversity with the livelihood prospects of present generation as well as the protection of future generation.

Conclusion

It is a truth that today Gujarat faces a major growth dilemma. On the one hand we notice dynamic economic growth with a new vision to reach the stage of high mass consumption while on the other hand we are heading towards a threatened future due to huge environmental damage. Today we dream together for livelihood security, energy security, economic security, ecological security and national security. For that we have to take in to account (PESTEL) factors, political factors, economic factors, social factors, technological factors and legal factors. Our policy should be socially, economically and environmentally sound. With a bunch of green initiatives the government of Gujarat has tried to create an (ecotopia) – a world in which environment, human society and individual all are treated well and help to persist long in the future. But for that we have to make a choice between "Techno-Centric Growth" and "Eco-Centric Growth". Dreaming up an eco-centric type of growth is not an easy task. For that we badly need a shared responsibility of all the players; polluters, regulators and regulated community. The players must cooperate to increase efficiency, transparency and accountability. Sustainable is not a fixed state of harmony but rather a process of change in which the exploitation of resources, the direction of investments, the orientation of technological development and institutional changes are made consistent with present as well as future needs. The green initiatives of government of Gujarat is not only an effort to set out a blueprint for sustainable development but it is also an endeavour through which we can bring an era of peace, prosperity and security where both present generation as well as future generation will enjoy in the years to come.

References and Notes

1. Ricklefs R.: The Economy of Nature - A Text in Basic Ecology, W.H.Freeman and Company, New York, 1997. P 601

2. Kahn M.: Green Cities: Urban Growth and Environment, Washington D.C: Brooking Institution 2006

3. Hardin, G.: 'Tragedy of Commons' Science 162, 1968, P.1243-8

4. Bob Williams: Greening the Economy, Interpreting economies and ecology to make effective change. Routledge and 2010 P 21-35.

5. Edwin Zaccai: Sustainable Consumption, Ecology and Fair Trade: Routledge 2007. P 57-60.

6. G. J. Paton: Seeking Sustainability, on the prospect of an ecological liberalism, Routledge 2011 P 91-110.

7. W.M. Adams: Green Development Environment and sustainability in a developing world, Routledge 2009 P 26-56.

8. C.K. Prahlad: Fortune at the Bottom of the Pyramid: Eradicating Poverty through Profit. Wharton School Publishing, 2004.

9. Our Common Future – The world Commission on Environment and Development, Oxford University Press -1987.

10. Sheetal Shukla: Sustainable Development of the Coastal Environment of Gujarat, V.D.M. Germany 2010.

11. Gujarat Pollution Control Board Annual Report 2010-11.

12. Socio-Economic Review of Gujarat: 2010-11, Directorate of Economics and Statistics, Government of Gujarat, Gandhinagar.

13. Controller & Auditor General Report: 2011-12.

14. Gujarat Human Development Report 2004, Mahatma Gandhi Labour Institute, Ahmedabad.

15. Environmental Sustainability Index for Indian States – Informing Environmental Action - Institute for Financial Management and Research, Center for Development Finance 2008.

Photo: Indira Dutta

Photo: Dr Natalie West Kharkongor

2.7 A 'clean' view through the 'clouds'? : Challenges to community participation and impact of tourism and development in Cherrapunjee and Mawlynnong in Meghalaya"

By Mirza Zulfiqur Rahman

The objective of this chapter is to bring out the local perspectives on the impact of tourism and related development on Cherrapunjee and Mawlynnong, as two separate case studies. The chapter focuses on the first level, overall development priorities and actions in Cherrapunjee and Mawlynnong by the government agencies, and then assesses the specific development priorities in terms of tourism and policy goals and objectives. The chapter aims to bring out local perceptions on the impact of tourism on these villages, be it positive or negative, and the dynamics of the coping mechanisms in the villages. The field research was done in Cherrapunjee, Mawlynnong and Shillong over 2012-13, a number of interviews and village group discussions were held with local stakeholders, such as village elders, village committee members, youth groups, church leaders, tourism agencies, local guides, taxi operators, media, academics and government agencies.

A 'clean' view through the 'clouds'?: Cherrapunjee

Sohra: The playground of the Rain Gods

Cherrapunjee, locally known as Sohra, is literally considered as the playground of the Rain Gods, where mere estimates of annual average rainfall has ceased to matter, rather the romanticism and the mysticism of the place has captured the imagination of people. This is true of the local people who inhabit 'Sohra' through its phases of verdant sunshine and incessant rains, and of the travellers from around the world who are drawn to 'Cherrapunjee' by its very name and the stories that they have heard about the place. These rolling hills attract people from all around the world, a lot of visitors apart from the regular flow of tourists, but adventurers, poets and writers, researchers and nature lovers.

The rolling Khasi Hills which nestles Cherrapunjee, described by the British as 'the Scotland of the East', now sits on a maze of limestone mines and rat hole coal mines, frequented by diesel fuming trucks ferrying the coal and limestone out of the place, and a huge ugly monolith cement factory has seemingly obliterated the many Khasi monoliths which had erstwhile dotted the countryside, the symbol of Khasi animist belief-system. The town of Cherrapunjee has grown bigger with more people settling in, and its rainfall intensity has decreased, due to the environmental changes that have occurred over time.

The road leading to Cherrapunjee away from the maddening traffic of Shillong, the capital city of Meghalaya, is one of the most beautiful hill roads in this part of the world, and is lined with local taxis and private cars and buses ferrying tourists. The impact of tourism is seen right from Police Bazaar in downtown Shillong, where taxi drivers jostle to attract tourists to visit Cherrapunjee, mostly on a day-visit basis. Most the tourists visiting Cherrapunjee make Shillong their preferred destination to stay overnight, and thereby a flourishing business of hotels, restaurants, shopping markets and taxi operators have emanated here, almost wholly controlled by local taxi owners and businessmen of Shillong and some investment from Guwahati in neighbouring Assam. The road to Cherrapunjee starts from Shillong, and so does the challenges and impact due to tourism.

Sohra: The two worlds of tourism

A closer look at the dynamics of tourism in Cherrapunjee, shows that the small town has distinctly two 'worlds' of tourism, completely two meanings of tourism, which operate simultaneously, but has very less in common, be it in modes of operation or in terms of impact on the place, its economy, environment and the local community. One is the 'Shillong driven' mode of tourism and the other is the 'local community driven' mode of tourism. It is the mix and the clash of these two diametrically opposite modes of tourism, which makes for the challenges that the community in Cherrapunjee is grappling today.

The 'Shillong driven' mode can also be termed as synonymous with the 'Meghalaya government driven mode' as the government tourism policymakers and the private business interests have marked out the contours of this mode of tourism in Cherrapunjee. This mode of tourism is characterized by day-visits to Cherrapunjee from Shillong, and the determination of specific tourist interest points, which can be covered in a single day. Here the 'tourism interest' is taken as what the government thinks will interest or capture the tourist attention, which are mainly in the nature of concrete dotted 'eco' parks, limestone caves and waterfall points, a cluster of them which have been identified and have been bandied around in colourful official tourism brochures of the Meghalaya state government, as the 'tourism circuit' of Cherrapunjee, as being all that the place can offer.

The main problem with the 'Shillong driven' mode of tourism is that it completely bypasses the local community stakeholders and there is minimal to almost no interaction of the local community with tourists coming to visit the Cherrapunjee 'tourism circuit'. This mode of conducting tourism is top-down and does not associate the aspirations or the opinion of the local communities of Cherrapunjee, is decided in the hallways of the tourism department in Shillong and the private business chambers of Shillong hoteliers. The worrisome part is that most of the tourism flow into Cherrapunjee come by the 'Shillong driven' mode and the window for the tourist is controlled by the private tour agencies, hoteliers and the taxi drivers, who decide on which 'tourism circuit' points to show and not to show to tourists in Cherrapunjee, also the duration a tourist spends there.

The other mode of the tourism is the 'local community driven' mode, and this has come about in the past few years, with the local villages taking up some of the mantle of demonstrating a bottom up approach to tourism development in the small town. This has been necessitated by the inflow of tourists to the villages of Cherrapunjee town, away from the government sponsored and publicized 'tourism circuit', largely owing to the absence of the means to facilitate such village based tourism activities by the government tourism department. The main driver for this mode of tourism came about with the tourists coming to visit the famous living roots bridges, especially the double decker living roots bridges in Nongriat village of Cherrapunjee. The government has come to take note of these sites in their brochures only recently, but they still do not have the facilitation measures in place for promotion of community based tourism activities here.

When we say that the 'local community driven' mode of tourism development in Cherrapunjee has been there for the past few years, it must also be noted that it is the 'elite within the local community', which has been controlling much of this activity. There needs a lot to be done in order to have a genuine bottom-up approach to tourism development in Cherrapunjee, especially in villages such as Nongriat and Tyrna, where such potential, and more importantly, motivation among people exists. At present, it is only a couple of local elite families in Cherrapunjee which have controlled the business of tourism in the villages, and this mode is fraught with challenges of economic and political rivalry vis-à-vis the 'Shillong driven' mode group of hoteliers and travel agents.

The local community has indeed moved a long way out of their roles as selling chips and biscuits to passing tourists at government designated 'tourism circuit' points, but a vast majority of them do not have the means to make much progress on their own, unless a substantive change in the tourism mode approach and development is facilitated by the government. A nominal percentage of tourists have been successfully attracted to the villages and the living roots bridges, trekking and caving options by local entrepreneurs, but the huge majority of the tourism traffic, is again flowing in the 'Shillong driven' mode of tourism development. There is an unsustainable investment pattern in Cherrapunjee, government driven tourism approach versus local community capabilities.

Sohra: The challenges facing the community

Mawsmai, about five kilometres from Cherrapunjee town, is a popular tourist point because of the Mawsmai limestone caves and the Seven Sisters waterfalls viewpoint, both being two important sites for the 'Shillong driven mode' of tourism that the Government of Meghalaya promotes. The 'sordar' or chief of Mawsmai elaka is dressed at his best for attending the opening ceremony of a large three star holiday property in Mawsmai, which is intended to cater to the flow of tourists to Cherrapunjee as a whole. He is invited to speak at the opening ceremony, apart from the businessmen of Shillong and high-ranking officials of the Government of Meghalaya tourism department. The new hotel property stands in complete contrast of the surroundings, veritably jutting out of the landscape, and definitely not in consonance of the local people's views and aspirations.

This is evident by the views of the sordar of Mawsmai, who feels completely out of place, in the grand gathering, and his presence is only symbolic of the local participation. He agrees that there will be some amount of employment to the local people, but at the same time mentions that he was not consulted before making such a big property in the place, otherwise he would have saved a lot of money for the builders, by suggesting them to build a smaller and more eco-friendly set-up. He points out that there could be many smaller places, which could have come out of the money that was spent to build this.

He thinks that his village or area does not need such a big place such as this, but the local people are amazed by this grandiose project, and even pay for entry tickets to enter and see the hotel property. The local people often come in large groups, happily pay twenty rupees per person at the gate of the hotel, to see the property and also visit the points, which are now inside the hotel, where they had clear views of the Seven Sisters Falls. The local villagers exclaim at disbelief at knowing the amount of money that the hotel charges to stay the night there, and then quickly starts calculating the amount of betel nuts they have to sell, in order to be able to pay for staying there, laugh and walk away. Conversations one has with the local villagers, gives a sense of disconnect felt by the villagers, but the big advertising hoarding of the hotel proclaims, 'We are Cherrapunjee'.

This is just one example of the challenges facing the community in Cherrapunjee, a tribal community living off barter trade mostly along the borders with Bangladesh, exchanging betel nuts for fish, pineapples for rice and so on and so forth. Most Khasi villagers do not have a sense of the value of Chapter money versus barter value of goods (their betel nuts and pineapples), and this is true again of many communities in Northeast India. The money economy that the tourism industry brings and thrives upon is something foreign to the villagers. The opposition to such blatantly unsustainable tourism infrastructure and 'development' activities in their villages, will only come from an understanding of the larger linkages of these with their livelihood and self-sufficiency in the long run. Till then the government agencies and the private business interests will have their own sweet run.

Another example of a smaller scale tourist holiday resort near the village of Tyrna and Nongriat, where the single decker and double decker living roots bridges are, is more at peace with the community and surroundings and employs a lot of local people in the resort, has encouraged homestays in the village and promotes them, definitely is in sharp contrast with the new hotel in Mawsmai. However, the people who visit here, do not get ample opportunity to interact with the villagers, nor does one get the feel of staying in the village, which is what it claims. An excellent place where such local village participation in sustainable tourism engagement can happen, is not exploited to its potential, simply because of the vision of the 'elite within the local community', who decides unilaterally.

There is no sense of discussion or real sense of participation, and whatever is seen is at a very cosmetic level. The local village committees are not talking about tourism, because it is not a all inclusive participatory affair, the mantle is taken upon themselves by the 'elite within the local community' to decide which brand of tourism should be implemented in the village, and never fails to take wholesome credit for any tourism 'development' in the village. A host of ego issues amongst these very 'elite within the local community' tourism stakeholders, keeps from bringing forward a discussion of the community, and each village is sharply polarized on the side of the families which have brought any semblance of tourism 'development' to their villages. This has led to interpersonal sense of conflict among guides, villagers who work as staff of these hotels.

The disunity amongst the villages of Cherrapunjee is the biggest hurdle towards initiating a dialogue on tourism and its operation, and at the same time, the tourism trends that we see in Cherrapunjee is slowly but surely impacting and veritably eating away on their social, cultural, economic, environmental and traditional coping mechanisms and support structures. The resilience of any tribal community is in its self sufficiency at the village level, and the pulls and pressures of the modern system of economic logic, through which tourism is being driven here, accompanied by the various ego and 'development' vision clashes among the 'elite within the local community', is testing the same resilience. The tourists who come from outside are viewed through varied prisms by different sections of villagers of the same village, depending on which side of the tourism stake the villager falls, and this is creating divides even within the village, which is a matter of concern.

Such a disunited situation locally conveniently falls into the lap of the government and business interests in Shillong and distant Guwahati, and they bring changes to the environment of the place, without any consultation with the local people. If the people of Cherrapunjee cannot stand up to show who they really are, it gives such hotels to claim that they are Cherrapunjee, and they are Shillong and so on. What is concerning is that there is no initiative to bring about any discussion among villages in Cherrapunjee, and the current model of development has become the norm, with a measure of impunity. The local villagers of Cherrapunjee are witness to the spectacular manner that their landscape has changed over the past decade or so, through tourism and other more destructively exploitative industries of coal and limestone mining, and there is evidently a sense of disconnect and of discontent. There is a wide disparity of wealth in Khasi society and this is stark in the village set-up, with contractors and tourism elite families dominating the economic payoff structure. The youth of Cherrapunjee, particularly, seem to take these developments in their villages, as being entirely normal course of events. The lack of communication is also being seen between the youth and the elders of the villages, which the elders term as threatening the traditional structure of Khasi society. The local villagers are sure footed and have a firm grip on the slippery steps leading to the living roots bridges, which many tourists find extremely difficult to negotiate, but are finding it hard to negotiate the steps of tourism policy engagement and community participation.

Sohra: The navigable pathways of unity and sustainable development

There is definitely hope for Cherrapunjee to stand up and take its own course of tourism development, but this has to start at the village level first and then spillover to the larger inter-community understanding of common challenges and intervention aspects. The realization that the brand of tourism 'development' that is being pushed by the government and other private interests, is not in the larger interests of the local community and that the ensuing impacts will not pick and choose villages in Cherrapunjee on the basis they have a tourism stake or not, but will impact the entire region, in terms of deeper social, cultural, economic, environmental ramifications. The trigger of such awareness and activism will not come overnight, but has its roots in the education opportunities available to local youth. Any change that will come in Cherrapunjee, will have to be grassroots based, in a bottom-up solution, and not external.

Natural resources are being plundered at will by contractors all over Meghalaya and the challenges run deep into the intricacies of politics of tribal identity and development. The state is also plagued by huge corruption, which has in many ways ensured that the concentration of capital and wealth is in the hands of a few. Community based tourism initiatives can be successful if they are really community driven, and not captured by the 'elite within the local community'. Sometimes the disunity factor in Khasi society seems overplayed by these very vested interests that seeks to control through such propaganda.

The role of the media, civil society, and the government is important in creating the adequate platforms of community participation in aspects of tourism operation and development, and a sustained engagement is required. One cannot expect unity among communities or villages overnight, and this will definitely take time, but must be initiated with a sense of local participation and belonging. The solutions require a long-term engagement, as time is needed for development activities and policies to be grasped, owned and informed by the local communities. The traditional institutions as well as the church can play a leading role in raising awareness and creating unity in Cherrapunjee.

A 'clean' view through the 'clouds'?: Mawlynnong

Tourism: A community wakes up

The family wakes up early at sunrise and young Labyaman gets ready with her even younger siblings Harvestfield and Richardofield to drive their baskets around their neighbourhood. It is like a car rally and soon other young kids join in steering with the rim of their baskets through the neat concrete pathways around their homes. Their objective is to clean the area near their houses from dry leaves and any other scattered items that may be lying around. This is apart from the normal routine of cleaning done by elders in the village, and this children troop is just out have some 'clean' fun. This is a morning scene at Mawlynnong, where a huge billboard, surprisingly or unsurprisingly put up by a cement company, wishes a hearty welcome to the 'cleanest village in Asia'.

Mawlynnong is a small village in Meghalaya, 18 kms inside from the state highway, now assigned to be the international highway through Dawki to Sylhet district in Bangladesh. The village is at the end of the arterial road and the vast plains of Bangladesh can be easily seen from any high point in the village. There are around 95 households in the village and the people belong to the War sub-tribe of the Khasi tribe. All the villagers are Christian by faith and are almost equally divided into two churches, one being the Church of North India and the other being the Protestant Church. The village livelihood is sustained by farming in their plots of land in the community forest adjoining their village, and the major crops are of betel nuts and betel leaves, pineapple, jackfruit, bay leaves, broomsticks and honey. The villagers work in their fields and regularly contribute to community work, which is a part of their daily community living. Their most favourite activity is fishing and they go in groups along trails only known by them to crystal clear streams with their fishing rods. These are the very paths, which lead to living root bridges, clear streams and gushing waterfalls that have opened up the village of Mawlynnong to their newest community activity, which is tourism. Mawlynnong is now known more by tourism than by their sweetest pineapples and the strongest betel nuts in the entire East Khasi Hills. The 'cleanest village in Asia' tag has ushered in tourism here.

Tourism: A Community Activity

Tourism is a community activity in Mawlynnong. Indeed, the very idea behind the sustenance of tourism as an activity in Mawlynnong and its 'unique selling point' has been the tagline given by various visiting journalists to this quiet village, which is the 'cleanest village in Asia'. What seems remarkable about this claim which has now become attached to the village's tourism brand, are not the questions of its validity and 'whether it is the cleanest or not in Asia', but the way that the village has come to use it.

The 'runaway' branding of this village as being the cleanest in Asia by what many like to call 'hit and run' journalists, has been taken by the villagers of Mawlynnong in a rather quiet and collected sense. There is no chest beating about this claim, as the sense of pride that comes from their community living in a clean and hygienic atmosphere, is innately natural to them. The tourism angle is just another welcome recognition to their traditional community living practices, and particularly for which their village has been known for among other neighbouring villages. The remarkable calmness in the community about this 'cleanest village in Asia' tag itself shows that the community has the will and inbuilt resilience to sustainably carry on their traditional living practices, which are clean.

A collective community decision, long back before any proper roads led to Mawlynnong, to systemically take out all the domestic animals to a designated rearing place outside their village, was one of the major factors that made the village maintain a clean living space. The picture perfect scenes of Mawlynnong and the uncluttered living spaces are the result of this community decision, which originally did not come out of any wild dream of 'cleanest village in Asia' tag prospects or of inviting tourists, but from an incident of a threat of disease from the domestic animals to the villagers and the children. Once taken, the decision was never reversed and it stayed like that. More than being physically clean in the living conditions, the added dimension of discipline and orderliness in the traditional community living practices of the villagers of Mawlynnong, make it all the more sustainable. All these aspects bring a refreshing feel to the village, and the colours of the place bear that freshness of the clean environment and living style.

The community came together to build a road to their village in the year 2003 and they made a jeepable road to the village with community labour and resources. Regular petitions by the village headman to the state government ensured that by the year 2004, the black topping of the road was done by the government funds, where the villagers also volunteered with their labour. It was only after this road was built, that the trickle of nature enthusiasts started visiting Mawlynnong. The flow of regular tourists from Shillong and other parts of India and the world started coming only by the year 2007.

The people of Mawlynnong have been in many ways connected to ideas from around the world, and the values and growth of this community has not been isolated due to lack of proper road infrastructure. Villagers from Mawlynnong participated in the First World War in the British Army, fighting for them in Europe. The village is close to the border-trading town of Dawki, which was an important connection for the British colonialists to Meghalaya and rest of Northeast India from Bangladesh through the Dawki Bridge. Mawlynnong was part of an active corridor for the Hynniewtrep National Liberation Council (HNLC) insurgents during the height of the Khasi insurgency, due to the unhindered access through the forests across to their insurgent camps inside Bangladesh.

The community in engaged in tourism collectively, even if majority of the villagers are not directly interacting with tourists on a regular basis. In other words, tourism has a bearing on the community life and thereby of all the villagers of Mawlynnong. The connected nature and relevance of the various activities of the villagers falling into the basket of tourism is being gradually realized by the people of Mawlynnong. The traditional village 'dorbars' or village committee has found the regular mention of tourism in their deliberations. The villagers have seen a remarkable impact on the village economy coming from tourism and thereby collective decisions and efforts to organize the basic tourism infrastructure in the village has been undertaken. The have been committees formed on tourism, with specific roles being assigned to villagers to ensure the smooth conduct of tourism activities in the village. A collective sense of ownership from the community towards the stakes and the responsibility of sustenance of tourism in the village have been seen through these organized efforts and community deliberations.

Tourism: A Community assesses the challenges

The people of Mawlynnong are simple minded with a simple livelihood and are ensconced in their particular way of life. The arrival of tourism as a means of livelihood and the flow of tourists to their village as a matter of daily life has indeed affected their individual and community lives in many ways. Most of them realize the tremendous potential of tourism to bring prosperity to their village and acknowledge the need for a regulated and sustainable flow of tourism in their village to make it be beneficial to all.

The community is aware of the changes and challenges that tourism brings to their village life as well as the challenges that they have to overcome in order to make tourism more organized, sustainable and profitable. The discussions that happen in the village about tourism mainly revolve around issues and questions of the latter kind. The village committee in Mawlynnong, locally known as 'dorbarshnong', has gradually started taking up issues relating to tourism and its development, and this reflects the importance assigned by the villagers to this new means of their livelihood and community activity.

Tourism in Mawlynnong springs with the cleanest village campaign and the major challenge starts with the aspect of cleanliness. The village, after it got the cleanest village tag, admits that it has been a struggle to organize resources to maintain the cleanliness at all times, given the pressure of the huge flow of tourism. On an annual average, at least 50 people visit Mawlynnong every day, which means there is a lot of pressure on litter management. A small team of young villagers from Mawlynnong, who are under the village committee, does an impeccable job of keeping their village free of any litter, but resources to support them are hard to come by, without any active government support. The village committee has to raise money from all the households to sustain this activity. Trash bins made of bamboo are placed at various points in the village, and because of heavy rain in the monsoon they have to be replaced every year, which is again an economic burden. The village committee has been grappling with the dwindling number of people being associated with this cleaning task, unable to support them financially for the work, and some committee members pay from their own pocket to keep this going.

Another aspect of this clean campaign is the adjoining village of Riwai, under the jurisdiction of which the famous living root bridge falls, and is one of the major tourist attractions. The people of Riwai do not care about keeping their village free of litter nor spend any money in engaging people to do that. This directly impacts upon the image of Mawlynnong as the cleanest village in Asia, as tourists consider the living root bridge as part of Mawlynnong itself, and the bridge itself is hemmed in with litter all along its sturdy and fascinating roots. Mawlynnong has not been successful in replicating their example of cleanliness with Riwai, even after meetings and persuasion over time. Riwai cites lack of resources to carry out such cleaning and maintenance work on a daily basis.

The community considers the lack of governmental support in developing the tourism infrastructure in the village as a major challenge. Most of the existing infrastructure catering to tourism has been on their own or through private funding from villagers who have done well in urban centres such as Shillong. A private entrepreneur from Shillong along with some resources from the village committee had helped build a community guesthouse in Mawlynnong, which remained the only proper tourist accommodation in the village. A government project for a tourist complex and a parking lot just outside the village was sanctioned but it has remained a non-starter, with only under 10 percent of work done, and now it has stopped completely. Villagers say that they were not consulted on the design of the government tourist complex, even after the village had allotted a large portion of land, and traditional design or material was not used in the building plan.

The village traditional lifestyle is accustomed to use of bamboo as building material with a lot of villagers are expert at bamboo design and architecture. The sturdy tree houses with beautiful natural and traditional design with bamboo and cane in Mawlynnong, is a testimony to this excellent but dying art. Most new houses are being built with cement, as bamboo buildings require regular maintenance, and the people who are well equipped with bamboo building are moving to learn masonry or are left with no work but to gather food in the forest. The young generation has not learnt this art of building with bamboo, and soon Mawlynnong will have none of these traditional bamboo and cane buildings and no people left who can create such fascinating architecture with natural building material.

Flowing from this, another big challenge is the huge number of day tourists and the accompanying number of polluting vehicles inside the village. Very few tourists can stay overnight in Mawlynnong, given the few options of accommodation and home stays, and therefore the village has to put up the with almost rampaging day tourists from Shillong. Most villagers prefer tourists who spend time in the village and also wished that there was adequate infrastructure to house more tourists. The villagers do not want the huge number of vehicles to come inside the village, which affects its peace and tranquility. The taxi drivers from Shillong bring tourists by the hordes and do not engage the local village guides to show around Mawlynnong, preferring to earn more by doing that on their own.

The villagers feel that they can control the number tourists when the proposed parking lot comes up outside their village, and they can charge an entry fee to enter the village. They feel that a sustainable and controlled level of tourism is only what they can handle as a village, given the limited infrastructure, and anything more than that creates problems. The village has to tackle tourists who are under the influence of alcohol, and who bring alcohol inside the village, and sometimes the situation goes into a confrontation. The village headman has issued directives banning the consumption of alcohol inside the village, but this cannot be enforced in totality by the managing staff of the village. Many villagers feel that this has a detrimental effect to the village decorum and to the children. The villagers acknowledge that it is the local Khasi tourists, which are difficult to handle in alcohol matters than tourists coming from outside Meghalaya, and this saddens them.

The Church brings to the table another major challenge, which advocates Sunday to be a total holiday in the village. Most of the restaurants and guides do not work on Sundays, when a large number of tourists come to the village. Gradually this issue has dominated discussions on tourism in the village, and most people are divided between religion and economic opportunities on a Sunday. Some villagers are open to working on Sundays and have started to take tourists around and open restaurants informally, and this has created a sense of uneasiness in the village, particularly between the villagers directly engaged with tourism and those who are engaged with their traditional occupation of farming. There is slowly a growing sense of 'unchristian' influence from tourism in Mawlynnong.

Tourism: A Community looks forward

Mawlynnong looks forward through these challenges, some it hopes to overcome in the coming times, some problems and challenges are yet unknown to this small community. For instance, the issue over Sunday as a compulsory church sanctioned holiday is something, which is facing the entire tourism industry in Meghalaya, and there are voices coming against it and some conforming to it. Mawlynnong has brought about a middle path in recent times, they work by rotation on Sundays, and the workforce in any family, which is directly related to tourism, goes to Sunday service at separate timings in the day. This is a sign of a resilient and dynamic community, which is setting a precedent for others to follow, and church leaders have come forward to acknowledge such a balance.

Mawlynnong, which has built a small but successful grassroots based bottom-up community led initiative in tourism is a model not just for Meghalaya, but for the entire Northeast to emulate. The 'communitization' initiative in Nagaland, for example, which includes tourism as a sector for empowerment of grassroots based community empowerment, is targeting the community values and unity in Naga society to make tourism a community run and owned initiative, but this is state government driven. Even without government assistance, Mawlynnong has come up on its own as a prime tourism destination, which is at the same time providing a new mode of employment to the villagers, as well as having a shared vision of a sustainable path of tourism development.

The indigenous knowledge systems of tribal societies in Northeast India have a lot to contribute to modern day knowledge and understanding. The villagers of the Khasi Hills, especially in the Mawlynnong-Riwai-Nowhet area has actively combined the indigenous knowledge and practice of growing living root bridges with tourism, and many villagers are initiating new living root bridges in their lands with increased prospects of tourism in mind, which takes years of human guiding of root growth patterns. It is an excellent example of how man has lived with nature in sustainable peace and contributed to each in many ways. Mawlynnong region has many living root bridges in nature-man building progress now, which reflects a continuum of community initiative binding with nature.

Mawlynnong is an excellent example of community resource management and governance through the active participation of the community. Its engagement with tourism brings forward an interesting case chapter, which posits the use of traditional community knowledge, adaptation and innovation techniques for overall community development and empowerment. The gains for Mawlynnong from tourism are now self-evident and soon neighbouring villages such as Riwai and Nowhet will be in a position to expand what Mawlynnong has started. The real success of the Mawlynnong example will be the community's ability and social persuasion on Riwai and Nowhet to understand the importance of preserving its natural resources and knowledge towards development.

However there has been no serious attempt at initiating such a dialogue between the communities, a general reflection of disunity between separate villages in Meghalaya.

Some political commentators in Meghalaya feel that the Khasi society is a disunited lot, and whatever sense of unity is within the unit of the village, and people cannot agree on anything outside their village affinities. Mawlynnong is no exception to this rule, as the villagers have been earlier resistant to dialogue with Riwai and Nowhet on their common problems. However, what marks the Mawlynnong community out of this general trend is the inclination and ability to discuss, listen and be open to ideas, thereby making it progressive and dynamic in character. This has led to a change in the attitude of the Mawlynnong community over time and its efforts at reaching out to other communities.

Mawlynnong has been able to strike a balance between tradition and modernity. The youth of the village have gone out to chapter and many of them plan to come back and contribute towards their village, and interestingly and what may seem obvious, many of them want to come back and be engaged in the tourism initiative. The parents realize that their children may become used to what they refer to as 'easy money' of tourism, as opposed to the 'hard money' of traditional farming in the community forests, and therefore they make it a point not to allow anyone to be involved in the tourism business in Mawlynnong before they attain the age of eighteen. They state that they want their children to be hardened farmers and learn the basic ways of their land and nature compulsorily, and only then they can serve judiciously and sustainably to the community.

The villagers of Mawlynnong know very well about how tourism has developed in Cherrapunjee, and they term that as being unsustainable and something that they do not desire for their village. They term the lack of unity and societal divisions in the many villages that comprise Cherrapunjee, to be the reason of their unsustainable tourism experience. Some people say that in the case of Cherrapunjee, each village does what it pleases and therefore does not take the other villages along with them, and therefore the society there lacks cohesiveness and is a fractured community. The Mawlynnong community is a close-knit one and they take pride in their unity and uniqueness of their village heritage and culture. The children are taught at a very young age about the village example of cleanliness and its importance and how it is bringing people from all around the world to visit their village. This imbibes a spirit of pride and participation in them.

The women of the village take a leading role in the community tourism initiative. They run all the major restaurants in the village and a number of women in a particular neighbourhood get together to help out in a particular restaurant and share the profits. The Khasi tribe is known to be a matrilineal society only in terms of property inheritance, but men generally dominate the household. However in Mawlynnong, this tourism experience of women working in groups has led to a new sense of empowerment and confidence. Women here take an active part in the deliberations of the village committee.

The tourist circuit in Mawlynnong has a lot to be explored, and there is the potential for growth in the coming future, and Mawlynnong seems ready for such a situation. The spirit of discussion and dialogue within the village and the method of collective decision making through the village committee ensures that preparedness to face any challenge. Mawlynnong is the new buzzword among tourists in Shillong, although the number one tourist destination remains Cherrapunjee, this is mainly because the taxi drivers sometimes do not give any information about Mawlynnong to the tourists on their own. The Mawlynnong community has not done any advertisements on their own to attract tourists from Shillong, and this has been a conscious decision to avoid a rush that they will not be able to manage. However, the Mawlynnong village committee plans to publicize their village in Shillong first and then in other parts of India in the near future.

Mawlynnong hopes to raise resources on its own for tourism development, as there has not been any government help forthcoming. Various commentators have described the tourism department of the Government of Meghalaya as being very corrupt and not interested in developing any tourism infrastructure, which is not near the main highway. They have spent a lot of resources on developing concrete parks and have neglected the village based community tourism initiatives. Most of the government attention is again on Cherrapunjee and the Meghalaya Tourism Development Corporation does not care to promote village-based tourism, unless the tourists have specific enquiries on Mawlynnong. It is some private entrepreneurs in Shillong and Assam, which promotes Mawlynnong on a regular basis. The taxi operators in Shillong do not want to publicize Mawlynnong on their own as they can make more money by doing trips to Cherrapunjee, easier to access and they can make more than one trip in a day in the high tourist season.

The village committee of Mawlynnong has some innovative ideas to raise resources for their village for tourism development. One of them is a system where a tourist to Mawlynnong can earn 'clean credits', based on the lines of 'carbon credits', by donating any amount of money to the village development fund, which in turn will help the village committee towards keeping the village clean and help plant more flower plants and trees. The village committee is planning an annual Mawlynnong village festival in order to publicize and showcase the tourism potential of the village, with innovative additions such as flower shows and promoting angling as a tourist activity, which is a local sport.

Mawlynnong village is located at a place where flourishing trading activity used to take place between the Assam and East Bengal in the past, and the proposed India-Bangladesh International Highway opening through the Dawki border post in the future. Mawlynnong is a small peaceful village with a healthy and sustainable tourism potential at the crossroads of future economic development in the region. The people of Mawlynnong realize that there will be challenges and change in the coming future, but are confident of guarding their unique tourism experience, which is based on their culture and traditions, on a sustainable manner. The real cleanliness of Mawlynnong village is in its spirit and character, and how it spreads its 'living roots' to strengthen other villages/communities.

Key Findings and Lessons to be learnt

Shillong, the capital of Meghalaya veritably controls most of the tourism flows and policy decisions, through the corridors of the tourism department and private business interests, which have amassed huge stakes in Shillong, and needs to do what it is doing in Cherrapunjee and Mawlynnong, in order to protect their commercial ventures in Shillong. They are also branching out, for example to Cherrapunjee, and have created assets there, which will ensure the continuation of such discriminative tourism policies in Meghalaya. There are similarities between the two case chapter areas, which relates to the lack of larger coordinated approach towards formulating tourism policies by the villages, as a result of disunity between the villages. Mawlynnong is only one excellent example of community based tourism initiative, with their ideas and innovations, but the neighbouring villages do not form a part of the same vision. The villagers of Mawlynnong have the benefit of being aware of the impact of tourism in Cherrapunjee, and hence are discussing tourism.

The government of Meghalaya does not have any plans to develop sustainable and community based tourism platforms in the state, while it is having its own tunnel vision agenda of developing mega tourism ventures in the state, and aiding private businesses. The commitment towards developing sustainable community based tourism in policy pronouncements are only at the level of conference presentations, while the ideas implemented on the ground do more damage than good to the community. There is no platform or mechanism in place for community voices to be heard by the department of tourism or the Government of Meghalaya, it is only a top-down 'development' strategy. The majority of tourism agencies that operate in Meghalaya are not sensitive about the need for eliciting community views on tourism at all, while individual taxi operators are concentrated on making a living out of ferrying tourists from one point to the other, covering only those mainstream touristy spots which the Department of Tourism in Meghalaya have almost an obsession with. The recent posters and brochures of living roots bridges by the Department of Tourism, only mean a day visit to the village, without any coordinated action plan to ensure that the villagers can create more avenues of tourism engagement on their own, or to assess such village tourism absorption capacity.

Tourism policy in Meghalaya - a brief analysis

The role of the tourism department starts with making the budget of the year and ends with submitting the expenditure reports of the year, and nothing is done in terms of policy intervention. The tourism department is only interested in controlling rather than facilitating the community to create more local stakes and benefits due to tourism. Therefore the policy impact of the tourism department is being seen across Meghalaya, be it in Cherrapunjee, Mawlynnong, West Khasi Hills, Garo Hills or the Jaintia Hills.

The tourism policy of Meghalaya seems to copy the tourism policy of neighbouring Assam, like many other copious government actions and policies. The proximity to Guwahati allows capital, control and policy direction to emanate from Assam. Many of the tourism stakeholders in Meghalaya are handling lot of investment from Assam business interests, and several top Congress politicians and ministers are involved in this. Some say that it would have been better if the tourism department, its policies and its sensitivities were similar to those of Assam, but unfortunately it is far worse than that. There is zero effort to reach out to the local communities and evolve understandings of local responses and inputs, but most of the tourism department's energies are directed at attending international tourism fairs and expositions, all by utilizing government money.

The civil society organizations and media in Shillong follow corruption issues in the tourism department just by the prism of general governmental corruption, which is huge in several departments, and the tourism debates gets lost in other 'important' issues. The Meghalaya Tourism Development Corporation (MTDC) and the Meghalaya Tourism Development Federation (MTDF) are working at separate levels and do not see eye to eye, and are basically at loggerheads, and nothing much has come forward from the Government of Meghalaya's perspective plan for twenty years, which was initiated in 2003, but most of the project planners and consultants were not local. The MTDF seems to be working at the local level more than the MTDC, but then the same trend of the few business houses claim that they are working with the community on issues of tourism, but in actuality, they only push their own agendas of tourism 'development', continues on.

Linking the case studies to policy: the road ahead

The two case studies demonstrate the need for a coordinated strategy on the part of the Government of Meghalaya to create platforms and mechanisms for local community responses to be heard by policymakers, and it cannot be left alone to the Department of Tourism, as both places require levels of intervention which transcends the mandate or capabilities of any one department of the government. The traditional knowledge of communities must be given precedence over bureaucratic top-down decisions, and a dialogue on tourism must start, preferably through civil society organizations. There must be some level of participation in local village dorbar meetings from the policymakers side, because the discussions have been happening on tourism and sustainable development issues in Mawlynnong village for example. The need to promote and project innovative ideas from villages such as Mawlynnong to other parts of Meghalaya such as Cherrapunjee, West Khasi Hills, Garo Hills and Jaintia Hills, and develop capacity within Mawlynnong to disseminate such ideas to neighbouring villages, and sustain it locally.

The awareness creation of tourism impacts in villages such as Mawlynnong, Riwai, Tyrna, Nongriat and other sites in Meghalaya through facilitation of civil society networks across Northeast India, and best practices and innovative ideas must be spread. The Government of Meghalaya necessarily does not have to bring in or fund all solutions, but it can be a facilitator, and must also be a participant observer, as it is critical for the implementation of such deliberative decisions. Any government mechanism on tourism at the village level, must work together with the traditional village dorbar system, and not seek to undermine it, as it is critical to promote traditional institutions, which have social acceptability and is a village level social asset. The desirable goals of accountability, transparency, collective decision-making, social audit and unity through a holistic sense of capacity building, will ensure the greater mobilization of resources and its effective utilization for community development. Tourism must be spread out to more villages in Meghalaya, developed in a carefully calibrated manner with community participation, have strong links to biodiversity and traditional knowledge conservation, and must not be aimed at substituting or replacing the traditional village economy and livelihood means.

2.8 Conservation Challenges and Prospects through Community Based Tourism (CBT) – A Comparative Case chapter of Laokhuwa-Burachapori Wildlife Sanctuaries, Assam

By Persis Farooqy

This Chapter explores the potential of Community Based Tourism (CBT) to play an important role towards achieving socio-economic development of local communities and conservation of their natural resources. Communities settled in the periphery of protected areas depend on these natural resources for their livelihood and subsistence. As population is increasing and so is this pressure, it can have a catastrophic effect on the overall biota. The objective of this Chapter is to bring out the challenges in the path of conservation and how Community Based Tourism has emerged as an active player in eliminating these challenges in two fringe villages of Laokhuwa Wildlife Sanctuary and Burachapori Wildlife Sanctuary in Nagaon district and Sonitpur district of Assam – Saath Nong Bogamukh and Dhania-Sisuati-Jhaoni, on the south bank of mighty Brahmaputra River. The local communities have been traditionally dependent on the sanctuary area for cattle grazing, collection of firewood and other NTFPs. There has been constant endeavour from Assam State Forest Department and some NGOs towards planning and promoting Community Based Tourism in order to strengthen conservation of the park. The major finding of this chapter is that both the sites have different level of potentiality for Community Based Tourism, however, emphasis on capacity building and improving the infrastructure is required. There is a need to develop local level institutions and a framework of rules and regulation for the promotion of Community Based Tourism, enabling the local community stakeholders to have a sustainable engagement.

Introduction

Forest is one of the most diverse ecosystems on our planet Earth and millions of people of tropical countries are dependent on it from centuries. It satisfies human need for food, shelter, medicine and timber and accounts for almost 25% of the terrestrial world. It also provides environmental services and maintains the ecological balance of nature. It is observed that deforestation is more common in developing countries than developed ones. Programmes like conventions, treaties and protocol at regional and international level are undertaken by the government to understand and work towards conservation of the remaining biodiversity. Declaration of protected areas is one such initiative. Every protected area has different background for its existence. Few came into being as an initiative for protecting natural resources while other were hunting grounds for the rich and powerful which are later preserved due to decreasing number of hunts. Communities' living in or near forests depend on forest products for maintaining their daily lives. However, with declaration of protected areas, they have faced turmoil in the name of law and governance. It has imposed restrictions on use and access of forest products that they have been enjoying traditionally (Mukul, 2007).

Bridging between tourism and conservation

Tourism is considered as one of the best way for addressing problems of employment, poverty and economic diversification initiatives in developing countries (GOI-UNDP, 2007). In the recent times, travelling to protected areas is among popular tourist destination. Thus there importance grew not just for tourism interest but also for keeping ecological balance intact. Also people living in urban spaces feel disconnected with nature as their lifestyle have become hectic and competitive. For many people relaxing and getting back in touch with is an excellent way of holiday to escape from hustle and bustle of everyday life (Kuenzi et al, 2008).

It is a matter of concern when expansion of tourism infrastructure and activities bring alteration in wildlife habitats. Sometimes it results in extinction of existing species or loss of biodiversity. Another threat in the pathway of conservation of protected areas is local communities indulging in illegal activities like poaching. Local communities are engaged in low level jobs in hotels and resorts which divert to engage themselves in illegal wildlife activities which cater more money within short span of time. In a way, they become irresponsive towards conserving the ecological assets of their locality.

With increased sense of environmental and social responsibility in tourism plus sustainability, Community Based Tourism is gaining popularity as part of strategies for conservation and development. Other primary purposes are cultural conservation, community and gender empowerment, poverty alleviation and income generation. It gives ownership of tourism assets to the community as it involves them in every aspect of planning. It also promote community pride (REST, 2003).It is a strategy to encompass a range of activities that collective contributes in improving conservation and development. It is observed that when local people participates in decision making, plan on investing resources and are able to achieve reasonable returns, the likelihood of their support and participation in conservation increases. On the other hand, if tourism provides low income to local participants who are engaged as employees, the linkage between tourism and conservation of natural resources is weak where huge profits from tourism is limited in the hands of powerful enterprises excluding the small local entrepreneurs. Thus participation of local communities in designing conservation actions which supports their livelihood is critical.

Presently the linkage between protected areas and tourism is one dimensional. It is important to realise that in a finite planet like Earth, resources used in linear pattern does not lead to sustainable development. Let us understand how it is with a hypothesis. There's a protected area where communities settled in its periphery. They are poor, limited occupational activities and dependent on NTFPs for their sustenance and livelihood as well. Having realized the potential of the area, the rich and powerful acquire land and set up tourism infrastructures. Locals are hired for building infrastructures and take up low status jobs later on. Returns are accumulated in few hands of owners of these enterprises and locals remain underprivileged. This may give rise to locals involving in unethical and illegal activities in the quest of acquiring wealth. The present status of Kaziranga National Park, Assam and threat to wildlife is deteorating as poaching has increased. However, such unlawful activities can't take place without involving either the administration or the locals. There are numerous resorts, hotels and dhabas mushrooming around the park. Few are within the radius of 5 kms of the park. This kind of situation gives rise to man-animal conflict and ultimately loss of wildlife.

There are successful examples of Community Based Tourism where communities have gained economically by providing alternative livelihood. In the work of Bill Tuffin, 2005, Ban Nalan is a village in Luangnamtha province of Laos which started tourism under the name of Nam Ha UNESCO Ecotourism Project. It is a small village with limited option for income. People are simple and poor. As the project started, it gave training and engaged villagers in tourism activities like lodging, cooking, selling food, selling handicrafts, and guides. Earlier villagers had limited income option and their economic condition was not good enough. With community's involvement in tourism, they were more confident and independent (Tuffin, 2005).

Field sites

Two villages namely Saath Nong Bogamukh and Dhania-Sisuati-Jhaoni were identified on the edge of Laokhowa-Burachapori Wildlife Sanctuaries for the present chapter. These two contagious sanctuaries cover an area of 70.1 sq km in Nagaon district and 44.06 sq km in Sonitpur district respectively (Ojah, 2012). They are separated by a stream of Brahmaputra, known as Kadam Nala. As Burachapori Wildlife Sanctuary is geographically isolated from mainland Sonitpur, the administration was handed over to Nagaon Wildlife Division. These sanctuaries fall in the buffer zone of Kaziranga Tiger Reserve. Being close to the river makes it a floodplain predominantly on the south bank of River Brahmaputra. It characterize as a unique combination of grasslands, woodlands and wetlands habitats. This landscape was rich in biodiversity and housed a number of mammals like tigers, deer, rhinos, elephants, wild buffalo, etc. Variety of avifauna and reptiles were also found. According to history, Lady Mary Curzon, the wife of Lord Curzon, the 36th Viceroy of India failed to spot any One-horned Rhinoceros on her visit to Kaziranga region of Assam. She insisted her husband to take initiative for conservation of rhinos in this area. Later, Balaram Hazarika, a noted animal tracker took her to Laokhuwa region where she saw a number of rhinos (Ojah, 2014). Tall grassland, a prime habitat for rhinos, still exists in Laokhuwa-Burachapori region.

Demography: Saath Nong Bogamukh is approximately 2 sq km consisting of 300 households with a population of 3200 people . This village is dominated by Bengali Muslim community. In Dhania-Sisuati-Jhaoni, there are approximately 200 households with a population of 1200 people . It occupies approximate 4.85 sq km area near Burachapori WLS as one of the fringe villages. This village is mainly dominated by Nepali – Gorkha community. This village do not have any health centre, thus they need to go to Bogamukh for treatment

Livelihood and Economy: The people I met in the villages of Saath Nong Bogamukh and Dhania-Sisuati-Jhaoni were very simple and their way of life is different from the complicated urban way of life. Most of the people depend upon agricultural activities for their livelihood. The villagers of the two villages generally cultivate paddy, vegetables and jute. They produce for their self-sustenance as well as for the market. Apart from that they also rear livestock that includes cows, goats and pigs. Some sell livestock produce in the market. Saath Nong Bogamukh, being a majority of Muslim community, villagers does not rear pigs. Within the villages, two or three small shops were seen. Other than the permanent market in Bogamukh, they buy stuffs from the local weekly bazaars called the Haats. In most households of Dhania-Sisuati-Jhaoni village, they own cattles, also known as Khuttis. They sell milk and by products in nearby market and in Bokakhat.

Transportation: Though the distance between both the villages is less than 2 kms, their means of transportation varied. Saath Nong Bogamukh has paved roads connecting up to NH 37 and thereafter is unpaved till Dhania-Sisuati-Jhaoni. Local transport like shared autos run but only up to paved roads. Villagers used country boats to go to Sonitpur district. The condition of boats is poor and posed risk of life of the travellers. They say that it is only by the grace of God due to which they haven't met any major accident till date in the river owing to the poor condition of their boats. The villagers were seen using mobile phones for communication. Provided the simple lifestyle and condition of the villages it was quite fascinating to see extensive use of mobile phones by them. Though electrification is

History of the village: Saath Nong Bogamukh is another small village situated on the periphery of Laokhowa Wildlife Sanctuary and Burachapori Wildlife Sanctuary. This village is around 60 years old and Bengali Muslims as the first settlers. They are predominantly into agricultural activities.

According to villagers of Dhania-Sisuati-Jhaoni, these villages are around 200 years old. Nepali community were the original settlers and they still exist. They used to own large dairy farms and let their cattle's graze in the sanctuary. However, as rules and regulations pertaining to national parks and sanctuaries became stricter, villagers were forbidden from grazing their cattle's inside the sanctuary. Gradually they started selling their cattle's and shift to other livelihood options (Ojah, 2014).

Views about Community Based Tourism: People from both the villages are enthusiastic about Community Based Tourism. Present mode of livelihood does not meet their daily demand. With the current economy structure of our country, price of basic commodities have shoot up sky rates. It has become difficult to support household needs like food, education and medical with their existing income.

Importance of chapter site for Community Based Tourism

For success of any business, it is essential to have advantage over the competitors. Though investment plays a determining factor for setting an enterprise, it cannot assure its lifetime. In case of the present chapter site, Community Based Tourism has potential to be a successful player in enhancing livelihood for the host community and promoting conservation of the sanctuaries. Firstly, as it is situated on the periphery of Laokhuwa-Burachapori Wildlife Sanctuaries, Saath Nong Bogamukh and Dhania-Sisuati-Jhaoni hold advantage over other nearby villages. Distance from both the villages to sanctuaries is short and can be covered by foot. Secondly, according to IRV (Indian Rhino Vision) 2020, Assam Department of Forest and Environment has embarked to increase the number of one-horned rhinos in Assam. On one hand, population of rhinos is increasing annually and on the other hand it has reduced due to rise in illegal activities like poaching. As per IRV 2020, the target for rhino population is 3000 and will be distributed in seven protected areas to provide long term viability. Laokhuwa-Burachapori Wildlife Sanctuaries is one of those selected sites for rhino translocation in near future (Ojah, 2014). Once the process of translocation is completed and opened for tourist, it will boost tourism in and around these sanctuaries.

Challenges to conservation:

In both the villages namely Saath Nong Bogamukh and Dhania-Sisuati-Jhaoni, challenges pertaining to conservation of biodiversity are more or less the same. Some of them are listed below:

•According to the history of Dhania-Sisuati-Jhaoni village, villagers used to own large herd of livestock and their livelihood was mainly selling milk and other milk products in nearby market place. Their cattles used free to graze in nearby forest. As time passed, the size of livestock's herd reduced. But still they are left to graze inside the forest.

•Wildlife disturbance can be due to visitor' intrusion upon wildlife from their visual presence to their movement, noise and behaviour. Tolerance level varies among different species and can affect their territoriality, feeding pattern, breeding seasons and behaviours. Unaccounted entry to the sanctuaries is dangerous. Since villages lie close to these sanctuaries, there are entry points for villagers who know the place quite well.

•Anthropogenic pressure on Laokhuwa-Burachapori Wildlife Sanctuaries is high even after restrictions imposed for conservation. Villagers are often found collecting firewoods and other forest products without seeking permission from the forest department.

•Human-animal conflict is common as both the villages are situated nearby. There are instances when villagers were attacked by wild buffalo while bringing their cattles from the forest.

•The EDCs of both villages trying to develop alternative livelihood and improve socio-economic of the villagers. The main constraints were non-inclusive method of decision making bodies and deficient of funds.

•Dhania-Sisuati-Jhaoni don't get enough attention from the district administration as the district headquarters is situated on the other side of Brahmaputra River. If there is any unrest in the village, they try to solve it in consultation with elderly villagers. For issues related to district authority, they need to travel to Tezpur.

After discussing challenges faced by the two contiguous sanctuaries namely Laokhuwa-Burachapori Wildlife Sanctuaries, Community Based Tourism has potential to drive them away. Few options have been listed below:

•**Homestay:** The architecture of house in Dhania-Sisuati-Jhaoni is unique and traditional. It is known as 'Sang ghor' in Assamese. It is usually a two storey house structure made from locally available resources like bamboo, thatch and wood. Tourist staying with community will give them greater exposure about the place, their culture and history.
In Saath Nong Bogamukh, it is mostly seen that the architecture of their house is modern and concrete. Thus homestay is not possible in this village.

•**Community lodge:** Due to high prospect of homestays in Dhania-Sisuati-Jhaoni-Sisuati-Jhaoni, community lodge are not promoted.
In Saath Nong Bogamukh, community lodge and community restaurant can be a viable option. Women usually remain indoors and interaction with outsiders is limited. However they can be involved in preparation of food for tourists. Village youths can work in the lodge and deliver services like guides, housekeeping, etc if they are given proper training.

•**Social acceptance:** In Dhania-Sisuati-Jhaoni, villagers are hospitable to their guest. They are educated and welcoming in nature. Women are equally privileged like men. Whereas in Saath Nong Bogamukh, it is observed that women are more conservative and remains indoors when guests arrive.

•**Village tracking:** In Dhania-Sisuati-Jhaoni, a village tracking route can carved out starting from Burachapori Forest I.B (Inspector's Bungalow) till EDC Entry Point office of this village till Kasodhora Beel inside the sanctuary. While tracking this route, one can witness the freshwater mangrove forest, flora found in the track and architecture style of Nepali houses. Another nature trail and trekking route starts from Dhania Range Office of Burachapori Wildlife Sanctuary and stretch towards Thulomkoli area through the unique Hijol tree vegetation. The trail proceeds towards the grasslands of Koroitoli where one can witness of the colonies of Bee-Eater birds in the sandy soil. Other grassland birds, snakes and mammals can be observed along with a variety of orchids. Then the trek moves towards Jhaoni region which lead to the river bank of Brahmaputra. The trek terminates in this point and returns to Dhania. But in Saath Nong Bogamukh, tracking route is not missing. Most of the house are pakka and do not display any traditional style of architecture.

•**Camping on the bank of Brahmaputra river:** Dhania village shares boundary with Brahmaputra River on the north and north-east direction. On the bank of Brahmaputra river, the location is marvellous for camp site during dry season along with ride on country boats. Due to less water in the river, the risk associated with depth of the river is minimal. Most of the villagers are good swimmer too. It is an excellent picturesque for nature and wildlife enthusiastic.

•**Other employment opportunities:** Along with existing resources, it is important to provide services to the tourists. Village youths are energetic and have in depth knowledge about their village and the forest learned from the older generation. They can be engaged as guides who take show around their village and also inside the sanctuary under the supervision of Forest department. Other prospects include cook, driver or housekeeping.

For the success of Community Based Tourism in the present chapter sites, besides the panorama that have been mentioned, the following must be taken care of during its planning and implementation.

✔ Infrastructure Zonation: To ensure maximum benefit to villagers settled in the periphery of protected area, there must be 'Infrastructure Zonation'. It will clearly allocate different area for Community Based Tourism which should be nearer to the sanctuaries than private hotels and lodge. Tourism infrastructure like homestays, community lodge, community restaurants, etc should be managed by community with ban on involvement of any private enterprise. It is also necessary to look through mistakes of other tourism enterprises at regional and international and precaution should be proposed. Currently, it is observed that tourism in and around protected areas has not benefited communities as much as enterprises owned by the rich and powerful.

✔ Constituting village level Community Based Tourism committee: To ensure maximum benefit and active involvement of the community, decentralization of responsibilities of tourism is crucial. A village level committee should be constituted which will be responsible for management and promotion of community based tourism in their respective villages. This committee should represent members of villages involved, their EDCs and Forest Department. Such village level committee should look into:

1. Be transparent in accounting and sharing benefits among its villagers
2. Organizing workshops on capacity building in the village with the objectives of Community Based Tourism and for feedback on quality improvement
3. Maintaining rotational pattern of allocating homestays
4. Proper disposal of waste generated from tourism activities
5. Maintenance of campsites and camping equipments like sleeping bags, tents, chairs, etc
6. Utilizing funds generated from CBT derived profits to develop village infrastructures/ common property resource

✔ Benefit sharing mechanism between villager and Forest Department: Presently, revenue generated from any tourist visiting Laokhowa-Burachapori Wildlife Sanctuaries directly goes to Forest Department. It is important to develop a mechanism of sharing income from tourism between Forest Department and local villagers where maximum benefit goes to villagers with only regulatory role by Forest Department.

✔ Rules and Regulations both for villages and visiting tourist (Do's and Don'ts): There are already national level and state level rules and regulation for promotion of ecotourism. However, to avoid any negative impact of Community Based Tourism in a site, it is important to frame site level rules and regulation. Such rules and regulations should be framed in consultation with local villagers. There should be two sets of rules and regulations or 'DOs and DON'Ts' – one for villagers so that visiting tourist don't experience anything negative because of villagers and second set for tourists so that the villagers don't experience anything negative because of visitors.

✔ Capacity building: Villagers should undergo training on group dynamics, book keeping, accounting, financial management and craft related activities. From the tourist point of view, hospitality is determining factor for survival of any tourism enterprise. Workshops on cooking, guiding, campsite management, etc should be organised.

Conclusion

The chapter conducted to understand challenges of conservation and prospect of community based tourism in and around Laokhowa-Burachapori Wildlife Sanctuaries revealed some interesting facts. Tourism haven't boom in this site on large scale but it is growing. In order to increase awareness among public, Forest Department have organised painting competition and trekking for children and photography trips on various occasions. As of now, no private enterprise on tourism has started in this area. Thus it is an excellent opportunity for the host community to establish themselves as a prominent enterprise dealing with tourism activities. Though the communities have never been associated with tourism activities earlier, they are positive towards the introduction and implementation of tourism. Both the villages showed different results based on same parameters on how tourism could be developed. As per the findings, it can be deduced that homestays will be suitable in Dhania-Sisuati-Jhaoni whereas community lodge has better prospect in Saath Nong Bogamukh. These communities also need to undergo skill development trainings for better management of the enterprise. Gradually their dependence on the sanctuaries will reduce as they will have disposable money to substitute forest resource. New opportunities in livelihood will bring development in their respective villages which will lessen the number of youths migrating to urban areas in search of employment. Transparency in profit sharing is important for sustainability of the enterprise. Strict legal penalties should be imposed if anyone found guilty for unaccountability. Through these small steps of involving community in income generating projects, their approach towards the forest and its conservation will increase. Success of Community Based Tourism extremely depends on the community as a unit. It is still left to understand on what ground the community bonding can be sustained to ensure Community Based Tourism's success.

References

- Government of India, United Nations Development Programme (2007) 'Biodiversity conservation through community based natural resource management' India
- Kiss, A. (2004). Is community-based ecotourism a good use of biodiversity conservation funds? TRENDS in Ecology and Evolution. pp232-237
- Mukul, S.A (2007) Bridging Livelihoods and Forest Conservation in Protected Areas: Exploring the role and scope of non-timber products, PhD Thesis, Bangladesh: Shahjalal University of Science and Technology
- Ojah, S, et al. (2012) 'Towards Participatory Management of Protected Areas: Some observations from the Eco-development Programme of Laokhowa and Burachapori Wildlife Sanctuaries of Assam'
- Ojah, S. (2014) 'Bringing back Rhinos to Laokhuwa Burachapori Wildlife Sanctuaries'
- Kuenzi, C and J. McNeely (2008), 'Nature Based Tourism', Global Risk Governance – International Risk Governance Council Bookseries, Vol 1, pp 155-178
- Potjana, S. (2003) 'Community Based Tourism Handbook', Responsible Ecological Social Tour – REST, Thailand
- Tuffin, B. (2005) Community based tourism in the Lao PDR: An Overview

Part 3: Business

3.1 CSR: A Tool to Create Sustainable Tomorrow

By A. Jayakumar and K.Geetha

Abstract

Businesses today operate in an increasingly resource constraint world and are exposed to an array of sustainability forces which will impact the way businesses will operate in the next two decades and beyond. With ever expanding global complex supply chain and diverse customers' base, companies will have to demonstrate the understanding of a full range of impact of sustainability. Many firms in India have taken the initiatives of CSR practices which have been meeting varying needs of the society. Moreover, over a period of time CSR in India has seen lot of changes. Now, more than ever with the coming of the new CSR regulation in India, we can expect a tremendous change in the development of the country. This Chapter considers the CSR as a tool of sustainability. This Chapter discuses about the concept of corporate social responsibility (CSR) and explains the some potential contribution to sustainable development because it brings incentives for corporations to act socially responsibly. The emergence of new CSR regulation in India and the nature and relationship of the concepts of CSR and sustainable development has been discussed in this Chapter.

Keywords: Corporate Social Responsibility, Sustainability, CSR regulation in India

1. Introduction

Globalization of Indian economy has led to a paradigm shift in the way corporate social responsibilities were performed in India. The way companies used to look at CSR activities has also changed from a philanthropic activity to more professional activity. Business enterprises are traditionally known as engines for driving the economic performance of an entity, its success being measured in terms of high returns on equity and its contribution to the development of the society and the nation's economic growth. The company gets everything from the society for its survival and it is the obligation of the enterprise to return positive attitudes towards the society. If the business organization fails to meet the expectations of the society, the society will punish the firm through their purchase behavior. Hence, the success of any business enterprise depends mainly on the ethical behavior of the enterprise towards the society.

2. Corporate sustainability

The term corporate sustainability first came to widespread acceptance in the World Commission on Environment and Development report in 1987 where it was defined as "development that fulfils the needs of the present without limiting the potential for meeting the needs of the future generations." It refers to building a society in which an appropriate balance between economic, social and environmental goals is developed. In order to achieve this goal, all three dimensions of sustainable development have to be satisfied, ie., economic, environmental and social dimensions (the well-known approach called triple bottom line). Integration of all three dimensions of sustainable development should be a condition for achieving long-term corporate sustainability.

Figure 1
Dimensions of Sustainable development

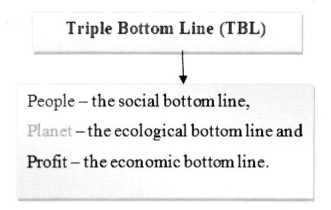

It prompts the corporations to take a more objective look at their impacts on people and planet, rather than focusing on profit motive alone. An increasing number of companies are adopting this new way of addressing the intangible concepts of CSR through TBL which focuses on data collection, analysis and decision making using economic, environmental and social performance information.

This broader coverage of Corporate Sustainability is also implied in the definition given by Pricewaterhouse Coopers which defines Corporate Sustainability as "meeting society's expectations that company adds social, economic and environment value from their operations, products and services". The report "The Business Council for Sustainable Development is released by the World Business Council for Sustainable Development during preparations for the 2002 World Summit on Sustainable Development in Hohannesburg defines sustainable development as a form of progress that meets the needs of the present without compromising the ability of future generations to meet their needs.

Corporate sustainability is understood as the ability of a company, through its governance practices, and market present to positively influence ecosystems, society and economic development.

2.1 Global driver of sustainability

There are four sets of drivers relating to global sustainability.

- The first set of drivers relates to increasing industrialization and its associated material consumption, pollution and waste generation.
- The second set of drivers relates to the proliferation and interconnection of civil stakeholders.
- The third set of drivers relates to emerging technologies that may provide potent, disruptive solutions that could render the basis of many of today's energy and material-intensive industries obsolete.
- Finally the fourth set of drivers relates to the increases in population, poverty and inequity associated with globalization.

In short, global sustainability is a complex, multi-dimensional concept that cannot be addressed by any single corporate action. Creating sustainable value thus requires that firms addressed each of the four broad set of drivers. First, firms can create value by reducing the level of material consumption and pollution associated with rapid industrialization. Second, firms can create value by operating at greater levels of transparency and responsiveness, as driven by civil society. Third, firms can create value through the development of new, disruptive technologies that hold the potential to greatly shrink the size of the human footprint on the planet. Finally, firms can create value by meeting the needs of those at the bottom of the world income pyramid in a way that facilitates inclusive wealth creation and distribution.

3. Corporate Social Responsibility

Corporate social responsibility (CSR) has come to the forefront of corporate and economic concerns because of the increasingly globalized nature of business and the so-called New Economy, a knowledge-based, technology-driven environment that has, among other things, affected an increase in stakeholders' access to information. "The premise of the corporate social responsibility movement is that corporations, because they are the dominant institution of the planet, must squarely face and address the social and environmental problems that afflict humankind."' As a mode of implementing human rights, labor, and environmental standards, CSR has long been discussed as a possible remedy to the inequalities created and exacerbated by globalization. It considers that a corporation is not just a self-centered profit-making entity, but that the company and its actions are also integral to the economy, society, and environment in which they occur. Directors and officers are becoming ever more aware that CSR may provide human rights, labor, and environmental protections to the communities in which they live and to the people they employ. The business case for such social responsibility among corporations is becoming clearer as globalization progresses.

It includes:

- Managing risks
- Protecting and enhancing reputation and brand equity
- Building trust and 'license to operate'
- Improving resource efficiency and access to capital
- Responding to or pre-empting regulations
- Establishing good stakeholder relationships with current and future employees, customers, business partners, socially responsible investors, regulators, and host communities.
- Encouraging innovation and new ways of thinking
- Building future market opportunities.

As such, a social responsibility policy can provide value as a strategic part of a firm's daily activities. Under a strategy that integrates socially responsible practices, a company's analysis of profit, return on investment (ROI), or return on equity (ROE) as the bottom-line should be replaced by a "triple bottom-line".

4. The Relationship between CSR and Sustainable Development

A well-implemented and strongly enforced CSR policy is a key to sustainable development. CSR is a comprehensive notion that takes into account economic, social, and environmental concerns and, at the same time, protects the interests of all stakeholders by requiring greater transparency. Inherent in social responsibility of corporations is the understanding among corporate managers that their business decisions must be made with consideration of a "wider range of constituents than shareholders, and thus they ought to consider the implications of their actions on employees, consumers, suppliers..., the community, and the environment." Stakeholders may also include civil society organizations and other non-governmental organizations (NGOs). This stakeholder view of a corporation's social responsibility requires a constant dialogue between corporate decision-makers and the company's various stakeholders.

 In the end, a well implemented and well-enforced CSR strategy that utilizes a constant dialogue with stakeholders should result in:

- ✔ Respect and care for the community of life,
- ✔ Improvement in the quality of human life,
- ✔ Change in personal attitudes and practices,
- ✔ Empowerment of communities to care for their own environments,
- ✔ Provision of a global framework for integrating development and conservation, and
- ✔ Creation of a global alliance.

All of these lead to long-term value creation for the corporation, its stakeholders, and the communities in which it operates. However, it is important to note that the implementation of a CSR policy will initially cause the corporation to incur additional costs with no immediate return. That is, the corporation may have to choose more expensive inputs and production techniques to protect the environment or pay laborers more and provide improved working conditions, all of which consume resources and detract from the bottom line by increasing operating costs. CSR may also require the corporation to forego certain opportunities that are not aligned with the company's values and principles as found in its CSR policy. But, "having a set of clearly stated values, principles and policies, and mechanisms for measuring performance and ensuring internal and external accountability for these" is crucial to the corporation's contribution to sustainable development in the globalized world.

Although CSR policies will vary among industries and among companies within those industries, three main areas that CSR policies will influence have been identified. First, CSR requires the implementation of socially responsible core business activities that minimize negative impacts and optimize positive impacts. This includes compliance with international standards concerning the environment, labor, and human rights. Companies can also be more proactive in controlling the risks and social costs associated with their activities. Second, companies should institute poverty-focused social investment and philanthropy programs such that their contributions to host communities and social causes become integral to the company's strategy. Third, CSR requires corporations to become engaged in public policy dialogues and institution-building with the goal of fostering an environment that is conducive to both profitable business and sustainable development.

CSR and Corporate Sustainability are two sides of the same coin. CSR defines the social responsibilities of a corporation which, if implemented, will lead to the corporation being sustained. It implies that CSR is a tool to achieve sustainable development and forms part of it.

Figure 2
General Models of CSR and Sustainability

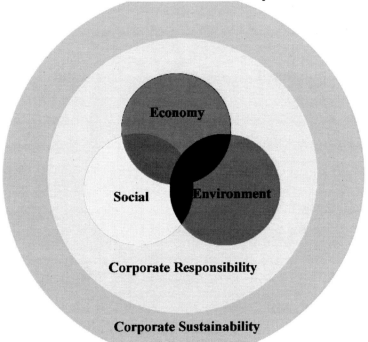

Source: Van Marrewijk (2003; p.107)

This model, corporate responsibility can be understood as the balancing of the economic, social and environmental roles that companies play when conducting business. Hence, CSR refers to when firms balance the three elements of sustainable development.

132

4.1 CSR in India

A company taking on a wider responsibility towards the local community is not a new phenomenon in India. Indian firms have a history of corporate paternalism and philanthropy which has affected expectations on CSR in India. As India has moved towards a liberalised and market-oriented economy, the public's expectations on corporate support have increased. This trend is common for developing countries since their laws and implementation of these laws are generallly not as strict as in developed countries when it comes to environmental issues or the protection of individuals. Also, the developing countries often lack a strong state and have weaknesses in social systems as well as in laws that regulate business conduct. Subsequently with time and growth of capitalist structure in India government has realized CSR as an effective tool to be used in the growth and alleviation of poverty due to huge power of influence that business houses hold over the population.

4.2 The New Regulation on CSR in India

The Government of India has adopted an inclusive growth strategy to implement CSR through corporate sector. The Indian Parliament passed the legendary bill making CSR mandatory for corporate. The regulation makes it compulsory for companies of a certain size to necessarily spend 2% of their profits towards CSR activities. Specifically the regulation states the following: All companies with revenue greater than Rs. 1000 Cr ($200M) or profits of 5 Cr must spend 2% of the average of the last 3 years profits, towards CSR activity. With the passing of this bill India has brought CSR from the backroom to boardroom and we can expect a positive change in all respects of the country.

4.3 The business benefits commonly linked with CSR and corporate sustainability approaches are outlined below:

 * **Licence to operate**: Possibly the crucial benefit for companies adopting CSR or corporate sustainability is preservation of their social licence to operate through enhanced reputation and social capital.

Enhanced reputation: It results from company focus on customer value, attention to employees and the environment, respect for the suppliers and good record on human rights. Investment in local communities normally attracts positive media attention and coverage in the local press where outstanding CSR or sustainability performance can lead to participation in high profile national/international events or awards. Overall, good corporate responsibility and sustainability performance increases a company's reputation strength and secures its social licence to operate.

Enhanced social capital: It results from investment on multi-stakeholder processes, international collaborations and community programmes. Strengthened relationships with international organisations, NGOs, local authorities and other regional bodies become an important dimension of social capital at company, regional and international levels.

- **Improved operational efficiency**

Improved risk control is attainable from transparency and broader awareness of financial, environmental and social risks. Enhanced risk management has a positive impact in operational efficiency and can result in significant direct cost savings depending on the size of the company and the sector in which it operates.

Increased efficiency could also result from:
- ✔ investment in technology to control environmental risks
- ✔ eco-efficiency which means making more from less by reducing ecological impacts.
- ✔ continuous improvement in supply chain processes
- ✔ improved human capital through talent attraction and retention and a motivated and participative work force.
- ✔ lower health costs from healthier employees

- **Improved investment opportunities**

Improved investment opportunities from Socially Responsible Investment funds set up specifically for investing in CSR and sustainability practising companies and from investors that take into account sustainability performance criteria.

- **New market opportunities**

New market opportunities arise from social innovation and green products and services. Social innovation refers to social learning and problem solving in areas ranging from improvements in human health, education, human welfare, environmental protection and energy saving instruments.

5. Conclusion

It can be concluded that in today's competitive world, Organisation cannot be successful without taking into account the social responsibility. Achieving corporate sustainability is one of the objectives of business enterprise and CSR has been an important ingredient of any organization to achieve corporate sustainability. Over the past several years, India has been updating its corporate law and legal framework to increase transparency, accountability, and align with international business standards and now with the emergence of the new CSR Regulation. India is looking forward to become a benchmark in terms of the CSR practices, being one of the 1st nations in Asia to come up with such regulation. More and more companies are discovering that integrating CSR strategies in their company strategies are only going to make their operations more profitable and sustainable. More CSR rating companies, CSR Consultancy agencies have been coming up, and this would bring new opportunities and development in near future. Hence, one can see the CSR as a major tool to create sustainable tomorrow.

6. References

- Andre Sobczak, GervaiseDebucquet and ChristelleHavard, "The impact of higher education on students' and young managers' perception of companies and CSR: an exploratory analysis", Corporate Governance, Vol.6, No.4, pp.463-474.
- Anu Singh Lather and Sona Vikas (2010), "Sustainable business Strategy or Eyewash for unethical business practices: A chapter of the CSR initiatives of Coca Cola India", Management & Change, Vol.14, No.2, pp.1-28.
- Capriotti, P., and Moreno A. (2009), "Communicating CSR, citizenship and sustainability on the web", Journal of communication management, Vol.13, No.2, pp.157-175.
- Du, S., Bhattacharya, C.B., and Sen, S. (2007), "Reaping relationship rewards from corporate social responsibility: the role of competitive positioning", International Journal of Research in Marketing, Vol. 24, No.3, pp. 224–241.
- Du, S., Bhattacharya, C.B., and Sen, S. (2010), "Maximizing Business Returns to Corporate Social Responsibility (CSR): The Role of CSR Communication", International Journal of Management Reviews, Vol.12, No.1, pp.8-19.
- Fergus, A. H. T. and Rowney, J. I. A. (2005), "Sustainable Development: Lost Meaning and Opportunity?", Journal of Business Ethics, Vol.60, No.1, pp.17-27.
- Jenkins, H. M. (2004), "Corporate Social Responsibility and the Mining Industry: Conflicts and Constructs", Corporate Social Responsibility and Environmental Management, Vol.11, No.1, pp. 23-34.

- Jeremy Moon (2007), "The Contribution of Corporate Social Responsibility to Sustainable Development", Sustainable Development, No.15, pp.296-306.
- Jones, M. T. (1999), "The Institutional Determinants of Social Responsibility", Journal of Business Ethics, Vol. 20, No.2, pp. 163-179.
- Jothi M (2011), "Competitiveness, sustainability and CSR initiatives of commercial banks in India: An empirical chapter of BSE listed commercial banks", The Alternative – Journal of Management studies and research, Vol.X, No.1, Oct–March 2011, pp. 21-37.
- Kailash Tuli, "Sustainable Business Strategy or Eyewash for unethical business practices: A chapter of the CSR initiatives of Coca Cola India", Management & Change, Vol.14, No.2, 2010.
- KailashTuli, "Sustainable Business Strategy or Eyewash for unethical business practices: A chapter of the CSR initiatives of Coca Cola India", Management & Change, Vol.14, No.2, 2010.
- Kamal Singh (2009), "Business Ethics and Corporate Social Responsibility – Time for action now", Effective Executive, Vol.XII, No.10, October 2009, pp.58-64.
- Kamal Singh, "Business Ethics and Corporate Social Responsibility – Time for action now", Effective Executive, Vol.XII, No.10, October 2009, pgs.58-64.
- Malvinder Singh (2007), "Corporate Social Responsibility- Contribution to sustainable development", Productivity News, Vol.45, No.3, May-June 2007, pp.52-54.
- Payne, D. M. and Raiborn, C. A. (2001), "Sustainable Development: The Ethics Support the Economics", Journal of Business Ethics, Vol. 32, No.2, pp. 157-168.
- Ruchi Khandelwal and Swarna Bakshi (2014), "The New CSR Regulations in India: The way forward", Procedia Economic and Finance, No.11, pp.60-67.
- Salzmann, O. et al. (2005), "The Business Case for Corporate Sustainability: Literature Review and Research Options", European Management Journal, Vol.23, No.1, pp. 27-36.
- Siebenhuner, B., and Arnold, M. (2007), "Organizational earning to manage sustainable development", Business Strategy & the Environment, Vol. 16, No.5, pp. 339-353.
- Signitzer, B., and Prexl., A. (2008), "Corporate Sustainability Communications: Aspects of Theory and Professionalization", Journal of Public Relations Research, Vol.20, No.1, pp. 1-19.

3.2 Application of Green Economics in Business and Rural India: methods and tools

Dr Natalie West Kharkongor

This chapter reflects the practical application of a new brand of economics, *Green Economics*, which is different from environmental economics and is on the way to be a remedy to our future problems. The operational mechanism of the existing economic systems clearly shows signs that the traditional economic tools and instruments are no longer effective. Hence, there is an urgent need for new economic models and derivatives in sustaining the existing resources. Relationship between mankind and environment has to be strengthened leading to innovative ways in tapping, using, and regenerating the limited natural resources. Surprisingly, we witness more of failures and crisis with the advancement in technology and knowledge. It is high time to diagnose the root causes of the problems and address them accordingly. In answering to these questions, role of Green Economics is significant. It focuses on value – in – use and not primarily on value – in – exchange, and gives importance to regeneration of individuals, communities and ecosystems rather than accumulation of wealth and assets. The section will focus on green and sustainable technologies adopted by most of the corporate in the Indian business. In addition, the section will also deal with eco – friendly technologies in rural India. The section will focus at length in how to give back to the system and not just taking from it.

Introduction

With the growing emphasis on green technology, several initiatives have taken place across various industry verticals. This section will look into the four emerging sectors viz. telecommunication, IT, automobile and banking, and the various green initiatives that have been taken up in such sectors, in the world. A mention is also made in the section about carbon credit. The section will focus on the green technologies adopted by the eight companies and banks in India viz., Airtel, Vodafone, Wipro, Infosys, Hero MotoCorp, Maruti Suzuki, ICICI Bank, IndusInd Bank in the four mentioned sectors. This is followed by the implementation of such green and sustainable initiatives in rural India.

Green Technologies in Four Global Emerging Sectors

Telecommunication is an important industry and is one of the pillars of the economy. With the advancement of technology, the world is more connected now, but at a price. The BTS towers, which provide the connectivity are one of the major consumers of electricity, and have a backup provided by diesel guzzling generators. Not only this, the mobile handsets add to the e-waste and contain hazardous and toxic substances. Of late, due to increasing awareness, several measures have been incorporated to offset this. First, solar energy and other types of renewable sources of energy are being increasingly used to power the transmission towers. Secondly, advanced batteries, which consume fraction of the energy consumed earlier, are used for providing the backup. Thirdly, operators are going in for sharing of mobile towers and other resources to lessen the number of mobile towers. Fourthly, greener data centers, and more energy efficient networking and telecom equipment are being used. Additionally, efforts are being made to make the mobiles and other equipment free of hazardous and toxic substances. Moreover, systems are also being put in place for proper disposal of the e-waste generated and also for the recycling of products.

Information Technology (IT) is an important sector, which has brought about a revolution. IT is the acquisition, processing, storage and dissemination of vocal, pictorial, textual and numerical information by a microelectronics-based combination of computing and telecommunications. The increasing dominance of computers, laptops, tablets, music players, scanners, printers, servers, other networking and storage equipment, in our lives, is due to information technology only. How these products and the IT services add to the emission, is something which is not unknown. However, importantly, this is changing. A lot of research and development is taking place which has lessened the impact of the technology on the environment. The datacenters which brought the digital revolution are being made greener. They are being increasingly powered by alternative sources of energy like solar energy, wind energy etc. and natural ways of cooling are being used to reduce the energy consumption by the cooling units. The networking and storage equipment too are being made more energy efficient. This is being coupled with smart building techniques, wherein sensors are being used to detect and reduce the wastage of electricity and water. Advanced technology has also resulted in smart grid technology, which increases the energy efficiency on the electricity grid and in homes and offices. Green IT has also enabled advanced video conferencing solutions which are being adopted by the corporate to reduce the emissions and spending due to air travel. Additionally, virtualization of servers is taking place to reduce the number of servers used. Moreover, IT has also made possible development of tools to calculate the carbon footprint, to monitor and control energy usage in homes and offices, besides providing utilities like ERP tools which aid a company to optimize their financials as regards to green concerns like energy efficiency, water, and waste and greenhouse gas emissions. Furthermore, several new systems and solutions have been put in place for effective traffic management. Initiatives have also been taken to reduce the use of toxic substances in IT products and to have better e-waste management and recycling solutions.

Not to be left behind is the automobile industry. Automobile industry designs, develops, manufactures, markets and sells motor vehicles and is one of the world's most important economic sectors. As per statistics, a total of 77,857,705 vehicles were globally manufactured in 2010. Adding to this, the number of vehicles already on road, the amount of fuel consumed is substantial. Apart from the fuel consumption, the vehicles also contribute to the pollution. Moreover, the manufacturing process too adds onto the greenhouse gas emissions.

Efforts have been made to make the automobile industry greener and more sustainable. These measures include, design and production of hybrid vehicles, electric vehicles, alternative fuel vehicles etc. These vehicles use electric energy or biofuels to power the cars, hence decreasing the use of conventional diesel and petrol. Other measures include greening the supply chain, wherein parts and components used for manufacture are procured from vendors who themselves adopt green practices, thus reducing the carbon footprint. Additionally, the vehicles manufactured are made in compliance with strict emission norms, to reduce the pollution and emissions. Moreover, other practices like carbon offsetting are also followed, wherein, a small fee is charged from the consumer to offset the carbon emissions incurred in the manufacturing process. This money is then used to fund other green projects or to plant trees. Furthermore, the government is also doing its bit in greening this sector by providing tax sops and other incentives for such green projects.

Banking is another important sector, which surprisingly contributes to the emissions equivalently. Daily electricity consumption, fuel consumption due to air and road travel etc. adds to the emissions. Moreover the huge amounts of section used results in the felling of trees. To make this sector more greener, one of the major initiatives has been the internet and mobile banking. Now, the banking transactions are being done through internet and mobile, and this has reduced the need for people to travel to bank. Secondly, core banking solutions have been implemented, which have minimized the amount of Chapter used, through the use of technology. The banks have also started sending customer banking statements through mail, further reducing the use of Chapter. Moreover, solar powered ATM's, and incorporation of smart building techniques in the office building has reduced the electricity consumption in a big way.

Apart from the Green technology and initiatives, the carbon credit policy also helps in minimizing the impact of technology on the environment by providing an incentive to invest in and adopt green technologies. A carbon credit is a generic term to assign a value to a reduction or offset of greenhouse gas emissions. A carbon credit is usually equivalent to one tons of carbon dioxide equivalent (CO2-e). A carbon credit can be used by a business or individual to reduce their carbon footprint by investing in an activity that has reduced or sequestered greenhouse gases at another site. Carbon credits are bought and sold in the international carbon market - much like any other commodity. Of the total number of carbon contracts signed in the world so far, India has the second largest portfolio with a market share of 12 percent, behind China which had a market share of 61percent. In India, the Delhi Metro Rail Corporation has been certified by the United Nations as the First Metro Rail and Rail based system in the world which will get carbon Credits for reducing Green House Gas Emissions as it has helped to reduce pollution levels in the city by 6.3 lakh tons every year thus helping in reducing global warming.

Green Technologies in India's Four Emerging Sectors

Telecommunication : Airtel which is one of the leading global telecommunications companies has launched a comprehensive program in saving energy. The main motive behind the entire program is to reduce energy and diesel usage leading to carbon emission reduction. One initiative of the program is the Green Towers P7 Initiative. It aims to cover 22,000 tower sites with a priority given to the rural areas. The program is for 3 years and at the end of the 3 years period it will bring down the diesel consumption of 66 million liters per year and carbon dioxide of around 1.5 lacs MT per year.

The Initiative includes the following:

· Alternate energy sources: Airtel has encouraged the use of clean energy solutions. These have proved to be the strong alternative to conventional sources of energy. The deployment of such alternate sources of energy at around 1050 sites has helped the company to save around 6.9 million liters of diesel and around Rs. 280 million.

· IPMS and DCDG: the installation of Integrated Power Management System

(IPMS) and the variable speed DC generators (DCDG) at around 900 sites has been able to reduce diesel consumption by 1.2 million liters and saved Rs. 47 million.

· FCU: The use of Free Cooling Units (FCU) in place of air conditioners at around 3400 sites has saved diesel consumption of around 4.1 million liters.

In addition to the Green Towers P7 initiative, Airtel has taken up other measures to reduce energy consumption such as:

· The installation of solar hot water generators at its main campus in Gurgaon for filling hot water requirement in the cafeteria.

· Lighting Energy Savers (LES) are installed across NCR region which has reduced energy consumption to the amount of 10 – 25% in the lighting system.

· The installation of Variable Frequency Drives at its campus in AHU (Air Handling Unit) has increased the efficiency of cooling system by 10%.

The above three measures have helped the company to save around 8.5 lakh units of electricity per year. The other measures taken up by Airtel are:

· The implementation of the 'Secure Print' solution which has saved about 8 MT of Chapter per annually. The drive of sending e- bills to the post – paid customers leads to the saving of 12,840 trees per year.

· BhartiInfratel, a subsidiary of BhartiAirtel has installed around 3 MWT of solar capacity which has generated more than 5 million units of electricity annually.

Vodafone, another leading player too has launched a series of green initiatives. It has introduced solar chargers and handsets that make extensive use of recycled plastic and have energy efficient features. They have reduced packaging material, and have introduced e-billing. They also collect handsets for reuse and recycling and have researched capacity to manage electronic waste.

IT Services

Wipro, an IT company and also a leading provider of IT services has taken up a number of initiatives leading to greener and sustainable environment. Some of the important measures are:

- *Ecological Sustainability*: This includes reduction in Green House Gases emission by:

✔ using alternative sources of energy for lighting like the LED lights

✔ implementing car – pool policy for employees

✔ reducing business commute

✔ generating wind/solar power in campuses

✔ running air conditioning plant on solar thermal

✔ by planting trees on unused campus land

- *Water Efficiency*: The use of Sewage Treatment Plans for recycling of water. The solid waste generated from treatment is converted to bio fertilizer for use in the campus garden. Approximately, 76% of waste generated is either recycled or composted.

- *E Waste Management*: Under e waste management, Wipro has adopted e waste take back program by following WEEE (Waste Electrical and Equipment) guidelines. Under this initiative, plastic and carton boxes are reused; the metallic parts are sent to European countries for treatment.

- *Elimination of Toxic Chemicals*: Under this initiative the Company has implemented 100% RoHS (Restriction on Hazardous Substances) compliant desktops and laptops and elimination of 21 hazardous chemicals. Additional products are free from toxic chemicals like PVC (poly vinyl chloride) and BFRs (Brominated Flame Retardants).

- *Greener and Ethical Supply Chain*: Under this measure, the suppliers are expected to supply products and services meeting environmental standards.

  Other initiatives are Clean Energy, Green IT Infrastructure, IT for green products and services.

Infosys, another IT giant too is not far behind. It has implemented database archival, and document sharing to minimize the use of Chapter. It has procured electricity through mini hydel plant, and has plans to install bio gas generation facility in its campus. Besides efficient building cooling solutions, smart power management tools, cloud computing solutions and greener data centers it also has effective waste management strategies in place.

Automobile

Hero MotoCorp has adopted a number of initiatives and tools in its organization to minimize the use of resources and to take care of the waste product leading to sustainable development. Some of the initiatives are:

· *Green Technology*: Hero MotoCorp has introduced a special painting process known as Acrylic Cathodic Electro Deposition (AECD) for the frame body. This new process leads to 99% paint transfer efficiency as well as minimizes effluents. The Company also used water soluble paint which is environment friendly ensuring quality and product.

· *Cleaner Processes*: Raw materials and chemicals are first tested on their impact on environment before introduced them in the process of production. Hero MotoCorp has eliminated the use of harmful substance like Hexavalent Chromium, Asbestos, and Phenolic Substances for many years now.

· *Green Roof program*: This program saves huge amount of energy by moderating temperature of roof and surrounding areas. It also helps in reducing storm water runoff volume and peak flow rate. In this way this eco – friendly method restores ecological and aesthetic value.

· *Green Supply Chain*: In the supply chain, the Company has launched two programs, The 'Green Dealer Development Program' for the front end and the 'Green Vendor Development Program' for the backend of the supply chain. In each of these programs, the partners are made aware of the importance of environmental issues as well as managing material resources, energy resource, industrial wastes, pollution and other effluents.

· *Rain Water Harvesting*: The Company has introduced Rain Water Harvesting at both its plants in Dharuhera and Gurgaon of Haryana, one of the driest states in India. In both plants, 16 rainwater harvesting catchments have been set up covering an area of 31540sqmts saving around 18 million liters of water annually.

Maruti Suzuki, another Indian automobile giant, has introduced fuel efficient engines, which gives greater mileage. They have also introduced vehicles which are factory fitted with dual fuel engines, and comply with European ELV norms, which mean that nearly 85% of the car is recyclable. They have strict adherence to BS III and BS IV emission norms and have brought reduction in landfill waste, reduction of groundwater consumption, reduction in CO_2 emission through processes like installation of solar panels, LED lights.

Banking

Reserve Bank of India acknowledges the term *green banking* in its publication, Policy Environment, 2009 – 2010. This report also provides the outlines for the implementation of Green IT in all areas of work in the financial sector. Subsequently, financial institutions are taking up a number of philanthropic activities under the CSR banner. In an emerging market such as India, projects which focus on clean production, good corporate governance, and sustainable energy are considered attractive business opportunities for the financial institutions.

The Indian financial institutions have incorporated sustainability by incorporating in their functions. They have embedded the concept of sustainability in their core business processes like decision making and risk management. Generally, in India, a separate organization or foundation is set up with the main purpose of giving back to the society. The main activities of such an organization relate to under privileged, education and social initiatives, partnering with an NGO or charity house, organizing employee engagement drives, in which employees donate part of their income, volunteer their time and share their knowledge for various community services.

Disclosure of sustainability performance helps in the ranking of financial situations based on global indices such as the Dow Jones Sustainability Index (DJSI), which tracks sustainable – driven companies worldwide on their financial performance. According to Ernst & Young Report, the steps that a financial services organization can take towards sustainability reporting are:

· develop a sustainable strategy

· identify a sustainability reporting roadmap

· develop and implement sustainability management systems

· assess sustainability relating to risk and opportunities

· obtain assurance on sustainability reports including on health and safety aspects

ICICIBank has promoted a number of green programs and technologies as part of giving back to the system. Some of these are:

· *Home Finance*: Under this program, the Bank offers reducing fees to customers who purchase homes in 'Leadership in Energy and Environmental Design' (LEED) certified buildings.

· *Vehicle Finance*: Under Vehicle Finance, the bank offers 50% waiver on processing fee on car models uses alternative mode of energy. These cars include Hyundai's Santro Eco, Maruti's LPG version of Maruti 800, Civic Hybrid of Honda, Omni and Versa, Reva Electric cars, Mahindra Logan CNG versions and Tata Indica CNG.

· *Instabanking*: This refers to Internet banking, i – Mobile banking, and IVR banking.This helps to reduce business commute.

ICICI Bank has also launched programs for employees such as follows:

· Fully utilizing power saving settings when in use and turning off lights and electronic equipments when not in use

· Use of CFLs bulbs

· Using online Webinars to save travel cost and time

· Use of car pool and public transport system

ICICI Bank has also initiated and promoted a program in making institutions, corporate, banks, and government agencies aware of environment issues like biodiversity, wildlife habitats and environment.

IndusIndBank, another local bank has initiatives like solar powered ATMs, thin computing, e-archiving, e-learning, e-waste management, Chapterless fax, energy conservation and also supports finance programs with incentives to go green. With the solar-powered ATM, the bank expects to save around 1,980 Kw of energy annually besides reducing carbon emissions by 1,942 kg. It also expects to save power bills of around Rs. 20,000 per year in urban areas, where it replaces diesel generators with solar panels.

Application of Green and Eco – Friendly Technologies in Rural India

India at present has promoted and facilitated a number of green and eco – friendly technologies in the rural sector. These technologies are implemented at the national level, regional level, and at the state level as given below:

At the National level:

· *SOLECKSHAW*: CMERI has developed a Solar Powered Electric three – Wheeled Vehicle, named as SOLECKSHAW. This vehicle transporting people through small distances, especially in busy streets of cities. It is an environment – friendly car since it is free from toxic emissions. The novelty of this invention is the use of Brushless Direct Current (BLDC) hub motor instead of Permanent Magnetic Direct Current (PMDC) motor. The electric drive has been separated by installing BLDC motor directly on to the front axle and the mechanical drive on the rear axle. This system has also eliminated the use of mechanical devices like spring loaded frictional plate and couplings.

· *Cabinet Dryer and Washing Unit for Ginger and Turmeric*: CMERI has developed an Improved Cabinet Dryer with higher drying rate. The availability of the sun is uncertain and hence the cabinet dryer serves as a useful device for preservation of ginger and turmeric produced by rural farmers. Likewise, CMERI has developed a continuous type washing unit where waste water is being filtered and re – circulated.

· *Cultivation of Medicinal and Aromatic Plants*: The cultivation and processing of aromatic and medicinal plants have enriched the bio – diversity of North Eastern Region as well as opening new opportunities for income generation in the rural sector. IIIM has developed and standardized cultivation and processing technologies in the case of rose, lavender, clarysage, rose geranium and others.

· *Low – Cost Oxygen Monitor*: The system is useful for measuring the oxygen percentage in the stack gas monitoring which in turn improves the combustion efficiency of the oil fired boilers used in various industries, ultimately to a cleaner and friendly environment The successful models taken by the State Science and Technology Councils in India are as follows:

Technologies for Water Purification and Waste Management

· *Plastic and hospital waste management system*: Four plasticand hospital waste disposal demonstration plants based on indigenously developed plasma incineration technologies were set up at ecologically fragile locations having tourist influx at Goa, A&N Islands, Himachal Pradesh & Sikkim and other locations in the states of Andhra Pradesh, Haryana, Uttar Pradesh and Tripura.

With a view to provide safe drinking water, *water purification technologies* are adopted to remove contaminants from drinking water. These technologies are installed in different states in India.

· *Pilot demonstration plant* for treatment of hard/brackish water based on indigenously developed Reverse Osmosis Technology was installed at UttarlaiAirforce Station, Barmer. The project is successful and has been providing drinking water to inhabitants of air – base as well as nearby villages.

· *A sea – water desalination plant* based on 2 – Stage desalination process development indigenously was installed in Nelmudar village, Tamil Nadu.

Distributed Energy Systems

In order to promote decentralized energy generation based on locally available resources, the following technologies are demonstrated at various places:

· *Bio – Diesel production plant* (100L/batch)set up at Orissa with IIT Delhi Technology.

· The Bio – Fuel Plant developed at JSS Academy of Technical Education, Bangalore has been installed at Utthan Center for Sustainable Development and Poverty Alleviation, UP & Raipur Institute of Technology, Raipur Chattisgarh.

· *Biomass Gasifier Project* using 30kg woody biomass per hour with 100% producer gas based engine has been installed at village Bagdora, Chattisgarh. The plant is operated by the Village Energy Committee (VEC). The plant is operating in the morning for commercial activity for 2 hours and in the evening for lighting purpose for 4 hours.

· *Biogas enrichment plant* to meet the electricity requirement has been installed at Rajasthan Go – SewaSangh, Jaipur, The plant has a biogas enrichment system used to get 95% Methane for power generation based on water scrubbing technology developed by IIT, Delhi.

· *Ferro Cement Roof Top Rain Water Harvesting Technology* constructed by Himachal Pradesh State Council of S&T, which was installed at Shimla.

At the Regional Level with Reference to North Eastern Region

In the North Eastern Region of India, the North – East Institute of Science & Technology which was established in the year 1961 has promoted a number of green initiatives. Some of the initiatives are as follows:

· *Agro practices of medicinal plants* like dioscorea, solaniumkhasianum, annatto, bhringaraj, kalmegh, punarnava, agechtachitrak, vedailota, and iswarmul which are used in treating diseases.

· *Bio – Organic Fertilizer*: It is an ecofriendly product of bioactive and organic compound. It enhances the soil fertility and plant growth, and it protects the soil and soil beneficial microbes. This fertilizer can be used for all types of cultivation.

· *VERMICOMPOST*: It is well recognized as an important organic manure for plant growth and development. It improves the physical conditions of soil, and helps in biodegradation of organic compounds and therefore improves the soil fertility.

· *Bacterial Culture for Crop*: It is a new formulation based on plant growth promoting rhizobacteria. It is used for all types of crops and it protects the plant from fungal diseases and enhances the microbial biodiversity. In this way, it increases crop yield.

· *Ceiling Board*: It is an environmental friendly product. The process is based on agricultural waste and by – products. Its main raw materials are agricultural wastes like paddy husk.

· *ACRYLAMIDE*: It is an environmental friendly product. It has a great demand a starting material for production of various polymers to be used as flocculating agents, stock additives and polymers for petroleum recovery.

· *Electronic Grade Potassium Silicate*: It is used for fixing TV tubes and screens. The product is an electronic grade and purity is very high. It is free from environmental hazards.

· *DEOILER*: It is used in oil industry for removal of oil from large volume of associate water effluent. It is an environmental friendly chemical and can remove as much as 90% of the oil present in the water.

· *Banana Fibers*: Fibers from banana pseudo stem can be used for manufacture of ropes and twines for packaging industry and also for manufacturing hessian clothes. It can also be utilized for making dolls, bags, table and door mats, baskets, and other products. Its process is eco - friendly with less disposal problems.

At the State Level with reference to Meghalaya

In the state of Meghalaya, the State Council of Science, Technology & Environment has adopted a number of green and eco – friendly technologies. The innovative technologies are:

· Improved Chula and Water Filtration

· Solar LED Lighting

· Stabilized Mud Block

· Fire Retardant & Life Extended Thatch Roof

· Low – Cost Sanitation

· Rain Water Harvesting

· Organic Chapter 10Composting

· Pedal Pump

· Hydraulic Ram Pump

· Low – Cost Oven

· Low – Cost Cold Storage

· Leaf Plate Making

· Chapter Re-cycling

There is no denying the fact that India has done a lot of work in saving resources, environment preservation and in giving back to the system, but there is a lot more for India to achieve in this regard. At present, there are no strict regulations that mandate sustainability reporting. However, certain measures are taken up by Government of India to make Indian corporations environmentally and socially responsible. One of such measures is a policy that will cause all PSUs, companies and financial institutions to invest 50% of their CSR funds in afforestation initiatives. Secondly, the Confederation of Indian Industry (CII) is coming up with a *green rating system* for the companies. Thirdly, the Institute of Chartered Accountants of India is working on a new set of rules on CSR. The urgency to adopt sustainability has been intensified with the launch of Sustainable Development Funds and Indices in India such as CRISIL, S&P ESG Index.

The chapter concludes by seeking suggestions from the other learned international speakers to address crucial issues of India like the recycling of huge amount of waste resource and empowering the law enforcement authority, which at present is weak.

References and notes:

1. Annual Report 2009-10, Department of Scientific and Industrial Research, Ministry of Science and Technology, Government of India.

2. State Science and Technology Program (SSTP), 2010, Ministry of Science and Technology, Government of India, New Delhi.

3. Annual Report, 2010, North Eastern Institute of Science and Technology, Jorhat, Assam.

4. Annual Report, 2006, RRL Jorhat Technologies, Assam.

5. Newsletter, September 2010, State Council of Science, Technology & Environment, Meghalaya.

6. Maruti Suzuki Sustainability Report 2009-10

7. Infosys Sustainability Report 2009-10.

8. Finesse, Financial Service Newsletter, Nov 2010-Feb 2011, Ernst and Young.

9. http://en.wikipedia.org/wiki/Automotive_industry

10. http://www.oica.net/category/production-statistics/

11. http://en.wikipedia.org/wiki/Information_technology

12. http://www.airtel.in/wps/wcm/connect/About%20Bharti %20Airtel/bharti+airtel/media+centre/bharti+airtel+news/corporate/pg-statement-from-bharti-airtel-green-initiatives

13. http://ibnlive.in.com/news/icici-goes-green-makes-offices-ecofriendly/861407.html

14. http://business-standard.com/india/news/for-banks-green-isnew-black/395561/

15. http://www.icicibank.com/go-green/Index.html

16. http://www.wiprogreentech.com/recycled_plastic_content.html

17. http://www.businessstandard.in/india/news/indusind-bank-launches-first-solar-powered-atm/81456/on

18. http://www.indusind.com/indusind/wcms/en/home/top-links/investors-relation/analyst-meet/QIPInvestorPresentationAugust2010.avsFiles/PDF/QIP %20Investor%20Presentation.pdf

19. http://www.epa.vic.gov.au/climate-change/glossary.asp#CAM

20. http://climatechange.worldbank.org/node/3828

21. http://www.delhimetrorail.com/whatnew_details.aspxid=LrHUclpDo3glld&rdct=d

22.http://www.vodafone.com/content/dam/vodafone/about/sustainability/reports/vodafone_sustainability_report.pdf

Photo: Dr Natalie West Kharkongor

3.3 Examining and analyzing corporate social responsibility (CSR) practices amongst small & medium sized enterprises (SMEs) in the leather industry of Agra, India

By Kanupriya Bhagat

This Chapter aims to examine and analyze Corporate Social Responsibility (CSR) activities amongst small-medium sized enterprises (SMEs) of the leather industry of Agra (India) by taking a qualitative research approach. SMEs in emerging economies such as India are responsible for supporting the local communities and CSR practices amongst them are under researched. Therefore, this chapter targets to bridge this gap in literature and tries to identify and examine the drivers behind CSR activities for SMEs.

Agra's labour-intensive leather industry mainly comprises SMEs-that are amongst the largest producer of leather shoes in the country, and contribute to the local economy significantly. Interviews with managers and owners indicate that CSR activities were found to be increasing recently. Global exposure to the international market and increased awareness of this subject was established to be the biggest driver for this change. Central CSR challenges are related to labour, and responses concern the well being of the workforce in contrast to the holistic change needed. Interview findings indicate that CSR in this context was understood as a form of corporate philanthropy that appears to be connected to social and cultural upbringing of individual managers/owners. It could also be argued that the participants are practicing some aspects of CSR unknowingly as they fail to recognize the connection between regulations and CSR. The results also revealed that CSR activities could be influenced by the age and gender of the manager but this was not investigated, given the limited scope of the chapter.

1. Introduction

In 1987, the World Commission on Economic Development (WCED) popularized the term 'sustainable development' in its well-cited report, *"Our Common Future"*. According to the WCED, sustainable development "is development that meets the needs of the present without compromising the ability of future generations to meet their own needs" (WCED 1987, pp. 43). The WCED stated that sustainable development required the synchronized adoption of environmental, economic, and equity principles. In the past, this concept was met with skepticism as it "challenged the deep-rooted assumption that environmental integrity and social equity were at odds with economic prosperity" (Bansal 2005, pp.197). However, with the growing social, economic and environmental challenged, people have come to accept this relationship.

Companies are an integral part of the world that surrounds them and over time organizations are realizing they "are not divorced from the rest of society. It is but one constituent part of society" (Bhagwat 2011, np.). The two are interdependent and responsible behaviour from an organization will have an exemplifying impact on the society and the environment on the whole. Simply put, an organization has an impact on its employees, customers and shareholders, on the city or region in which they operate, and on the ecosystem in which they exist. Therefore, the concept of corporate social responsibility (CSR) involves applying the concept of sustainable development to the corporate world. As an engine for social progress, CSR encourages the companies to live up to their responsibilities as global citizens. Hence, the concept of CSR is underpinned by the idea that corporations can no longer act as isolated economic entities operating in detachment from broader society. Traditional views about competitiveness, survival and profitability have been replaced by ethical and sustainable business practices (IISD[1]).

The concept of CSR itself is highly ambiguous in nature with no clear definitions. It is considered to be a subjective concept, open to interpretation by the practitioner. Hence, even though it has been around for several decades, scholars still consider it to be a "developing field of research" (Crane et al 2008).

History provides three phases in the development of CSR-
· **Phase 1** (1960-1990): Pre CSR phase - adoption of CSR was only in the form of environmental issues
· **Phase 2** (1990-2000): CSR initiation phase -CSR gained ground in corporate boardrooms
· **Phase 3** (2000-ongoing): early CSR mainstreaming (Katsoulakos et al 2004).

Phase 2 (after the definition of SD was popularized) saw the most growth in the development and adoption of this concept; however, it was exclusively focused on multinational corporations (MNCs) given their substantial global impact. It wasn't until the mainstreaming of this concept that people realized the collective impact of small and medium sized enterprises (SMEs) on the economy, society and the environment (Morsing and Perrimi 2009). Since then, the investigation of CSR practices amongst SMEs and drivers behind these practices has become an important field of research. Hence, this chapter will aim to provide an insight to SMEs and draw upon their CSR practices.

Similarly, CSR practices also tend to differ in developing and developed countries. CSR may vary depending on the country, social and cultural setting it is implemented in. Therefore, theories (like many currently being used) established in developed countries are likely to produce less effective results in developing countries (Khan 2008). CSR in emerging economies draws strongly upon cultural traditions, business ethics, and community which when mixed with "western perception" of CSR will produce ineffective results (Visser 2008). Thus, this chapter will focus on India (a developing country) to understand how CSR activities are practiced there.

The leather industry of India contributes to almost 10% of global leather requirement by exporting over US$ 2 billion worth of leather and leather products annually, 80% of which is produced by SMEs. India is also the worlds second largest footwear producer after China, producing over 2065 million pairs annually (IILF[2]). Within India, Agra is one of the largest producers of leather footwear, producing over 200 million pairs annually and exporting 95 % of their production to over 10 different countries globally (Aggarwal 2004). This region is known for its rich culture and craftsmanship, which can be dated back to the 16th century when the Mughal Empire ruled this region (Aggarwal 2004; Kumar 1997 in Sarkar 2010). Since then, Agra has been a center for cottage industry, comprising of family run production units operating from home and therefore not influenced by MNCs.

The leather industry of Agra comprises of shoe manufacturing and leather trading. Slaughterhouses and tanneries do not exist in this region. Given the impact this industry has globally, CSR practices are highly significant. However, during my research; little or no empirical data could be found that investigates CSR practices in this industry.

The aim of this chapter is to try and bridge this gap in literature by examining and analyzing CSR activities amongst the SMEs of the leather industry of Agra. This chapter will focus on 3-research question, which will help fulfill the objectives of this chapter:

1. How is CSR understood amongst the SMEs of the leather industry of Agra?
2. How have regulations impacted CSR practices amongst these participants?
3. What effects does globalization have on CSR practices?

This chapter will focus on two main aspects of CSR that were identified in literature and are likely to effect CSR practices – regulations and globalization. Additionally, bulk exporters of footwear are the sample size of this chapter. They are likely to possess knowledge of global trade as they have adhere to international protocols. Moreover, since they are dealing with international clients on a regular basis, globalization is likely to affect their perspective about CSR practices. Hence, this chapter will specifically focus on these two aspects and distinguish the effects they may have on CSR practices. Lastly, given the subjective nature of this concept, the prevalence of cultural and religious ethos amongst people, and limited time and resources, a qualitative approach to research was taken in the form of semi-structured interviews and document analysis.

2. Literature Review

The source of literature is mainly from academic research Chapters and some industry reports associated with CSR and the leather industry.
Five strands of literature have derived upon doing research: -
(i) Understanding CSR
(ii) CSR in emerging economies
(iii) CSR in India
(iv) CSR amongst SMEs & SMEs in India
(v) Leather Industry impacts & CSR.

This literature review aims to start with the broad introduction to CSR and then narrow down to the specific industry in question.

2.1 Understanding CSR:

The most important aspect to understanding this concept is recognizing the relationship between CSR and sustainable development. It has been well established that the businesses and the environment are interdependent but this relationship has been severely analyzed given the pressing global problems such as climate change, poverty, human rights violations and HIV/aids (Kolk and Tudler 2010). Thus, different types of firms are increasingly called upon to play a positive role, and contribute towards SD by practicing CSR.

In history, the concept of social responsibility can found as early as 1930 when Wendell Wilkie " helped educate the businessman to a new sense of social responsibility" (Cheit, 1964, p. 157, citing historian William Leuchtenburg in Carroll 1979). However, the modern era of social responsibility is marked from 1953 when Howard R. Bowen Published "Social Responsibilities of Businessman" as many scholars believed this to the first distinctive book about CSR (Carroll 1979, Garriga and Mele 2004). Following Bowen, many concepts and definitions have been produced over time and yet both the corporate and academic world find it difficult to generate an appropriate CSR definition (Dahlsrud 2006, pp1, Kraus and Brtitzelmaier 2012, pp.283). Some scholars have even gone as far as saying that "we have looked for a definition and basically there isn't one" (Jackson and Hawker, 2001 in Dahlsrud 2006, pp1). Similarly, empirical researchers were also unable to distinguish whether CSR is good for business or not. This particular question has dominated CSR research from the last 30 years. (Crane et al 2008). Van Marrewijk (2003) suggests that there is an abundance of definitions and concepts but they are often biased towards certain interests that eventually hinder the development and implementation of this concept on a wider scale. However, this claim cannot be supported by any empirical data (Dahlsrud 2006). Upon doing research to establish a definitive definition, research suggested that different authors explain this concept differently. Some argued that CSR is an excellent tool to market the firm and should therefore be led by marketers (Lantos 2001), while others use CSR to enhance the company's brand (Lewis, 2003). Others argued that firms should be socially responsible because that is the right way to behave (Novak 1996; Trevino and Nelson 1999). The confusion about what CSR really is has also contributed to cynicisms towards this concept itself (Wan-Jan 2006, pp.107). One of the biggest arguments against CSR was presented by neoclassical economists who claiming CSR to be a dangerous concept that "threatens the foundations of market economy" (Friedman, 1970; Henderson, 2001, 2004 in Wan-Jan 2006, pp.107).

Hence, for the sake of this research, CSR should be understood "not as concept, construct or as a theory but as a field of scholarship" (Lockett et al 2006 in Crane et al 2008). Bibliometric analyses of CSR literature also suggest "despite its identifiable set of core concerns, not to mention its relatively long history, CSR is still a developing field of research" (Crane et al 2008). Finally, Lockett (et al 2006, pp 133), after chaptering CSR literature for 10 years concluded, "CSR knowledge could best be described as in a continuing state of emergence. While the field appears well established (overall profile in management journals, increasing significance of other CSR literature in emerging knowledge), it is not characterized by the domination of a particular theoretical approach, assumptions and method" (Lockett et al 2006, pp.133). However, to define this concept, the researcher has adopted two most commonly used definition of CSR- (both these definitions were found to have the maximum frequency count in a chapter conducted by Dahlsrud 2006).

The EU Commission describes CSR as -"A concept whereby companies integrate social and environmental concerns in their business operations and in their interaction with their stakeholders on a voluntary basis" (European Union Commission in Dahlsrud 2006, pp.7), whereas, the World Business Council of Sustainable Development define CSR as "the continuing commitment by business to contribute to economic development while improving the quality of life of the workforce and their families as well as of the community and society at large." (Corporate Social Responsibility: Meeting-changing expectations, **pp.3** WBCSD).

To understand this concept better, Brown and Fraser (2006) presented three broad approaches to social and environmental accountability (SEA): the business case, stakeholder-accountability and critical theory approaches. Over the years, SEA has become an integral part of CSR. Liberal notions of CSR have placed great emphasis on "voluntary, partnership and market based approaches to tackling social and environmental problems and managing conflict" (Newell 2005, pp. 543). Therefore, reporting these actions play a vital role in enhancing CSR.

 These approaches are based on fundamentally different understandings of the business–society interface, which, in turn, leads to quite different views about why and how (if at all) the field should be developed. These three fields are explained briefly below:

· Business Case Approach: As the label indicates – this approach views CSR and SEA initiatives primarily from the perspective of "what's in it for business and shareholders?" (Brown and Fraser 2006). O'Dwyer (2003) implies that businesses tend to "ignore, deny or gloss over conflicts of interest in business–society relationships". Therefore, the focus of business case approach is to identify and pursue forms of CSR and SEA that result in 'win–wins' for both business and wider stakeholders.

· Stakeholder-Accountability Approach: This approach views large corporations as "quasi-public institutions" and seeks to promote a more open, transparent and democratic society (Gray et al., 1996). It promotes the idea that various stakeholders have 'information rights' which must be acknowledged for decision-making purposes and to protect against potential abuses of corporate power. This approach also proposes that groups such as employees, consumers and local communities have a 'right to know' (Swift 2001) and to then apply rewards and sanctions through 'exit', 'voice' or 'loyalty' options. Stakeholder accountability is also increasingly viewed as a process "in which people and records must interact to achieve accountability"(Yakel 2001, p. 234).

· Critical Theory Approach: The critical theory or 'radical' approach is essentially a critique of the stakeholder-accountability approach to CSR and SEA. Supporters of this approach are doubtful about the potential for 'real accountability' in the absence of radical change in capitalist society (Brown and Fraser 2006). Under this approach, CSR/SEA is expected to expose the basic contradictions and exploitative aspects of the capitalist system. It also suggests that environmental degradation and social inequities should be highlighted for CSR to SEA to work (Brown and Fraser 2006).

Another important aspect of this concept is the assimilation and application of CSR. From the industrial revolution until the 1970s, social objectives were considered to be government responsibility. It was not until 1970-1980 that social movements and NGO activity led to the "mobilization of public opinion demanding from corporations to demonstrate a socially responsible stance" (Bichta 2003, pp.9). Today, while there is broad unanimity that CSR is a business-driven approach and that the main focus of CSR development is the business sector, attention must also be paid to the development and application of this concept within the framework of other stakeholders, such as governments (Albereda et al 2008). Over the last decade, governments have joined other stakeholders in assuming a relevant role as drivers of CSR (Moon 2004) and adopting public sector roles in strengthening CSR (Fox et al. 2002). Countries like the UK, Denmark and Sweden have been amongst the pioneers in this aspect as they have managed to develop and implement policies that foster CSR (Bhave 2009). However, little empirical evidence could be found for the same in developing countries (like India).

The World Bank has identified four principal public sector roles in relation to CSR that are mandating, facilitating, partnering and endorsing roles (see Table 1 below)

Essentially, 'intelligent' government action is needed to ensure that businesses contribute towards SD (Cowe and Porritt 2002 in Bichta 2003).
This just gives a brief introduction to the role government might play towards promoting CSR. This role will be further discussed below.

2.2 CSR in emerging economies:

Literature suggests that CSR may vary depending on the country, social and cultural setting it is implemented in. Empirical evidence has already shown that CSR perception and practice in Europe differs from that of the United States (Matten and Moon 2005). This is majorly due to the fact that both countries share different cultural norms and institutional structures and political legacies (see for e.g. Doh and Guay 2006, Matten and Moon 2005). Hence, considering that CSR can be viewed as a social construction (Dahlsrud 2006) and CSR activities are sensitive to even subtle differences within developed countries- it is highly likely for it to be different in emerging economies. Khan (2008) argues that majority of the studies conducted on CSR are based on the western perspective of CSR that does not fit the Asian countries

(India for example). Thus, it is now imperative to question whether the time has come to develop CSR research from an emerging market perspective (Khan 2008).

Visser (2008) also draws upon the cultural traditions in emerging economies and how that influences their CSR activities. He suggests, "CSR in emerging economies draws strongly on deep-rooted indigenous cultural traditions of philanthropy, business ethics, and community embeddedness. Indeed, some of these traditions go back to ancient times" (Visser 2008. pp. 481). Moreover Frynas (2006, pp.17) also suggests that most of the CSR activities in emerging economies are "driven by the external demands in developed countries and foreign multinational firms spear heading CSR activities".

If we consider one of the most popular models-Carroll's classic CSR pyramid (1991) comprising economic, legal, ethical, and philanthropic responsibilities is almost entirely based upon research conducted in an American context (Visser 2008) and therefore, cannot be applied in an emerging economy context. A good example of this was a chapter conducted by Zabin (2013), who applied Carroll's CSR pyramid in Bangladesh's ready-made garments factory and discovered similar results- economic and philanthropic responsibilities triumphed legal and ethical responsibility. Figure 2 (see below) below illustrates this point and highlights the different priorities firms may face in developed and developing countries respectively.

Frynas (2006) in his chapter concluded that motives for CSR and actual CSR practice in emerging economies tend to have a "peculiar local flavor". Often, the local socio-economic needs of a developing country are so great that philanthropy is an expected norm. Commonly, many companies are also found to have been supporting entire communities in the absence of local government (Visser 2008). Therefore, philanthropic responsibilities often take over legal and ethical responsibilities in an emerging economy (Frynas 2006; Visser 2008)- suggesting CSR activities are practiced differently in developing economies and CSR definitions generated in developed counties cannot be expected to produce appropriate results when used in a developing country setting.

Similar trends can be found in the public sector initiatives as well. Examples of developing country public sector initiatives can be found in all categories mentioned above in section one (i.e. mandating, facilitating, partnering and endorsing roles), however, they are present on a local and regional level only. Rich body of experience is present at subnational level in many developing countries, which are unexplored (Fox et al 2002). Moreover, trade and investment promotion were found to be two main drivers CSR initiatives by public sector agencies in developing countries, for example, the public sector is now beginning to encourage the local producers to meet requirements of voluntary CSR standards such as SA8000 (Fox et al 2002).

Additionally, by providing higher minimum social and environmental standards, the CSR agenda encourages innovation. For example, anecdotal evidence suggests that the CSR agenda on child labor in developing countries has encouraged public sector labor inspectorates in some developing countries to step up their compliance activities. Lastly, consumer demand was also found to be an important driver of CSR practices in developing countries (Fox et al 2002).

Section 2.2 (above) explains how CSR is practiced differently in emerging economies. It also highlights the different drivers behind CSR activities, which is essential to understand how CSR might be practiced in India.

2.3 CSR in India:

The concept of CSR in India has been a well-established tradition in number of organizations, especially family owned business who posses a strong community ethos, however, this practice might not necessarily be coined as CSR. Historically, culture has been a significant influence, impacting on business and government and society relationships (Shrivastava and Venkateswaran 2000; Khan 2008). India has seen four phases of CSR. Changes in CSR activities can clearly be noted over time. Additionally, this also highlights that the concept of CSR is in fact not new.

Additionally, Kumar et al. (2001: 1-6 in Balsubramanian et al 2005 .pp 80) identified four models of social responsibility that currently operate in India (i.e. fourth phase)
(i) The Gandhian model- "Voluntary commitment to public welfare based on ethical awareness of broad social needs"
(ii) The Nehru model –"State-driven policies including state ownership and extensive corporate regulation and administration"
(iii) The Milton Friedman model-"Corporate responsibility primarily focused on owner objectives"
(iv) The Freeman model- "Stakeholder responsiveness which recognizes direct and in direct stakeholder interests" (Balsubramanian et al 2005 .pp 80)
However, while these four models help clarify different approaches, they are not mutually exclusive. Organizations may see an overlap between two or more approaches or multiple orientations may occur (Balsubramanian et al 2005).
Over the years India has evolved in the field of CSR. Today, companies in India participate to address various issues such as healthcare, education, rural development, sanitation, microcredit, and women empowerment. To mention a few examples- CII (Confederation of Indian Industry) in partnership with UNDP has set up India Partnership Forum to promote multi stakeholders approach to CSR. Additionally, Social Development Council (SDC) also set up by CII, ensures corporate participation

in social development and provides an institutional base for social activities of the corporate sector and finally, Progress, Harmony and Development chambers of commerce and Industry (PHDCCI) has major interventions in family welfare and rural development which promote CSR (Gautam and Singh 2010).

Moreover, analysis of surveys (such as Singh and Ahuja 1983, Partners in Change 2000, Karmyog CSR rating 2007-08) in Gautam and Singh (2010) suggest that even though many companies have adopted CSR in their business approach, "CSR seem to be in a confused state" (Gautam and Singh 2010, pp.50). Independent companies adopt and define CSR in their own way, which might be incomplete given the limited resources and understanding towards this subject. The end result being that all activities undertaken in the name of CSR are mainly philanthropy, or an extension of philanthropy (Gautam and Singh 2010, pp.50). Similarly, Mehra (et al 2006 in Khan 2008) argues even though CSR is now gaining popularity in this country, "mainstreaming CSR in the corporate process and achieving consistency in actions remains to be achieved" (et al Mehra 2006 in Khan 2008, pp.44). It is also evident that CSR is boosted by international exposure at the local, national and international level (this might include exports, conferences, globalization, advanced technology) (Chapple et al 2003; Khan 2008; Chambers et al 2003). According to Chapple (et al 2003), the multiplier effect of international operations on stakeholders, the need for domestic companies to establish themselves as good citizens in the international market and institutional changes occurring due to globalization is the reason behind this change. Similarly, failure to provide consistent pressure on businesses by local authorities (such as NGOS, domestic government and third parties) also forces the businesses to rely on external bodies (i.e. international governance), which is again considered to boost CSR practices (Sawhney 2004 in Khan 2008)

Chambers (et al 2003) on the other hand concludes that only two percent of Indian companies actually produce dedicated CSR reports (Chambers et al. 2003, pp. 12), he further distinguishes that out of this 2%, 47.2% produce "medium" extent reports (i.e. three to ten pages) and only 36.1% produce "extensive" reports (i.e. over ten pages-optimal level) (Chambers et al. 2003, p. 11). Similarly, KPMG conducted a survey in 2013 to mark the evolving trend of CSR reporting in India and concluded with an average quality score of 42 out of possible 100 for all CSR reports, indicating that there is need to significantly improve the quality of CSR reporting in India. Additionally, this survey also mentioned that 39 per cent of N100 companies with separate CSR reports have simply repeated the information presented for earlier reporting years.

As mentioned above, government legislation plays a vital role in facilitating CSR. In India certain initiatives have been taken by the government to do the same. For example, according to Minister for Corporate Affairs, Mr Salman Khurshid, the Indian government is in process of developing a system of CSR credits. This is similar to the system of carbon credits, which are given to companies for green initiatives (Berad 2011, pp. 102). Additionally, the concept of CSR in India is governed by clause135 of the Companies Act, 2013, which was recently revised on 29 August 2013. Under this clause, now companies with an annual turnover of INR 10 billion (GBP 98.3 million) and more, or a net worth of INR 5 billion (GBP 49.2 million) and more, or a net profit of five crore (approx. 500,000 BBP) and more are now required to set up CSR Committee of their board members, including at least one independent director from the fiscal year 2014-2015. The Act now encourages companies to spend at least 2% of their average profits in the previous three years on CSR activities (PWC handbook).

Lastly, Sharma, Sharma and Kishor (2013) in their chapter conclude, "there has been an clear transition from giving as an obligation or charity to giving as a strategy or responsibility. The review of the case studies and work done on CSR by companies in India suggests that the CSR is slowly moving away from charity and dependence and starting to build on empowerment and partnership" (Sharma, Sharma and Kishor 2013 pp. 61).

This section explores how the concept of CSR is understood and practiced in India. It also highlights the drivers behind these activities and how they can be improved. Therefore, this section is essential in analyzing the data collected to determine how CSR is practiced and understood in India.

2.4 CSR amongst SMEs and SMEs in India

There is a growing unanimity in literature that SMEs demonstrate distinctive characteristics, which make them unique and, therefore, the content, nature and extent of their participation in CSR and ethics is likely to be different than that of large corporations (Jenkins, 2006). So far, large corporations have dominated research on CSR and SMEs have received relatively little attention compared to the CSR in large corporations (Moore & Spence 2006; Jenkins 2006). Similarly, Moore and Spence (2006), in their research also argue, "there is no area of research into responsible business practice and SMEs which we could claim is well addressed, there are some areas which have been investigated to some extent" (Moore and Spence 2006, pp. 220). According to them, "current literature reviews tend to focus on one literature and hence run the risk of missing significant contributions to the broad area of responsible business practice and SMEs" (Moore and Spence 2006, pp. 220). Additionally, majority of the research does not refer to social and ethical issues associated with businesses or responsible business practices that might help address these issues.

Morsing and Perrimi (2009) and Pandey (2007) both have emphasized the importance of SMEs in a country, be it UK or India. MNCs do have a large impact on the society and the environment, however "'smallness' of the individual SME is not proportional to the collective 'grandness' of SMEs" (Morsing and Perrimi 2009, pp.2), which subsequently suggests that SMEs do have an impact on the society and the environment and CSR practices amongst them is a necessity.

In developing countries like India, as some authors like Leutkenhorst (2004 in Srinivasan 2011) highlight the contribution of SMEs towards employment generation. SMEs tend to increase employment by using more labor-intensive production processes, which in turn leads to a more unbiased income distribution. In developing countries where disparity level in income is high and the industrial growth has not been widespread and uniform, the role of the medium, small and micro enterprises in creating employment is quite relevant (Srinivasan 2011).

The contribution of SMEs to the economic development of India is well documented in an academic Chapter published by Pandey (2007). Their contribution in the total corporate sector is as follows: 40% of the total volume of production, 80% of employment, 60% of the exports and 92% in terms of enterprises. The SMEs contribute 7% of India's GDP. As per the Third All India Census of Small Scale Industries conducted in 2004, the SMEs have increased from about 80,000 units in the 1940s to about 10.52 million units. In the sports goods and garments sector their contribution to exports is as high as 90% to 100%. They constitute 90% of the industrial units in the country and also contribute to about 35% of India's exports (Pandey, 2007). Therefore, their existence and contribution cannot be overlooked.

In recent years, CSR in SMEs in India has been gaining increased attention from practitioners, NGOs and international agencies, but not from scholars. Very little empirical data was found upon doing research, which specifically targeted SMEs of India, however, the few that were found are mentioned in this section. In a comparative chapter conducted on CSR practices of Dutch Multinationals and SMEs operating in India, it was found that while large multinationals had established a CSR policy, CSR was not institutionalized amongst SMEs (CREM, 2004). The reasons attributed to the lack of institutionalization of CSR include limited resources to do CSR, lack of pressure from the customer or NGOs to do CSR and finally, the inability to see any direct benefit in doing CSR (CREM, 2004). Furthermore, anecdotal evidence in India on SMEs implies that the ethical or social orientation of the firm is a byproduct of the ethical and social stand of its owner. While the ownership structure is likely to vary (see section iii (CSR in India) for the four CSR models that operate in India), it is likely that the government norms that apply to large corporation may not be relevant in the case of SMEs (Srinivasan 2011).

Studies also show that limited resources and understanding of the subject has led the managers of many SMEs to believe that compliance to the government laws can be seen as being socially responsible. Similarly, SME owners were also found to assume that philanthropy and CSR are one and the same. (Srinivasan 2011; Gupta, Sukhmani and Kalra 2012). Since many of the SMEs are at a stage where they are struggling to establish themselves and do not have the manpower or resources to address these issues, they tend to ignore them (Revenkar, 2004 in Srinivasan 2011). Gupta (et al 2012) concluded the lack of financial support to be one of the main drivers to be discouraging CSR amongst SMES. Additionally, studies also suggests, SMEs are unable to see any clear benefits by following or practicing CSR and therefore, very few companies had social reports, codes of conduct or stated ethical practices (see Srinivasan 2011,Gupta, Sukhmani and Kalra 2012, Neilson and Thomsen 2009). In a chapter conducted by the UNIDO (2008) on CSR perceptions and activities in SMEs in five industrial clusters in India, it was found that regardless of the geographical region they were operating in or originated from, SMEs tended to behave similarly towards CSR. Many of them considered 'taking care of their employees internally' and 'being involved in community welfare' as their CSR responsibility (Srinivasan 2011, pp.59). This might also suggest that these activities were considered as a norm and not CSR practices.

One of the most recent developments in this field was the revised CSR clause of the new Company Act in 2013. By requiring companies with a minimum net profit of 5 crores INR (500,000 GBP, to spend on CSR activities, the Company Act is likely to bring in many SMEs into the CSR fold. This change will encourage (in some cases force) SMEs to adopt CSR activities despite their limitations (PWC handbook)

This section highlights how CSR is practiced and understood specifically amongst the SMEs and SMEs of India. It highlights the gap in literature and suggests that even though SMEs play a crucial role in the economy of India, CSR practices amongst them are under research. This section provides the background of information needed to understand the position of SMEs in India and what is being done to encourage CSR amongst them.

2.5 Leather Industry Impacts and CSR

Leather is considered to be one of the first manufactured material in history and over the years it has outgrown its practical purpose to become a luxury item. Lucintel (2013), in their report estimated that this industry to likely to reach a revenue of $91.2 billion by the year 2018 with a CAGR (compound annual growth rate) of 3.4%, over the next four years. This shows the growing demand of leather and its products in the world, which sequentially makes CSR practices amongst them highly significant.

Majority of leather and leather products are manufactured in developing country (SINET - Sustainable Industrial Networks and Its applications on Micro Regional Environmental Planning, 2007) and like other developing countries, the leather industry occupies a prominent place in the Indian economy in view of its substantial export earnings, employment potential and growth. The table below (Table 3) highlights key aspects of the Indian leather industry.

Table 3: Source- SINET 2007; Kulkarni 2005

Indian Leather Sector: A profile
· India is the largest livestock holding country 21% large animals and 11% small animals
· A source of 10% global leather requirement
· The industry exports US$ 2 billion worth of leather and leather products i.e. 50% of production
· The industry employs more than 2.5 million people
· 80%of the total produce by value in the Indian leather sector originates from small and medium enterprises
· In 2003, Out of a total of US$ 2094 million of exports of leather and leather products by India, footwear and footwear components accounted for US$ 750 million, i.e. more that one third.
· Enormous potential for future growth (domestic as well as exports)

The Indian leather industry is spread in about six key segments:

(i) tanning and finishing
(ii) leather footwear
(iii) footwear components
(iv) leather garments
(v) leather goods
(vi) saddlery and harness

The footwear segment and saddlery and harness segment have the highest share of the household, tiny and cottage industry sector (India FTAs and MSMEs). India is also the worlds second largest footwear producer after China, producing over 2065 million pairs annually (IIFL). Footwear industry of India is also known to be the second largest employer in the country (Aggarwal 2004).

Three states namely Uttar Pradesh, Tamil Nadu and West Bengal contribute sizable proportion of employment for the footwear industry. Together they back four-fifth of total employment generated (Sarkar 2010). Situated in Uttar Pradesh state, Agra is one of the largest footwear manufacturing center of India, which caters to both the domestic as well as international markets (Aggarwal 2004). The leather industry of Agra mainly comprises of shoe manufacturing (i.e. sourcing the leather and producing the shoe). There are no legal slaughterhouses or tanneries in this area. Figure 3 (see below) highlights the three Indian states and Agra on the map of India- giving a clear idea of the location being chapter in this research project.

Agra has seen a long history of rich culture and craftsmanship, which can be dated back to the 16th century when the Mughal Empire ruled this region (Aggarwal 2004; Kumar 1997 in Sarkar 2010). Since then, Agra has been a center of cottage industry production, based on family run production units operating from home. As the production volume increased over the years, these individual units converted into organized units, there by improving working standards and conditions. About 25% population of Agra city is directly or indirectly earning their livelihood through this industry (Aggawal 2004). This industry supports approximately 60,000 skilled workers and provides employment to over 100,000 people. SMEs in Agra produce roughly 200 million pairs of footwear, which satisfies approximately 53% of the domestic requirement of the footwear (Aggarwal 2004, India's FTAs and MSMEs; IILF).

Exports of footwear began as early as 1950 to several East Asian countries but only after 1955 the export orders from communist blocks became very important to Agra. One estimation showed that by 1963, 13% of all shoe traded in Agra was with Russia and its satellite countries (Lynch, 1969 in Sarkar 2010). The industry developed considerably from the 1970s s with a change in the organization of the production, marketing, invention of new technology for methods of construction and use of raw materials for producing the footwear (Aggarwal 2004). With a view to assist house hold artisans, cottage and small scale units in marketing of shoes and providing financial, technical assistance, the Uttar Pradesh Leather Development Corporation (LAMCO) in collaboration with the national government and organizations like, Bharat Leather Corporation (BLC) and Bhartiya Charm Udyog Sangh played a crucial role in the development of this sector by providing technical and financial assistance. They also sold their products in the country through their network, which boosted the distribution and demand of the product (Aggarwal 2004). The following table (see Table 4) shows the illustrative growth of the modernization of the footwear industry: -

Table 4: Growth of footwear industry. Source: Aggarwal 2004

S.N	Year	No. Of Mechanized Units	No. Of Semi Mechanized Units
1.	1970	10	50
2.	1980	15	85
3.	1990	25	120
4.	2000	40	180
5.	2005	50	200

Agra's footwear industry can be divided into two major groups. First, organized and mechanized footwear units that produce largely for exports and other units those are producing largely for domestic market (Sarkar 2010). Furthermore, these producers can further be broken can be broken down into 60 exporting units, 200 larger domestic units, 200 smaller domestic units and 4,500 home based units (Ganguly, 2008). Among 60 exporters, there are 10 exporters whose capacity of footwear production are more than 3000 pairs per day and they employ 800 or more workers (Sarkar 2010). Today, firms exporting their product are mainly family business or partnership firms. A few larger ones are private limited companies. This cluster does not have any presence of corporate sector or MNCs but shoes from Agra is supplied to several MNCs around the globe (Aggarwal 2004; Sarkar 2010). Hence, this research project is based on SMEs of the leather industry of Agra, specifically focusing on the 8 big exporters (employing over 800 workers), which contribute to roughly 40% of the shoes produced from this region.

Furthermore, Agra's competitiveness lies on its abundantly available skilled artisan labor. Labor is mostly of local origin although migration from neighboring districts and other states cannot be ruled out (Aggarwal 2004; Sarkar 2010). Traditionally, workers learned the skills from forefathers while working at home as an apprentice in home enterprises or under master artisan in workshop from a young age. However, in recent years workers can only start an apprenticeship from 15 years of age due to restrictions on child labour in workshops. This has created a labour shortage in the industry due to the growth in the production and lack of skilled workers to manufacture the products. In order to address this issue companies are now supporting CFTI (Central Footwear Training Institute), which is now the official training institute to train workers (Sarkar 2010).

Lastly, this section provides an insight of the leather industry in India and Agra specifically, which is highly significant since the whole research project is based on this industry.

3. Discussion and Conclusion

This Chapter will integrate the body of literature presented in Chapter 2 with the findings from Chapter 4. From the wide range of results displayed above, it is clear that there are different drivers of CSR that influence CSR practices amongst the SMEs of the leather industry of Agra. This section will aim to summarize these findings with the help of previous literature mentioned in chapter two. Together this will help answer the research questions and fulfill the objectives of this chapter.

Every research question will be answered separately and at the end future implication of his project will be provided.

3.1 How is CSR understood amongst the SMEs of the leather industry of Agra?

CSR is a highly susceptible concept, which may vary depending on the country, social, and cultural setting it is implemented in. Literature review clearly suggests that CSR is influenced by several subtle cultural norms, institutional structures and political legacies (see for e.g. Doh and Guay 2006, Matten and Moon 2005) and therefore, it is likely to differ in every country and industry it is practiced in. Visser (2008) proposes, "CSR in emerging economies draws strongly on deep-rooted indigenous cultural traditions of philanthropy, business ethics, and community embeddedness. Indeed, some of these traditions go back to ancient times" (Visser 2008. pp. 481). Similarly, if we consider one of the most popular models-Carroll's classic CSR pyramid (1991) comprising economic, legal, ethical, and philanthropic responsibilities, in a developing country setting economic and philanthropic responsibilities will always triumph legal and ethical responsibility (Zabin 2013).

Participants in this chapter understand CSR practices in a similar way. During the interviews majority of participants only associated CSR to taking care of their workforce and people in need (BPL people) by mentioning the various voluntary steps they take and all the government regulations they follow. However, other government regulations and activities related to ethical and legal responsibilities of a business were ignored. This suggests that participants feel that CSR practices only involve being responsible for their workforce and helping people in need (BPL people). This could be due to the cultural traditions of philanthropy or it could be due to the fact that the shoe making industry is very labour intensive, so the workers wellbeing will directly impact the quality of their product. If the same is compared to Carroll's CSR pyramid (1991), economic and philanthropic responsibility triumphs legal and ethical responsibility amongst the participant of this chapter.

Anecdotal evidence in India also implies that the ethical or social orientation of the firm is a byproduct of the ethical and social stand of its owner. (Srinivasan 2011). In this chapter all participants were respective decision makers in their company and most of them owned family businesses passed on from generation. Hence, their cultural and social upbringing is likely to affect the choices they make. Their choice of CSR practices may very well be the byproduct of their perception and cultural upbringing.

Studies also show that limited resources and understanding of the subject has led the managers of many SMEs to believe that compliance to the government laws can be seen as being socially responsible. Literature also indicates that regardless of the geographical region they were operating in or originated from, SMEs tended to behave similarly towards CSR (UNIDO 2008). Many of them considered 'taking care of their employees internally' and 'being involved in community welfare' as their CSR responsibility (Srinivasan 2011, pp.59). Parallel results were found in this chapter, where government regulations (both national and international) were followed as a norm. Moreover, when all the results are put together, a predictable pattern of CSR activities can be seen. Participants follow all the regulations (national and international) and almost everyone either donates money or is associated to charities that help BPL people. Suggesting that all SMEs in this region follow a similar pattern.

Gupta (et al 2012) also concluded the lack of financial support to be one of the main drivers to be discouraging CSR amongst SMES. Additionally, studies also suggests, SMEs are unable to see any clear benefits by following or practicing CSR and therefore, very few companies had social reports, codes of conduct or stated ethical practices (see Srinivasan 2011,Gupta, Sukhmani and Kalra 2012, Neilson and Thomsen 2009). Results suggest that the former is true to a certain extent; however, over time participants of this chapter are realizing the merits of practicing CSR. As mentioned in the pervious section, they understand "win-win" situations of CSR and further implementing these concepts. They mentioned several incidences when CSR activities have helped them maintain the quality of their product, which in-turn helps them retain their clients.

Therefore, overall CSR practices in this particular chapter overlap between three models mentioned by Kumar (et al 2001) - the Gandhian model, the Nehru model and the Milton Friedman model. The diagram below (see Figure 8) tries to map CSR activities against the three models to determine which models exists amongst the participants of this chapter. CSR practices in this dissertation is mainly influenced by regulation and owners personal objectives, whereas, globalization is responsible for increasing awareness and influencing these activities in the long run.

Half of the firms CRS activities are influenced by regulations and owners personal objectives. Participants also took upon voluntary commitments to public welfare in the form of philanthropy (The Gandhian model), while some firms (firms 2 and 3) where influenced by all three models.

3.2 How have regulations impacted CSR practices amongst these participants?

Government legislations play a vital role in facilitating CSR practices in developing countries. Literature advocates that trade and investment promotion were found to be two main drivers of CSR initiatives by public sector agencies in developing countries (Fox et al 2002). Additionally, by providing higher minimum social and environmental standards, the CSR agenda encourages innovation. For example, anecdotal evidence suggests that the CSR agenda on child labor in developing countries has encouraged public sector labor inspectorates in some developing countries to step up their compliance activities. (Fox et al 2002)

The data presented with two sets of regulations-international and national- which had a significant effect on CSR activities. It suggests that participants followed all the regulations as norm or a way of doing business. It could also be argued that participants indulge in CSR activities unknowingly. Many participants failed to recognize the relationship between regulations and CSR practices. Therefore, government plays a vital role as it has the power to facilitate CSR practiced amongst the SMEs. If regulations are enforced, participants are likely to abide by them to continue producing shoes.
CSR agenda is also encouraging innovation in this case chapter. For example, all legal tanneries have now been shifted to government allocated clusters with state of the art pollution treatment plants. The government has also established education and training centers to educate the local workforce to help decrease the labour shortage. These training centers also sponsored by companies directly, actively involving them in to produce more skilled labour. Data also indicates that national government has always been supportive towards the shoe manufacturers in Agra. Since the beginning the participants were given tax incentives to promote trade and production and now the government is enforcing schemes like "CSR credit" and revising company act of 1948 to include CSR activities. Therefore, on the whole a progressive approach of CSR legislations is seen where the national and international government are formalizing CSR practices over time.

3.3 What effects does globalization have on CSR practices?

Past literature suggests that most of the CSR activities in emerging economies are "driven by the external demands in developed countries and foreign multinational firms spear heading CSR activities" (Frynas 2006, pp.17). It is also evident that CSR is boosted by international exposure at the local, national and international level (this might include exports, conferences, globalization, advanced technology) (Chapple et al 2003; Khan 2008; Chambers et al 2003). According to Chapple (et al 2003), the multiplier effect of international operations on stakeholders, the need for domestic companies to establish themselves as good citizens in the international market and institutional changes occurring due to globalization is the reason behind this change. Similarly, failure to provide consistent pressure on businesses by local authorities (such as NGOS, domestic government and third parties) also forces the businesses to rely on external bodies (i.e. international governance), which is again considered to boost CSR practices (Sawhney 2004 in Khan 2008). Lastly, consumer demand (in this case- international brands) was also found to be an important driver of CSR practices in developing countries (Fox et al 2002).

On the whole, globalization was greatly responsible for majority of the CSR practices that take place amongst the partakers of this chapter. Data indicates that only 8 firms in this region trade with over 10 countries globally. Alliance with international firms exposes these participants to international trade fairs, conferences and legislations that are significantly responsible for increasing awareness regarding CSR. It was seen that the participants adopt latest technology and business practices to establish themselves as global citizens and exports their products in the global market. Participants also went as far as saying that if it wasn't for international regulations they would never have known about CSR.

In this case, demand of the international buyers was another major factor that encouraged CSR. Participants were seen following every demand their respective buyers had, for example, ISO certifications that require audits varied in different countries and buyers operating from USA required an additional "security audit". It was seen that manufacturers dealing with clients in USA went through an additional audit just to satisfy their customer. This goes on to suggest that customer demand plays a vital role in promoting CSR. In this case, majority of the customers are international buyers, which makes globalization an important aspect of CSR activities.

3.4 Summary:

In a comparative chapter conducted on CSR practices of Dutch Multinationals and SMEs operating in India, it was found that while large multinationals had established a CSR policy, CSR was not institutionalized amongst SMEs (CREM, 2004). However, in this chapter it is evident that CSR has evolved over time and is in fact establishing itself amongst the SMEs of the leather industry of Agra. In the past this concept used to be practiced as philanthropy and because it was the "right thing to do". It has been seen that this sense of philanthropy still exists in some cases. Participants till date go out their way to help BPL people in the form of charity and donations; nevertheless, these practices have become more formalized since the mainstreaming of the concept from 2000s. Global exports of these products from Agra have proved to be instrumental in bringing about this change and raising awareness.

All the policy documents provided and interview transcripts were analyzed to determine the extent of CSR activities amongst the participants of this chapter. It was found that participants of this chapter were doing CSR activities unknowingly. If all the policies and activities are collated, data suggested that in order to be ISO certified; participants investigated and assessed the social, economic and environmental aspects of their company, which is in line with the CSR definition mentioned in chapter 2 of this dissertation. Furthermore, the effects of globalization and regulations were also found to be interrelated in several cases. Globalization gave rise to awareness, exposure and exports, which encouraged domestic producers to export and follow international protocol. As mentioned above, these exports also forced all the participants to be global citizens and adhere to all the rules and regulations (for e.g. ISO certificates, REACH standard leather) laid out by their international customers. It could also be argued that protocols regarding CSR developed in developed countries sets a chain reaction that effect the CSR practices in developing country due to trade that takes place between the two countries.

On the other hand, being a developing country, India faces significant structural challenges that effect CSR practices amongst SMEs. For e.g. illiteracy amongst labour and corruption amongst policy makers were two problems mentioned by participants that obstruct the development of CSR practices, nevertheless, as time is passing the national government is becoming more aware and implementing policies that will have a positive effect on the CSR practices amongst the SMEs. It was also found that if a business case approach to CSR is advocated, it is likely to generate more interest in this subject. As mentioned in the previous section, participants seek "win-win" situations, which has occurred in some cases and generated greater interest and understanding of this field. Some examples of this could be seen when participants invested in projects like solar power plants and leather waste recycling by converting scrap leather into handicraft goods. The main reasons behind these projects were to generate income and lower the production costs.

Lastly, as Sharma, Sharma and Kishor (2013) conclude in their chapter, "there has been a clear transition from giving as an obligation or charity to giving as a strategy or responsibility. The review of the case studies and work done on CSR by companies in India suggests that the CSR is slowly moving away from charity and dependence and starting to build on empowerment and partnership" (Sharma, Sharma and Kishor 2013 pp. 61). CSR practices amongst the SMEs of the leather industry of Agra are likely to have a similar future.

3.5 Implication for future research

This aim of this chapter was to provide an insight on how CSR is practiced and understood amongst SMEs taking the leather industry of Agra as a case chapter. However, given the limited amount of time and resources, this chapter was based on a very specific sample size and interview questions. In future, more participants in multiple industries and cities could be investigated to determine the CSR trends amongst the SMEs of India. Different research design in the form of surveys and questionnaires could also be used to target a larger sample size.

Questions related to religion were absent from the interview but given the strong cultural and religious influence that prevail in the society- it is likely to have an effect on a participants perception on this concept which in turn will have an effect on their CSR practices. Relationship between age/sex of the participant and their understanding of CSR should also be investigated to determine the different drivers behind CSR activities.

Lastly, this chapter did not investigate individual company policy reports, as the participant did not voluntarily provide them. In future, individual company policies along with their annual reports could be analyzed to generate a deeper understanding of this concept.

On the whole, even though this chapter gives a minute insight in this broad field of research, it could be used as a basis of future research.

3.6 Implications for sustainable development

As mentioned in chapter 1 of this dissertation- the concept of CSR involves applying the concept of SD in the corporate world. In current socio-economic scenario the concept of CSR has become widely integrated with business ethic in all parts of the world, though, the need of CSR is even more urgent in developing countries where economic inequalities are more prominent and both ecology and society are vulnerable to human induced environmental hazards (Dodh et al 2013).

India is a developing country with similar economic, social and environmental problems and in several instances corporations (SMEs and MNCs) have played a dominant role in addressing issues of education, health, environment and livelihoods through their CSR involvements across the country. Therefore, investigating these CSR practices will help scholars and policy makers understand the drivers and motives behind these practices, which could then be used to promote effective and efficient ways to do CSR.

In this chapter it was established that SMEs of Agra in the leather industry do have a significant impact on the society, economy and environment in which they exist. As mentioned earlier, collectively these 8 companies produce over 40% of the shoes manufactured from this region and trade globally with over 10 countries. Hence, investigating CSR activities amongst them will have a significant impact on the society and environment at large. Moreover, CSR activities amongst SMEs in developing countries are under researched; especially this industry has never been examined despite its significant impact. Therefore, this chapter examines and analyzes the drivers behind these CSR activities, on the basis of which SD could be promoted in future.

3.7 Concluding remarks

This chapter clearly demonstrates that CSR practices differ in developing country than developed countries. In developing countries CSR is influenced by strong cultural and religious traditions of philanthropy, business ethics and community embeddedness where economic and philanthropic responsibility are always likely to overpower legal and ethical responsibilities. Similarly, CSR practices also tend to differ between MNCs and SMEs. SMEs tend to be more community oriented and the owner's social and ethical orientation will almost always influence a SMEs operations. This dissertation proves both the points.

A strong sense of community embeddedness and philanthropy was seen amongst the participants of this chapter. CSR still existed in the form of philanthropy in some cases; however, it is getting formalized over time. Participants were now more aware of the concept and its advantages. They now actively participate in promoting CSR, even though most of them are not aware of it. While globalization plays a significant role in promoting CSR, government involvement cannot be ignored. Given the structural challenges (corruption, illiteracy, economic disparity) faced by India as a developing country, legislations can be seen as a guidance tool. Despite the inconsistency in knowledge amongst the participants, legislations can act as a balancing tool and therefore, I feel should be the primary mode used to navigate future CSR activities amongst the SMEs of India.

References and Bibiliography

1. Aggarwal. (2004). DIAGNOSTIC chapter REPORT FOR LEATHER FOOTWEAR CLUSTER, AGRA. Available: http://www.ediindia.org/DSR/Foot %20wear%20cluster,%20Agra%20_DS_.pdf. Last accessed 20th February,2014.
2. Balasubramanian, N. K., Kimber, D., & Siemensma, F. (2005). Emerging Opportunities or Traditions Reinforced. Journal of Corporate Citizenship,2005(17), 79-92.
3. Berad, N. R. (2011, March). Corporate Social Responsibility–Issues and Challenges in India. In International Conference on Technology and Business Management March (Vol. 28, p. 30).
4. Bhave, A. G. Experiences of the Role of Government in promoting Corporate Social Responsibility initiatives in the private sector.

5. BLC leather tech, Available: http://www.blcleathertech.com/testing-services/reach-testing.htm. Last accessed 29th April, 2014

6. Boeije, H. (2002). A purposeful approach to the constant comparative method in the analysis of qualitative interviews. Quality and quantity, 36(4), 391-409.

7. Brown, J., & Fraser, M. (2006). Approaches and perspectives in social and environmental accounting: an overview of the conceptual landscape. Business Strategy and the Environment, 15(2), 103-117.

8. Bureau   Veritas.. Available: http://www.bureauveritas.co.uk/wps/wcm/connect/bv_couk/local.   Last accessed 29th April, 2014.

9. Burr, V. (1995) An Introduction to Social Constructionism. London: Routledge

10. Carroll, A. B. (1979). A three-dimensional conceptual model of corporate performance. Academy of management review, 4(4), 497-505.

11. Chahoud, T. (2006). Shaping Corporate Social Responsibility (CSR) in India– Does the Global Compact Matter?.

12. Chambers, E., Chapple, W., Moon, J., and Sullivan, M. (2003), CSR in Asia: A Seven Country chapter of CSR Website Reporting, International Centre for Corporate Social Responsibility, University of Nottingham, Nottingham: UK.

13. Chapple, W., Moon, J., & Sullivan, M. (2003). CSR in Asia: A seven country chapter of CSR website reporting (pp. 09-2003). International Centre for Corporate Social Responsibility.

14. Crane, A. (Ed.). (2008). The Oxford handbook of corporate social responsibility. Oxford Handbooks Online.

15. CREM Report. 2004. Corporate social responsibility in India: Policy and practices of Dutch Companies. Amsterdam.

16. Dahlsrud, A. (2008). How corporate social responsibility is defined: an analysis of 37 definitions. Corporate social responsibility and environmental management, 15(1), 1-13.

17. Dodh.P , Singh.S and Ravita. (2013). Corporate Social Responsibility and Sustainable Development in India. Global Journal of Management and Business Studies.. 3 (6), p681-688.

18. Doh, J. P., & Guay, T. R. (2006). Corporate Social Responsibility, Public Policy, and NGO Activism in Europe and the United States: An Institutional-Stakeholder Perspective. Journal of Management Studies, 43(1), 47-73.

19. Fox T, Ward H, Howard B (2002), Public Sector Roles in Strengthening Corporate Social Responsibility – A baseline story, The World Bank.

20. Friedman M. 1970. The social responsibility of business is to increase its profits. The New York Times Magazine 13 September, p 32–33, p 122–126.

21. Frynas, J. G. (2006). Introduction: corporate social responsibility in emerging economies. Journal of Corporate Citizenship., 6(24), 16-19.

22. Ganguly, S. (2008), 'Agra – Centre of the Indian Footwear Industry', World Footwear, March- April.

23. Garriga, E., & Melé, D. (2004). Corporate social responsibility theories: mapping the territory. Journal of business ethics, 53(1-2), 51-71.

24. Glaser, B. G., & Strauss, A. L. (1967).The discovery of grounded theory.New York: Aldine.

25. Gray R, Owen D, Adams C. 1996. Accounting and Accountability – Changes and Challenges in Corporate Social and Environmental Reporting. Prentice-Hall: London.

26. Guba, E., & Lincoln, Y. (1994). Competing paradigms in qualitative research. In N. Denzin & Y. Lincoln (Eds.), Handbook of qualitative research (pp. 105-117). London: Sage.

27. Gupta, S., & Kalra, N. (2012). Impact of Corporate Social Responsibility on SMEs in India. Asia-Pacific Journal of Management Research and Innovation,8(2), 133-143

28. IILF. (2013). Indian Leather Industry. Available: http://www.iilfleatherfair.com/leatherfair/leather_industry.php. Last accessed 20th February,2014.

29. India Corporate Responsibility Reporting Survey 2013

30. India's FTAs and MSMEs. India's Free Trade Agreements and Micro, Small and Medium Enterprises A Case chapter of the Leather Industry. Available: http://www.twnside.org.sg/title2/FTAs/General/MSMES/FTAs_MSME_India_Leather_vol_III.pdf. Last accessed 20th February,2014.

31. ISO standards. Available: http://www.iso.org/iso/home/standards/management-standards.htm. Last accessed 29th April, 2014

32. Jenkins, H. 2006. Small business champions for corporate social responsibility. Journal of Business Ethics, 67: 241–246.

33. Kelle, U. (1995). Theories as heuristic tools in qualitative research. In I. Maso, P. A. Atkinson, S.Delamont, & J. C. Verhoeven (Eds.),Openness in research: The tension between self and other (pp. 33 – 50). Assen: van Gorcum.

34. Kelle, U. (2005). "Emergence" vs. "forcing" of empirical data? A crucial problem of "grounded theory" reconsidered. Forum: Qualitative Social Research, 6 (2), Art. 27. Retrieved July 4, 2011, fromhttp://www.qualitative-research.net/index.php/fqs/article/viewArticle/467/1000

35. Kolk, A. & van Tulder, R. 2010, "International business, corporate social responsibility and sustainable development", International Business Review, vol. 19, no. 2, pp. 119-125.

36. Kraus, P. & Brtitzelmaier, B. 2012, "A literature review on corporate social responsibility: definitions, theories and recent empirical research", International Journal of Management Cases, vol. 14, no. 4, pp. 282-296.

37. Lantos GP. 2001. The boundaries of strategic corporate social responsibility. Journal of Con- sumer Marketing 18(2): 595–630.

38. Lewis S. 2003. Reputation and corporate responsi- bility. Journal of Communication Management 7(4): 356–394.

39. Lockett, A., Moon, J., & Visser, W. (2006). Corporate Social Responsibility in Management Research: Focus, Nature, Salience and Sources of Influence*.Journal of management studies, 43(1), 115-136.

40. Lucitel. Available: http://www.lucintel.com/Search.aspx. Last accessed 29th April, 2014

41. Mack, N., Woodsong, C., MacQueen, K. M., Guest, G., & Namey, E. (2005). Qualitative research methods: a data collectors field guide.

42. Mackenzie, N., & Knipe, S. (2006). Research dilemmas: Paradigms, methods and methodology. Issues in educational research, 16(2), 193-205.

43. Matten, D., & Moon, J. (2008). "Implicit" and "explicit" CSR: A conceptual framework for a comparative understanding of corporate social responsibility.Academy of management Review, 33(2), 404-424.

44. Miles, M. B. & Huberman, A. M. (1994) Qualitative Data Analysis: an Expanded Sourcebook, Thousand Oaks, Calif., Sage.

45. Moore, G. & Spence, L. 2006. Editorial: Responsibility and small business. Journal of Business Ethics, 67(3): 219–226.

46. Morse, J. M. (2001). Situating grounded theory within qualitative inquiry. In R. S. Schreiber & P. N. Stern(Eds.),Using grounded theory in nursing (pp. 1 – 15). New York: Springer Publishing Company.

47. Morsing, M., & Perrini, F. (2009). CSR in SMEs: do SMEs matter for the CSR agenda?. Business Ethics: A European Review, 18(1), 1-6.

48. Newell, P. (2005). Citizenship, accountability and community: the limits of the CSR agenda. International Affairs, 81(3), 541-557.

49. Nielsen, A. E., & Thomsen, C. (2009). CSR communication in small and medium-sized enterprises: A chapter of the attitudes and beliefs of middle managers. Corporate Communications: An International Journal, 14(2), 176-189.

50. Nordstom, C. (1997): A Different kind of war story. University of Pennsylvania Press, Philadelphia.

51. Novak M. 1996. Business as a Calling: Work and the Examined Life. The Free Press: New York.

52. O'Dwyer B. 2003. Conceptions of corporate social responsibility: the nature of managerial capture. Accounting, Auditing and Accountability Journal 16(4): 523–557.

53. Oliver.P. (2006). The SAGE Dictionary of Social Research Methods.Available: http://srmo.sagepub.com/view/the-sage-dictionary-of-social-research-methods/n162.xml. Last accessed 29th April, 2014.

54. Pandey, A.P. 2007. Indian SMEs and their uniqueness in the country. MPRA Chapter No. 6086. [Online]. Available: http://mpra.ub.uni-muenchen.de/6086/. Accessed on 20th February 2014

55. PWC. (2013). Handbook on Corporate Social Responsibility in India.Available: http://www.pwc.in/en_IN/in/assets/pdfs/publications/2013/handbook-on-corporate-social-responsibility-in-india.pdf. Last accessed 20th February,2014

56. Ragodoo, N. J. (2009). CSR as a tool to fight against poverty: the case of Mauritius. Social Responsibility Journal, 5(1), 19-33.

57. RINA. Available: http://www.rina.org/EN/istituzionale/presentazione.aspx. Last accessed 29th April, 2014

58. Robert Thornberg , Informed grounded theory, 2012, Scandinavian Journal of EducationalResearch, (56), 3, 243-259

59. Sarkar. A Case chapter of Footwear Industry in India . Available: http://www.ihdindia.org/Formal-and-Informal-Employment/Chapter-4-A-Case-chapter-of-Footwear-Industry-in-India.pdf. Last accessed 20th February,2014.

60. Sharma, S., & Kishor, R. S. J. EMERGING TRENDS IN CORPORATE SOCIAL RESPONSIBILITY IN INDIA-A DESCRIPTIVE chapter.

61. Shrivastava, H., & Venkateswaran, S. (2000). The business of social responsibility: the why, what, and how of corporate social responsibility in India. Egully. com.

62. Srinivasan, V. (2011). India: CSR and ethics in MSMEs in India. In Ethics in Small and Medium Sized Enterprises (pp. 55-63). Springer Netherlands.

63. Swift T. 2001. Trust, reputation and corporate accountability to stakeholders. Business Ethics: a European Review 10(1): 16–26.

64. Thomas, D. R. (2006). A general inductive approach for analyzing qualitative evaluation data. *American journal of evaluation*, 27(2), 237-246.

65. Trevino LK, Nelson KA. 1999. Managing business ethics: Straight Talk about how to Do it Right. 2nd ed. John Wiley and Sons: New York.

66. Van Marrewijk, M. (2003). Concepts and definitions of CSR and corporate sustainability: between agency and communion. Journal of business ethics,44(2-3), 95-105.
67. Visser, W. (2008). Corporate social responsibility in developing countries. The Oxford handbook of corporate social responsibility, 473-479.
68. von Glasersfeld, E. (2002). 1 Problems of Constructivism. Radical constructivism in action: Building on the pioneering work of Ernst von Glasersfeld, 3.
69. Wan-Jan, W. S. (2006). Defining corporate social responsibility. Journal of Public Affairs, 6(3-4), 176-184.
70. WBCSD. (.). Corporate Social responsibility. Available: http://www.wbcsd.org/work-program/business-role/previous-work/corporate-social-responsibility.aspx. Last accessed 20th February,2014.
71. Yakel E. 2001. The social construction of accountability: radiologists and their record-keeping practices. The Information Society 17: 233–245.
72. Zabin, I. An Investigation of Practicing Carroll's Pyramid of Corporate Social Responsibility in Developing Countries: an Example of Bangladesh Ready-made Garments.

Photo: Indira Dutta

Part 4: Nature and Environmental Change and Justice

4.1 Working with Nature, not Against it

By Ranjit Barthakur

A new way of looking at nature is now being developed - the new model seeks to integrate the real value of nature into its thinking. It understands how nature provides a wealth of resources and services that we currently take for granted and count as "free", and that it is as vital to invest in these services. It is not about just taking notice of the market price of natural resources: it is also about assigning value to the services provided by nature and are finding ways to make what was once the invisible value of nature's resources and services apparent in development mod els. Indeed future development opportunities which create wealth will be enhanced by helping to increase nature's health and services, not by continuing to deplete nature as has happened to date.

In order to work with nature, a holistic approach is needed, The first step is to be aware of how we depend directly or indirectly on natural ecosystems. There is a need to understand the natural cycle that they are an integral part of – the food cycle, water cycle or the carbon cycle. There are also inter-cycle linkages which need to be understood. For example, while an agricultural farming business or economy may consider itself to be within the food cycle, it is also linked to the water cycle through its water requirements, and to the carbon cycle through its energy requirements and fertilizer usage.
Intra and inter cycle linkages and implications need to be clearly understood to develop strategies on how we can work with nature.

Lets take each of the cycles and understand them better, and also highlight some examples of 'working with nature' in these cycles.

The food cycle is the natural cycle for companies that are in agricultural farming, animal husbandry, food processing and food retailers. There is significant potential for working with nature for such businesses to create economic and reputational value. One of the key opportunity areas is food waste. There is potential for greater use of waste in anaerobic digestion (AD) on farms. Farms with AD facilities would benefit from lower energy costs, reduced waste disposal costs, increased energy security, and could tap into the market for selling energy back to the grid. Using livestock waste (e.g. manures and slurries) and other farm waste (e.g. poultry litter) as feedstock for AD avoids costs of dealing with it more traditionally like sending it to landfills. Conversion of farm waste to energy saves greenhouse gas emissions associated with the alternative production of energy, reduces emissions of methane from manures and agricultural residues and can deliver air and water quality benefits. In Germany there are 7,400 AD plants, which are generally operated by farmers and primarily used to produce electricity, around 2,500 MW in total. Peterborough City Council recently awarded a five year contract to green energy company Biogen to collect a projected 6,000 tonnes of household food waste annually. The food waste will be sent to Biogen's anaerobic digestion plant near Rushden in neighbouring Northamptonshire; the biogas produced by the food waste is used in a combined heat and power engine to produce electricity which is piped to the national grid, heat which is used back in the process, and biofertiliser for crops.

There are significant opportunities that are linked to the water cycle. From the perspective of their internal operations, companies can move towards water neutrality by optimising the reuse and recycling of water thereby better managing waste-water, so as to minimise intake of fresh water and mitigate risks associated with water stress. There is a strong linkage between energy and water – the more efficient you are with water use, the more energy you will save. You will require less energy to pump fresh water and to treat water.

Energy savings through wastewater reuse, heat recovery exchangers and demand reductio n can decrease operating costs. In the textile sector the advent of waterless dyeing has brought water use reductions of up to 97% and energy use reductions of up to 89% compared to conventional dyeing. India's pulp and Chapter industry is currently very water inefficient, withdrawing 150-200 m3 water per tonne of Chapter compared to the global best benchmark of 20-30 m3 per tonne. Our analysis shows that by 2030 a 26% reduction on 2030 Business as Usual (BAU) levels is possible with off -the-shelf water and energy efficiency technologies, and by consolidating small, inefficient plants. In total, more than 1 billion m3 of water can be saved, equivalent to the annual domestic water consumption of 35 million people, roughly 3% of the Indian population.

Finally, in the carbon cycle, there are opportunities to gain advantages by better understanding the carbon footprint across the entire lifecycle. For example, for light bulbs, 96% of the carbon footprint is in the consumption phase of the life cycle. Hence light bulb innovation is focused on energy efficiency through more energy efficiency products like CFLs and LEDs. On the other end of the spectrum, 73% of the carbon footprint of milk is in the 'raw materials' stage related to use of grazing land for cattle, cattle feed, methane emanating from the cattle, etc. Similarly, those producing orange juice would look at distribution closely, while those producing potato chips would look at production closely.

In order to measure how effectively an economy is working with nature, we suggest that there should be an index or a rating system. Once the baseline score is defined, then this performance assessment can be done on a periodic basis so that progressive ecological performance can be measured. Once ecological performance is measured, it would then be important to translate ecological performance in economic terms, as economic based evaluation is the most accepted performance evaluation approach.

Economies and companies are not only embracing this concept of working with nature individually, but are also collaborating together in this area. The drivers for this collaboration could be related to advocacy, geographic aspects, product based, or mitigation or offsetting opportunities.

Working with nature radically cuts the resource and natural capital impact of the development model making it more sustainable.

4.2 Green Groundwater in India: The chapter of Developed Technologies for Groundwater Conservation

By Ashok Kumar Maurya

Introduction

The aim of the Green Groundwater is to help reduce groundwater consumption and maintain both the quantity and quality of the available groundwater. The call to 'save water' has been echoing universally in recent times in view of the rapid depletion of groundwater resources throughout the world. Groundwater resources have, in fact, virtually reached a nadir so much so that it may not be possible to provide hygienic and potable water for the people in any country in the near future. In India too, groundwater constitutes a key resource for agriculture and farm irrigation. According to the Central Ground Water Board, in 2009, 91 per cent of the total groundwater was consumed for agricultural purposes, and only 9 per cent for domestic and industrial use. Over the last few decades groundwater, as it covers 60 per cent of the total irrigated area in the country. It is estimated that about 70 per cent of the nation's foodgrain production comes from irrigated land in which groundwater plays a dominant role (Gandhi and Bhamoriya, 2011). However, despite the significance of groundwater as a major resource, especially for agriculture and irrigation, it has not been controlled by government regulation and no stringent rules have been implemented to prevent over-use of groundwater. Instead groundwater usage is presently only a part of highly decentralised private activities and the groundwater revolution has, by and large, gone unnoticed.

Rainwater harvesting and artificial groundwater recharge

Rainwater harvesting and artificial groundwater recharge constitute effective green groundwater schemes for groundwater conservation. Both the Government of India as well as the states have been promoting these schemes for ensuring green groundwater development. In fact, the Government of India started a large number of major and medium irrigation projects for energy generation and irrigation immediately after Independence, but due to ineffective policy implementation and general apathy on the part of the implementing agencies, most of these projects have either failed to take off or do not cover the targeted irrigation areas. Thus, lack of proper implementation of the concerned projects constitutes one of the most important reasons for the failure of surface water management and the increasing and unchecked use of groundwater resources. The conservation of rainwater would, therefore, entail an effective alternative plan for conserving water in all types of geographical locations ranging from hilly area to the coastal regions. Further, both efficient surface water management and use of appropriate technology are important for saving groundwater resources and improving their quality.

The Government has been focusing on schemes of groundwater recharge through rainwater harvesting and maximum utilisation of irrigation water by putting in place technologically advanced systems like drip and sprinkler irrigation methods. The availability of surface water also depends upon the quantum and nature of rainfall. Rainwater harvesting can obviously help in conserving a large amount of rainwater, which, in turn, can be used for domestic purposes and for irrigation and groundwater recharge. However, in the area of rainwater harvesting too, lack of effective management prevents effective water conservation, encouraging wastage by allowing a large part of the rainwater to flow away into rivers and drains. It is thus imperative to ensure effective management and technology usage for saving and conserving water as part of the Green Groundwater project. A heartening development in the generally grim scenario, however, is that the Indian Government has started treating this project as a major emerging issue because of its importance in tackling the threats to groundwater as a whole. This is reflected in the various policies and schemes introduced by the Indian Government to promote sustainable green development in the country.

Criticality of groundwater as a resource

The widespread dependency on groundwater has increased the water crisis in India as a large area of the country is being highly exploited for accessing this resource. The weather conditions in India and the surrounding regions are largely uneven and uncertain. A large part of India often faces uneven and erratic rainfall. This factor is also responsible for the need to augment irrigation facilities for agriculture and to control the unchecked exploitation of groundwater.

During the initial stage of groundwater development in the 1950s, groundwater mining was dominated by traditional dug wells, with the depth of each of these wells being not more than 30 feet. The use of physical energy involving both humans and animals was often resorted to for lifting the water, and constituted over 60 per cent of the methods used for irrigation. Sometimes, well irrigation and tank irrigation were also used conjunctively for hydrological purposes (Jeet, 2005). In the 1970s, the second phase of groundwater development saw the considerable growth of dug-cum-bore wells (Singh, 2003). The depth of these wells increased from 50 to 100 feet and the use of centrifugal pumps became common. The extent of the irrigated areas also increased slightly and cropping shifted towards water-intensive crops. During the mid-1970s, with the advent of the Green Revolution, institutional credit became easily available for the construction of wells, and the number of wells increased substantially by the late 1970s. During the third phase of groundwater development beginning in the mid-1980s, the use of submersible pumps signaled a change in the technology used for groundwater withdrawal as the depth of the wells increased to beyond 400 feet in many parts of India. Water extraction also increased rapidly due to the grant of subsidies on electricity, illegal use of unmetered electricity supply, easy credit availability and the commercialisation of agriculture (Singh, 2003). This led to a rapid decline in both the water table and the quality of water, increased frequency of drying wells, and rising costs of well investments and operations. The concomitant increase in groundwater use also resulted in a speedy decline in the groundwater table in several parts of the country (Dubash, 2002). The number of shallow wells doubled roughly every 3.7 years from 1951 to 1991, with the total crossing 18.5 million wells nationwide and accounting for over 50 per cent of the irrigated area (Moench, 2003).

Figure 1: Groundwater Fluctuation and Net Irrigated Area by Sources of Water

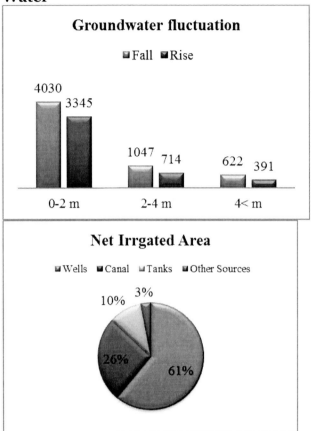

Note: Calculations based on availability, utilisation and stage of development of groundwater resources in India (as in 2009) and Net Irrigated Area by the sources of irrigation (2007-08).
Sources: Central Groundwater Board, 2013; and Ministry of Agriculture, Directorate of Economics and Statistics, 2013.

Figure 1 shows that the fall in the water level in observation wells is much higher than the rise of the water level. It is also important to note that 61 per cent of the irrigated area currently falls under groundwater resources as compared to 26 per cent the canal command area. Further, as mentioned earlier, a large quantity of the extracted groundwater is used for irrigation purposes, and the participation of other alternative irrigation sources is comparatively much less than that of groundwater, which is why the former have failed to play a significant role in agriculture activities. According to the Central Ground Water Board (CGWB) (2009), 26 per cent of the *Blocks/Mandals/Talukas* fall under the critical categories in terms of groundwater exploitation. The condition of groundwater resources seems to be even more precarious in agriculture-dominated states such as Punjab, Haryana and Rajasthan, wherein the incidence of over-exploitation is very high and the situation pertaining to groundwater depletion is fast becoming critical. According to the CGWB, over 80 per cent of the blocks/assessment units have been over-exploited in Punjab, with the corresponding figures being 70 per cent in Rajasthan and 74 per cent in Delhi. In the states of Haryana, Tamil Nadu, and Karnataka too, the corresponding percentages are very high, at 59, 36, and 26, respectively. Groundwater extraction has obviously increased noticeably in India over the six decades since Independence. Official statistics and estimations indicate a rapid growth in the area irrigated with groundwater while the numbers of tubewells, dug wells and energised pump sets have increased drastically over the corresponding period (World Bank, 1998).

After the Green Revolution, the Government's policies have made subsidies and credit extensively available to farmers in the interest of promoting food security and inclusive growth (Singh, 2003). These factors have also influenced power pricing and technological changes, which have strong linkages with groundwater development and use. In addition, these policies have brought significant gains to the farmers in terms of free electricity for pumping of water and the distribution of subsidised electric and diesel pumps for use in their agricultural activities. Further, the Government has also given subsidies for the drilling of tubewells besides providing irrigation facilities in the form of public tubewells. However, this does not obliterate the fact these policies have promoted intensive groundwater utilisation, leading to a sharp increase in groundwater use, bordering on over-exploitation. A large number of studies have also shown that the rise in groundwater use has resulted in a speedy decline in the groundwater table in several parts of the country (Dubash, 2002). This is especially true of the water-scarce regions wherein the fall in the water table has been much more alarming and rapid than in other states. In Rajasthan and some parts of Gujarat, for instance, the decline in the groundwater has been recorded at the rate of 1 to 5 meters per year under different conditions. If this trend continues, there would be irreparable loss of this vital resource, leading to serious socio-economic and environmental challenges, which would also put the implementation of the Green Groundwater project in peril.

Artificial groundwater recharge through rainwater harvesting

The Government of India constituted the Artificial Recharge of Groundwater Advisory Council on 17 April 2006 for ensuring that the groundwater level is maintained at an ideal level. Across India, groundwater depletion due to its excessive exploitation is, therefore, a burning issue, which underscores the need for promoting artificial groundwater recharge as one of the major and effective alternatives for the conservation of groundwater resources. Artificial recharge is a process whereby the groundwater reservoir is augmented at a rate exceeding that under natural conditions of replenishment. Under the artificial recharge system, unnatural forces are used to fill water in the aquifers. The natural process of the replenishment of groundwater reservoir is sluggish and unable to maintain the groundwater balance when over-exploitation takes place, which disturbs the groundwater storage, causing it to be severely depleted. Artificial recharge can be effectively achieved by augmenting the natural movement of surface water into the groundwater reservoir through the construction of suitable civil structures. Both the source of the surface water and the prevalent hydro-geological conditions thus constitute important factors for attaining artificial groundwater recharge in a particular area. As regards surface water management, rainfall is an important input factor for artificial recharge. Artificial recharge and rainwater harvesting also constitute important options for combating the water crisis by increasing the water supply as they are environment-friendly and do not require much land, which is why they also do not cause any displacement of population. Rooftop rainwater harvesting has been adopted in urban and hilly areas for facilitating the availability of water for domestic use and recharge. It is an easy method for storing rainwater through constructed surface or sub-surface tanks. On the other hand, most of the urban areas depending on groundwater supply are facing the problem of water scarcity. India has a large coastline with a large percentage of the population residing along it. Saline sea water ingress has also been observed due to large-scale groundwater development at places along the coastline. This has resulted in deterioration of fresh groundwater aquifers. Suitable recharge techniques therefore need to be adopted in order to protect the fresh ground aquifers along the coast and water-scarce areas.

Figure 2 shows the current status of groundwater recharge through both rainfall and artificial sources, during both the monsoon and non monsoon seasons. While the rate of groundwater recharge increases during the monsoons, even in the non-monsoon season, recharge is possible through unexpected rainfall and artificial recharge from other sources of surface water though the ratio of the recharge would be less than that during the monsoons.

Figure 2: Annual Groundwater Recharge from All Sources and from Rainfall

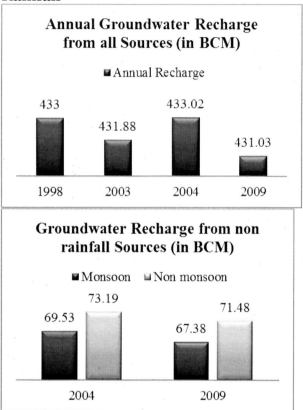

Source: Various issues of the Groundwater Year Book.

The present scenario pertaining to groundwater recharge does not show any conclusive trends. There is no positive progress with regard to groundwater aquifers even as the groundwater exploitation rate is increasing day by day. An analysis of the data for the years 2004 and 2009 on groundwater recharge from non-rainfall sources indicates that during the non-monsoon season, the quantity of water is higher as compared to the monsoon season. This also demonstrates that Government policies and schemes have proved to be effective in bringing about a positive change in groundwater development and that a large amount of surface water has been successfully converted into groundwater through artificial recharging. However, the figures for 2009 show a decreasing trend as compared to 2004 with regard to groundwater recharge through non-rainfall sources. The reason for this could be the high degree of rainfall during the 2004 monsoon, which led to a notable increase in the availability of surface water.

Here, it may be observed that the groundwater recharge through rainfall during the non-monsoon period shows a more positive picture in 2009 as compared to that in 2004. Hence, the success of groundwater recharge depends on the quantum of rainfall and its effective conservation through rainwater harvesting.

Artificial Recharge of Groundwater through Dug Wells (Dug Well Recharge Scheme)

The Dug Well Recharge Scheme is being jointly run by the CGWB, the state governments concerned and Non-government Organisations (NGOs) in the different hydro-geological and agro-climatic regimes of the country. The evaluation of the projects under this scheme reflects the importance of conservation and groundwater recharge in controlling the decline in ground water levels, augmentation of resources, and increased sustainability of wells besides mitigation of groundwater quality problems. As per the latest groundwater resource assessment carried out by the CGWB, jointly with the state level Groundwater Departments, out of 5,723 assessment units (Blocks/*Talukas*/*Mandals*) across the states, the position of 1615 units is in a critical situation due to groundwater exploitation. Among all the critical units, 839 units are over-exploited, 226 units are critical, and 550 units are in a semi-critical condition. In many areas in the critical units, hard rock aquifers have been found that have limited storage potential and are facing acute problems in terms of over-exploitation and depletion of groundwater resources. About 80 per cent of these groundwater-stressed areas are located in the hard rock area in the states of Andhra Pradesh (AP), Gujarat, Karnataka, MP, Maharashtra, Rajasthan and Tamil Nadu, wherein a rapid decline of groundwater levels has been observed on a long-term basis. The Dug Well Recharge Scheme, which is a state sector scheme, is primarily being implemented in these areas. It has been phased across a span of over three years, and is being taken up during the Eleventh Plan period at an estimated cost of Rs. 1798.71 crores.

Table 1 Number of Dug Wells Owned by Farmers Proposed for Rain Runoff Recharge

Name of State	Total Number of Districts	Total Numberof DugWells
Madhya Pradesh	17	3,60,088
Karnataka	19	1,54,493
Andhra Pradesh	21	7,37,436
Gujarat	21	5,58,536
Maharashtra	11	3,28,322
Tamil Nadu	27	12,50,730
Rajasthan	31	10,65,051

Source: www.cgwb.gov.in, Accessed on 17 May 2014.

The Dug Well Recharge Scheme is also slated to be implemented by the respective state governments in association with Panchayati Raj Institutions (PRIs), the CGWB, the National Bank for Agriculture and Rural Development (NABARD), and some NGOs, among other organisations. The objective of this scheme is to set up 4.455 million of the existing irrigation dug wells for the identified beneficiaries. Artificial groundwater recharge through the existing dug wells is thus expected to significantly improve the groundwater situation in the affected areas. The dug well schemes are also anticipated to increase the sustainability of wells during lean periods and to improve productivity of the overall irrigated agricultural area and the availability of drinking water, as also the socio-economic conditions and quality of life of the people in the affected areas. In the fluoride-prone areas, this scheme is also slated to enhance the quality of the groundwater. This scheme would thus help in the creation of an effective institutional framework, spreading of awareness and capacity building of beneficiaries, besides augmenting the overall involvement of the community in water resources management in the affected areas.

Need for technological improvements in minor groundwater irrigation

Technological improvement can go a long way in reducing the demand for water in agriculture. This includes the implementation of demand side management practices including minor irrigation technologies such as drip and sprinkler methods, which constitute the key interventions for conserving water and improving crop productivity. In the case of the drip irrigation system, water is supplied directly to the root zone through a network of pipes and emitters, while the sprinkler irrigation system operates in the same way as rainfall, by pushing in air through nozzles, which subsequently break into small water drops and fall on the field surface. While the drip irrigation system prevents water losses through conveyance (Dhawan, 2002), evidence shows that as much as 40 to 80 per cent of water can be saved and water use efficiency can be enhanced by up to 100 per cent through the use of a properly designed and managed minor irrigation system as compared to the conservation of only 30-40 per cent of water under conventional practices (Sivanappan, 1994). However, the adoption of effective minor irrigation practices necessitates technical and economic efficiency, and two additional preconditions, that is, technical knowledge about the nature of technologies and their accessibility through the promotion of institutional support systems (Namara, *et al.*, 2005).

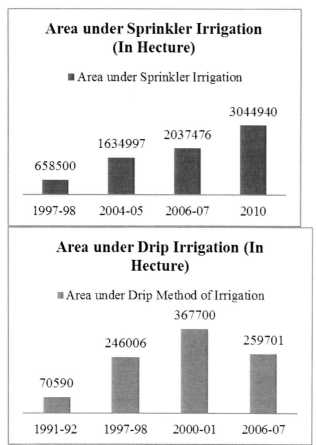

Sources: Census of Minor Irrigation (Various Issues) and International Commission on Irrigation and Drainage (2012).

The development of the drip irrigation method in India was initially very sluggish but its spread increased significantly after the 1990s due to the introduction of various promotional schemes by the Government of India and by governments in states like Maharashtra. The launch of these drip irrigation methods also led to an increase in the total irrigated area from a mere 1500 hectares in 1985 to 70,589 hectares in 1991-92, and subsequently to 2,46,000 hectares in 1997-98, and though there was a slight decrease in the total area under drip irrigation in 2006-07, it eventually covered a total of 2,59,701 hectares. In 2003, 78 per cent of the drip irrigation methods in operation functioned as part of schemes implemented by the Government of India. However, According to the Report of the Task Force on Micro-irrigation, a large number of institutions, commercial organisations, universities, large public and private sector companies, and NGOs, among others, in the country, have been using drip irrigation for their farms or crops, covering a total estimated area of about 1,00,000 hectares. This area is not reflected in the estimates made by the various government departments.

The sprinkler irrigation method is a relatively old system as compared to the drip irrigation method as far as Indian farmers are concerned. The sprinkler method was introduced in India during the mid-1950s for plantation crops like coffee and tea (Narayanamoorthy, 2009). Over the years, the sprinkler irrigation method has been extended to large areas in states like Haryana, Rajasthan, Madhya Pradesh (MP), Maharashtra and Karnataka. The gross area under sprinkler irrigation increased from 6, 58,500 hectares in1997-98 to 30, 44,940 hectares in 2010. According to the National Committee on Plasticulture Applications in Horticulture (NCPAH), the total area under irrigation using the sprinkler method is estimated to have increased to 1.63 million hectares since the advent of this technique for irrigation, which is almost 300 per cent higher than the present area under the drip method of irrigation. The adoption of the sprinkler irrigation method has, however, not been equally distributed across all states; it is mainly focused in the central and the northern part of the country. In 2004-05, the states of Haryana, Rajasthan, West Bengal and Maharashtra accounted for 70 per cent of the total area in the country irrigated by the sprinkler irrigation method (Narayanamoorthy, 2009). The total reported area under sprinkler irrigation in India is also much higher than that under drip irrigation. One of the International Commission on Irrigation and Drainage reports of 1998 provides a lot of information about the sprinkler method, but does not mention where and what crops are being cultivated under this method. It is thus imperative for agencies involved in promoting minor irrigation to make all efforts to publish data on the development of micro-irrigation in terms of crop composition, area by states, districts and different size classes, and area by state-promoted schemes and other schemes. This would help one analyse the underlying factors influencing the irrigation technique being used in a particular area and also suggest possible ways and means to increase the adoption of such water-saving technologies.

Conclusion

It may thus be concluded that the quantity of groundwater resources has reached a critical stage in India. The implementation of the Green Groundwater project is, therefore, essential for ensuring groundwater conservation. Although some effective technologies for groundwater recharge and irrigation have been adopted in India, they need to be implemented to a much wider extent than has currently been achieved. Even public investment and awareness about these technologies among the people are much below the desired level. For instance, the progress of water harvesting methods and groundwater recharge is far from satisfactory while even the sprinkler and drip irrigation methods being employed do not cover a significant target area. It is thus necessary to ensure the appropriate usage of natural resources and stop their over-exploitation for attaining green development in India. Groundwater is a vital component of the green development project because human life is not possible without water. Hence, in order to facilitate green groundwater development in future, there is no alternative but to save and conserve groundwater resources.

References

Dhawan, B. D. (2002), "Technological Change in Indian Irrigated Agriculture: A chapter of Water Saving Methods", Commonwealth Publishers, New Delhi.

Dubash, Navroz K. (2002), "Tubewell Capitalism: Groundwater Development and Agrarian Change in Gujarat", Oxford University Press, New Delhi.

Gandhi, Vasant P. and Vaibhav Bhamoriya (2011), "Groundwater Irrigation in India Growth, Challenges, and Risks", India Infrastructure Report, IDFC Foundation, New Delhi.

Jeet, Inder (2005), "Groundwater Resources of India: Occurrence, Utilisation and Management",
Mittal Publications, New Delhi.

Moench, Marcus (2003), "Groundwater and Food Security in India", in Kamta Prasad (ed.), *Water Resources and Sustainable Development: Challenges of the 21ˢᵗ Century*, Shipra Publications, Delhi, pp. 148-67.

Namara, R.E., B. Upadhyaya and R.K. Nagar (2005), "Adoption and Impacts of Micro-irrigation Technologies: Empirical Results from Selected Localities of Maharashtra and Gujarat of India", *Research Report 93*, International Water Management Institute , Colombo, Sri Lanka.

Narayanamoorthy, A. (2009), "Drip and Sprinkler Irrigation in India: Benefits, Potential and Future Directions", in Upali A. Amarasinghe, Tushaar Shah and R.P.S. Malik (eds.), *India's Water Future: Scenarios and Issues, Strategic Analysis of National River Linking Project of India Series 2*, International Water Management Institute Colombo, Sri Lanka.

Singh, Dalbir (2003), "Groundwater Markets and Institutional Mechanism in Fragile Environments", in Kanchan Chopra, C.H. Hanumantha Rao and Ramprasad Sengupta (eds.), *Water Resources, Sustainable Livelihoods and Eco-system Services*, Concept Publishing Company, New Delhi, pp. 311-340.

Sivanappan, R. K. (1994), "Prospects of Micro Irrigation in India", *Irrigation and Drainage System*, Vol. 8, No. 1, pp. 49-58.

World Bank (1998), "India—Water Resources Management Sector Review", *Groundwater Regulation and Management Report*, The World Bank and Government of India, (Ministry of Water Resources [MoWR], Washington DC and New Delhi.

4.3 Towards a People Centred Afforestation Programme for North East India

By Abhijit Kumar Bezbarua

The area under forests is widely accepted as an important indicator of the environmental health of any nation. While the National Forest Policy of 1988 aims at keeping a third of India swathed by forests and trees, the country has just 24% of its geographical area under such cover now. The National Afforestation Programme (NAP) is the leading programme for expanding the jungles of the country, apart from regenerating its degraded forest areas. It is being funded by the Ministry of Environment & Forests through the National Afforestation & Eco-development Board (NAEB). Since the commencement of the 10th Plan in 2002, various afforestation projects had been implemented across the nation. The project components are executed by village based Joint Forest Management Committees (JFMCs). Such committees work under the aegis of Forest Development Agencies (FDAs), which have been formed at the level of the Forest Divisions.

This model of development is relies upon the Forest Department, which controls and guides the involvement of communities living in the project areas. The works have to be undertaken in accordance with the guidelines and circulars issued from time to time by the Ministry of Environment & Forests of the Government of India. This Chapter seeks to develop an alternative paradigm for the afforestation of hill areas in North East India, wherein the planning and implementation of works are led by local communities. The can supplement the existing efforts while keeping the local ground realities in mind and optimizing the utilization of public funds. The writer was empanelled by NAEB as an Evaluator during the 10th Plan period (i.e. the years from 2002 to 2007). The Chapter has been developed based on his experiences covering many of the hill states of North East India.

Introduction

The overall environmental health of any nation (or any part thereof) is determined by a large number of factors. The extent and quality of the forest cover as a percentage of the geographical is one of the more important indicators of such environmental conditions. Forest cover enhances the supplies of water, fire wood, small timber, fodder, medicinal plants etc. used by the fringe dwellers, many of whom are marginalized tribal communities. In consideration of the vital role of forests, the Constitution of India has the following provisions:

- Article 48A ('Directive Principles of State Policy') mentions that 'the state shall endeavour to protect and improve the environment and to safeguard the forest and wildlife of the country'.

- Article 51A ('Fundamental Duties') states that it shall be the duty of every citizen of India '(g) to protect and improve the natural environment including forests, lakes, rivers and wildlife and to have compassion for living creatures'.

The National Forest Policy of 1988 aimed at bringing one third of India's geographical area under forests and tree cover. In its Approach Chapter to the 10th Plan (2002-07), the Planning Commission had fixed the target of increasing such forest/ tree cover to 25% of the geographical area by the end of the Plan period (March 2007) and to 33% by the end of the subsequent Plan period (i.e. by March 2012).[1] However, the country has been able to keep just 24% of its geographical area under forest and tree cover as stated in the biennial 'India State of Forest Report 2013' (released on 8th July 2014).[2] In addition, substantial forest area has been diverted for non-forest use. Between 1980 and May 2004, about 9.21 lakh hectares of forest land had been diverted for non forestry uses. In addition, forest land aggregating up to 1.14 lakh hectare had been diverted after May 2004 till March 2012.[3] Hence, there is a pressing need to expand forest cover through planned interventions.

Moreover; the management of the nation's forests has attracted the attention of the judiciary at the apex level. In fact, the Supreme Court of India started playing a

---

1   Ministry of Environment & Forests, Government of India: 'Annual Report 2004-05', Page No. 75

2   'The Hindu', Wednesday, July 9, 2014, Page No.10

3   Comptroller & Auditor General of India: 'Compensatory Afforestation in India', Report No. : 21 of 2013, Page No. 3

proactive role in the matters of forest policy and governance from 1995 onward. In the Godavarman case (T.N. Godavarman Thirumulpad v/s Union of India related to large scale illegal felling of trees in Gudalur, Tamil Nadu), the Supreme Court issued interim rulings related to aspects such as tree felling, operations of saw mills, violations of approvals for forest diversion, de-reservation of forests and matters related to compensatory afforestation. In 1996, the Supreme Court put a stop to all on-going activity like functioning of saw mills and mining within any forest in the country that was being carried out without the approval of the Government of India.[4]

On-going Government Interventions

In view of the above imperatives, the Government of India and the State Governments have been taking measures to increase the area under forests and to regenerate degraded forest lands. Some of the programmes being operated for improving forest / tree cover include:

- National Afforestation Programmes (NAP)

- National Mission for a Green India

- Compensatory Afforestation Programme

A brief description of the above schemes is furnished below.

(a)National Afforestation Programme (NAP)[5,6]

The NAP is the main programme of the Government of India for increasing forest and tree cover in India, including the regeneration of degraded forest areas. It was launched in 2002 (i.e. at the outset of the 10th Plan period) by merging four existing schemes, viz. Integrated Afforestation and Eco-Development Projects Scheme (IAEPS), Area Oriented Fuelwood and Fodder

---

4   Barik & Darlong: 'Natural Resource Management Policy Environment in Meghalaya Impacting Livelihood of Forest Poor', Centre for International Forestry Research (CIFOR) Bogor, Indonesia Page No. 19

5   National Afforestation & Eco-Development Board: 'National Afforestation Programme, Compendium of Operational Guidelines and Circulars', November 2003

6   National Afforestation & Eco-Development Board: 'National Afforestation Programme Revised Operational Guidelines, 2009'

Projects Scheme (AOFFPS), Conservation and Development of Non Timber Produce including Medical Plants Scheme (NTFP) and Association of Scheduled Tribes and Rural Poor in Regeneration of Degraded Forests (ASTRP).

The funding of this programme is routed through the National Afforestation & Eco-development Board (NAEB) which functions under the Ministry of Environment & Forests, Government of India. This body is responsible for promoting afforestation, tree planting, ecological restoration and eco-development activities in the country. The planning and implementation of this programme is carried out in accordance with guidelines periodically issued by NAEB. Since the commencement of the NAP, various afforestation projects had been implemented across the nation. The project components are executed by village based Joint Forest Management Committees (JFMCs). These committees work under the supervision and control of Forest Development Agencies (FDAs), which have been formed at the level of the Forest Divisions.

(b) National Mission for a Green India[7]

The National Mission for a Green India (GIM) is one of the eight Missions under the National Action Plan on Climate Change (NAPCC). GIM acknowledges the influences that the forestry sector has on environmental amelioration through climate mitigation, food security, water security, biodiversity conservation and livelihood security of forest dependent communities.

It will focus on the quality of forests (density of forest cover) and ecosystem services, with an emphasis on biodiversity, water and improved biomass while treating carbon sequestration as co-benefit. GIM also aims to focus on democratic decentralization by treating the village based Gram Sabha (Village Institutions in 6th Schedule Areas) as the grass roots level institution to facilitate implementation of the Mission activities at the village level. Further, it also aims to create a new cadre of community youth as foresters.

---

7   Ministry of Environment & Forests, Government of India: 'National Mission for a Green India', March 2011

(c) Compensatory Afforestation Programme[8]

Whenever forest land is to be diverted for non-forestry purpose, the Forest (Conservation) Act 1980 requires that compensatory afforestation be taken up on forest land, preferably in lands contiguous to the affected forests. The above Act also requires that funds for raising compensatory afforestation etc are to be realized from the user agencies requiring such forest land on the basis of the rates fixed by the State Forest Department. Such rates are site specific and vary according to the species, type of forest and site.

Afforestation Programmes in NE India

The North Eastern (NE) region of India consists of eight states of the country. It may be noted that these states account for a quarter of the forest cover in India[9], while having about 8% of its geographical area. The above mentioned afforestation schemes are being implemented in the region through the various State Forest Departments. However, the NE Region has several distinguishing features that set it apart from most other states of India. These factors have an impact upon the forestry operations being carried out in the states.

Under Article 244(2) of the Constitution of India, special provisions have been kept in the 6th Schedule for the administration of the tribal areas in Assam, Meghalaya, Tripura and Mizoram. These include the formation of District Councils or Regional Councils for the protection of tribal communities. Such Councils have been vested with powers to make laws for 'the management of any forest not being a Reserved Forest'[10]. Thus, in the areas covered by these Councils, the role of the State Forest Department is limited to the management of Reserved Forests.

Further, in most parts of the region (excluding the valley areas of Assam and parts of Tripura); land has not been surveyed and 'settled' for determining land revenues as elsewhere in the nation. In fact, in most hill states of the region, land belongs to the community, clan or the individual as per the customary practices. Usually, the State

---

8   Comptroller & Auditor General of India: 'Compensatory Afforestation in India', Report No. : 21 of 2013

9   Forest Survey of India: 'India State of Forest Report 2013', Page No. viii

10   As provided under Paragraph 1 (b) of the Third Proviso of the Sixth Schedule related to 'Powers of the District Councils and Regional Councils to make laws'.

Government has limited powers to acquire land for developmental purposes – including for afforestation projects.

Another factor is the widespread prevalence of 'shifting (jhum) cultivation' in the hill states of NE region. As a percentage of the state's area, the areas under current and abandoned jhum range from 2% in Meghalaya to 17% in Nagaland.[11] This excludes lands with dense and open scrub, scrub dominated forests etc. that may have been caused by such practices. Shifting cultivation lands remain the most dominant form of land use in many North Eastern states and it has a larger extent than settled agriculture and horticulture. A view has emerged that shifting cultivation has deteriorated and has become ecologically unsuitable because of the shortening and unsustainable management of the forest-fallow phase of the shifting cultivation cycle.[12]

It may be noted that various afforestation works have a limited impact in the region. In fact, as per the latest State of Forest Report of 2013, the region has registered a decline of 627 km^2 of forest cover as compared to its forest cover recorded in 2011.[13] Nagaland, Tripura, Manipur and Mizoram have recorded high loss of their forest cover in relative terms as per the above Report.[14] Hence, there is a necessity to develop a new approach to accelerate the regeneration of forest and tree cover in the NE region.

Limitations of the Current Approach

The present model of afforestation relies upon the State Forest Departments for planning and implementation of works. The department controls and guides the involvement of communities involved in the projects. The works have to be carried out in accordance with the guidelines and circulars issued by the Ministry of Environment & Forests, Government of India. Hence, there are many limitations in the current approach of the Government for forest regeneration. At best, it is able to maintain the forest cover of the country despite the pressures on account of population growth and developmental activities. However, the present cover (24.01% in 2013) is considerably

---

11 Department of Land Resources, Government of India: 'Wastelands Atlas of India, 2010', Page No. 37

12 Ministry of Environment & Forests: 'Report of the Inter-Ministerial National Task Force on Rehabilitation of Shifting Cultivation Areas', 2008

13 Forest Survey of India: 'India State of Forest Report 2013', Page No. viii

14 Ibid, Page No. 17

lower when compared with the stipulation of the National Forest Policy of 1988 to increase the forest / tree cover of India to 33% of its land area.

The main limitations of the present approach of afforestation, *especially* in the North Eastern region of India, are summarized as follows:

· Top down uniform model of afforestation;

· Low levels of community involvement;

· Non-availability of land;

· Choice of species used;

· Flow & Utilization of Public Funds for Afforestation; and

· Sharing of Benefits.

The discussion given below is based on the writer's experience of evaluation of schemes like the National Afforestation Programme (NAP), Tree Plantation under Twenty Point Programme (TPP) and the erstwhile Grants-in-Aid scheme providing assistance to voluntary agencies for tree plantation (VA Scheme). Further, readily available secondary information has been referred to wherever needed.

Top down Uniform Model of Afforestation

The State Forest Departments are officered at the higher levels (Forest Division and above) by personnel of the Indian Forest Service (IFS), which is one of the three all-India services. In this aspect, this department stands out amongst almost all the other state level departments. Except for the Administration and Police, none of the other state level departments (like Public Works, Agriculture, Health, Education, Rural Development etc.) have a similar all-India cadre of officers working from the district (divisional) level upward.

The above structure of the Forest Department has facilitated a top down uniform model of afforestation through schemes like the National Afforestation Programme (NAP), which is being entirely funded by the Centre. For the implementation of the NAP, the Government of India had laid down the operational guidelines in May 2002. Such guidelines cover aspects like planning (including micro-planning), proposal formulation, funding, monitoring and evaluation. The National Afforestation & Eco-development Board (NAEB) issued circulars periodically whereby these guidelines were modified or supplemented.

Despite the fact that the nature of forests varies widely in the country, the guidelines fix the same amount of funds for afforestation throughout the country for the same daily wage levels. For example; if a degraded forest had to be regenerated, an amount of Rs. 9,750/- was fixed as the permissible cost for 'Aided Natural Regeneration' with 200 plants per hectare, based on a daily wage level of Rs. 75/-.[15] If the number of plants or wage rates differed, then the above permissible cost was subject to pro rata variation. Thus; even in spite the wide variation of costs like labour, planting materials, maintenance etc.; the permitted costs were uniform throughout India for different work components for afforestation.

Low Levels of Community Involvement

The NAP guidelines provide for the development of micro-plans to carry out afforestation at the village level. These micro-plans form the basis of the planning exercise for the district afforestation works. Such plans are to be prepared by the village based Joint Forest Management Committees (JFMCs), which are constituted by including all able bodied and willing adult members of the village. In addition, the works are to be implemented by the JFMCs through their members who are to be paid a daily wage.

However, in most villages of the region, the villagers were unable or unwilling to prepare the micro-plans by themselves. Usually, these plans had to be framed by the field level officials of the Forest Department in consultation with their superiors and after the necessary community feedback. Further, the implementation of afforestation works was found to be usually done as a departmental exercise through the engagement of labourers, who are shown to be paid through the JFMCs.

NAEB had envisaged that the community involvement would avert the need for fencing off the areas where plantation works are carried out. In fact, the concerned guidelines specify that fencing costs are not to exceed 5% of the plantation cost in usual circumstances. In practice, the need for fencing has been repeatedly voiced by the Forest Department officers, who often state that the allocation for fencing works is low

---

15   National Afforestation & Eco-Development Board: 'National Afforestation Programme, Compendium of Operational Guidelines and Circulars', November 2003, Page Nos. 8-9

under NAP and that their field staff cannot protect the young trees from straying cattle belonging to the local villages due to this factor. This indicates the low level of community participation in the planning and implementation of afforestation works. In recognition of the issue, the Revised Operational Guidelines of 2009 state that 'If the local edapho-climatic and biotic factors require fencing beyond the stipulated 5% costs, the same may be supplemented by additional funds admissible for problem lands ... or by additional funds under other schemes'.[16]

Unsurprisingly, the Mid Term Evaluation of NAP projects carried out on a national basis by the Indian Council of Forestry Research and Education, Dehra Doon has observed that 'communities should be involved in micro-planning and project implementation activities'.[17]

However, the execution of the 'Entry Point Activities' under the NAP seems to be guided by the public requirements. These activities are carried out in the project villages to gain the cooperation of the local communities. It is seen that many useful assets like water supplies, ponds and fisheries, concrete steps, community halls etc. have been built in the project villages after duly consulting with the members of the project village.

Non-availability of Land

The NAEB has stated that plantation works under NAP are to be carried out within recorded forests or in adjoining lands (such as community land, revenue waste land, village common land, degraded jhum land etc.) using the watershed or catchment area approach. Clusters of compact blocks measuring 20 hectares or more can be taken up. The major part of project area was expected to comprise of degraded forests, pastures and community lands. Strip plantations can be carried out in two rows or more along roads, canals or railway lines.[18]

---

16 National Afforestation & Eco-Development Board: 'National Afforestation Programme Revised Operational Guidelines, 2009', Page No. 8

17 Indian Council of Forestry Research and Education:'Mid Term Evaluation of the NAP Schemes implemented through FDAs', June 2008, Page No. vi

18 National Afforestation & Eco-Development Board: 'National Afforestation Programme, Compendium of Operational Guidelines and Circulars', November 2003, Page Nos. 6-7

However, if works were undertaken within Reserved Forests, then the villagers will not be able to avail of usufruct benefits such as firewood, fodder, fruits etc. Hence, there was a disincentive to undertake the regeneration of degraded forests located within the protected areas.

Nationally, the availability of land was cited as a major gap area by the Planning Commission in its discussions on the 10th Plan[19]. Under the Revised Operational Guidelines for NAP finalized in 2009, the requirement of block size has been reduced to 5 hectares. Smaller areas could be taken up if the JFMC agreed to extend additional voluntary support required for regeneration and maintenance of a smaller area.[20]

As discussed previously; in the hill states of the North Eastern region, land usually belongs to the community or to individuals as per customary laws. Apart from the Reserved Forests and Protected Forests, the Forest Department has a limited role. Further, in states like Meghalaya, Tripura and Mizoram, the management of forests (excluding reserved forests) has been kept under the ambit of the District or Regional Councils formed at the sub-state levels under the Constitution of India. Hence, in the hill states, the Forest Department faces additional hurdles in finding available land for carrying out afforestation projects.

Choice of Species Used

The choice of species used in afforestation is usually guided by the Forest Department officials. As the Mid Term Evaluation of NAP projects, carried out by the Indian Council of Forestry Research & Education, had observed, 'However, area selection for treatment and choice of species for plantation have followed departmental decisions as these are still being viewed by foresters and communities alike as forte of the technocrats'.[21] For their own reasons; the Forest Department and commercial growers usually choose to raise hardy tree species that grow comparatively quickly, and which command higher market demand and prices mainly for their woody biomass.

---

19 Comptroller & Auditor General (CAG): 'Environment Audit Report', Report No. 17 of 2010-11, Page No.13

20 National Afforestation & Eco-Development Board: 'National Afforestation Programme Revised Operational Guidelines, 2009', Page Nos. 3-4

21 Indian Council of Forestry Research and Education:'Mid Term Evaluation of the NAP Schemes implemented through FDAs', June 2008, Page No. 19

Consequently, out of India's total estimated forest plantation area, nearly 45% is composed of fast-growing, short-rotation species such as *Eucalyptus grandis, E. tereticornis, Acacia auriculiformis, A. mearnsii* and *A. nilotica*. Teak (*Tectona grandis*) accounts for about 8% of the total plantation area. Other commonly planted hardwood species are *Albizzia* spp, *Azadirachta indica, Casuarina equisetifolia, Dalbergia sissoo, Gmelina arborea* and *Hevea brasiliensis* (rubberwood). Pines and other conifers make up about 10% of the total forest plantation estate.[22] On the other hand, the needs of the fringe village communities are better served by species endowed with larger crown biomass, which can perform functions for maintenance of life support systems, hydrological and nutrient cycles and form the most important source of production of biomass for use as fuel, fodder, manure, fruits etc.[23]

The NAP guidelines provide for the use of improved technologies like clonal seedlings, root trainers, hormonal treatments etc. to encourage a wider variety of species and to improve the planting stock. Additional funds up to 25% of the plantation costs can be utilized for adopting such improved technologies. However, the existing limitations like skills and know how available at the field level prevented the effective utilization of funds in this direction. In addition, it has been observed that 'the NTFP (Non Timber Forest Product) species still constitute a minority in the plantation programmes'.[24]

Flow & Utilization of Public Funds for Afforestation

The flow of funds for the forestry sector originates from the budgets of the Government of India and of the various State Governments. In addition, externally aided projects are being operated for afforestation works. The major sources include NAP, Green India Mission, Compensatory Afforestation, Finance Commission grants etc. The plan outlays and expenditures incurred through the NAEB / Green India Mission during the 11th Five Year Plan period have been tabulated below.

---

22   International Tropical Timber Organization: 'Encouraging Industrial Forest Plantations in the Tropics', 2009

23   Dr. Vandana Shiva: 'Monocultures of the Mind', Palgrave Macmillan, 1993, Page No. 34

24   Barik & Darlong: 'Natural Resource Management Policy Environment in Meghalaya Impacting Livelihood of Forest Poor', Centre for International Forestry Research (CIFOR) Bogor, Indonesia Page No. 32

Table -1: Outlays & Expenditures on schemes of NAEB, NAP & Green India Mission

Financial Year	Rs. in Crore	
	Plan Outlay	Expenditure
2007-08	359.23	422.05
2008-09	398.62	370.71
2009-10	386.62	354.97
2010-11	352.00	353.93
2011-12	330.00	334.92
Total for 11ᵗʰ Plan	**1,826.47**	**1,836.58**

Source: Ministry of Environment & Forests: 'Outcome Budget for FY 2012-13', Page Nos. 52-53

From the above table, it is seen that the average annual expenditure incurred on the above schemes was over Rs. 367 crore per annum – i.e. just over Rs 1.00 crore a day for the entire plan period. This figure excludes funds from the Finance Commission award, external sources, compensatory afforestation and state budgets. The magnitude of the funds available from the above sources is given below[25].

- The Thirteenth Finance Commission award for the forestry sector was Rs 5,000 crore for a five year period starting from FY 2010-11, of which 25% was allocated for forest development and infrastructure.

- Compensatory afforestation funds ranged between Rs 1,000 crore and Rs 1,500 crore per annum during the 11ᵗʰ plan period, with such funds being available for mandatory compensatory afforestation in lieu of diverted forest area for non-forestry purpose, catchment area treatment, strengthening the protection and management of forests, infrastructure development and maintenance of older plantation etc.

- Externally aided projects were being operated in 11 states in the above plan, with their combined annual outlays ranging between Rs 500 crore and Rs. 600 crore per annum.

---

25 Planning Commission: 'Report of the Sub-Group-I on Forestry' [Constituted under Working Group for Forestry and Sustainable Natural Resource Management for the 12ᵗʰ Five Year Plan (2012-17)]

The present budget for FY 2014-15 makes a total plan outlay of Rs. 2043.00 crore for the Ministry of Environment & Forests; of which Rs. 1169.20 crore has been earmarked for 'Forestry & Wildlife'. The plan outlay for some schemes for the FY 2014-15 is given as follows:

National Afforestation Programme (NAP)	Rs 318.15 crore
Green India Mission	Rs 80.00 crore
Intensification of Forest Management Scheme	Rs 68.25 crore (*)

(*) for forest infrastructure, boundary demarcation and management of forest fire

It may be noted that a substantial part of the above funds are allocated to the North Eastern states. For example, the Thirteenth Finance Commission had awarded Rs. 1676.72 as grants-in-aid for forests – i.e. 33.53% of its total award. Similarly, the funds released to these states under NAP formed 18%, 16% and 20% of the total funds released by NAEB in the first three years of the 11th Five Year Plan.[26]

While the availability of funds is substantial, as indicated at above; there have been some issues with the utilization of funds as well as with the timely release of funds. The following examples are cited in this connection:

- The Comptroller & Auditor General of India (CAG) has observed that the NAEB had sanctioned Rs. 47.03 to Voluntary Agencies (VA) and State Forest Departments (SFDs) / Forest Development Agencies (FDAs) for implementing 647 projects under its 'Grants-in-Aid scheme for providing assistance to voluntary agencies for tree planting' (VA Scheme). Only 3.6% of the projects sanctioned to VAs and 23% of the projects sanctioned to SFDs / FDAs could be completed. In over three fifths of the above projects sanctioned to VAs (352 out of 560 cases), only one instalment was released as the NAEB did not receive Utilization Certificates, Progress Reports and other documents from the VAs. The CAG has stated that 'the possibility of misuse / fraud could not be ruled out'.[27]

---

26 Indian Council of Forestry Research and Education: 'Forestry Statistics of India – 2011', Page Nos. 67 and 69

27 Comptroller & Auditor General of India: 'Environment Audit Report', Report No. : 17 of 2010-11, Page Nos. 13-16

- Regarding fund flows under the NAP from the NAEB to FDAs, the Mid Term Evaluation carried out for the programme on an all India basis had observed that 'Most of the FDAs have reported delay in transfer of funds from NAEB, New Delhi office. This delay is more pronounced in release of 2nd and subsequent instalments'.[28]

- The progress of compensatory afforestation (CA) is marked by low achievement on the ground and poor utilization of funds as pointed out by the Comptroller & Auditor General of India. The pertinent details are furnished below.

As per Supreme Court order and forest laws, the Government is to collect funds from projects intending to use forest lands. These funds are based on rates set for different classes of forests, called the Net Present Value. These funds were then to be spent on greening other available lands in lieu of the forests handed over. In April 2004, the Ministry of Environment & Forests notified the Compensatory Afforestation funds Management and Planning Authority (CAMPA) to administer such Compensatory afforestation funds. Since the CAMPA was not made operational, the Supreme Court had intervened and formed an ad-hoc body in May 2006.

After examining the utilization of compensatory afforestation funds, the Comptroller and Auditor General of India has observed[29] that 103,382 hectares of forest land had been diverted for non-forest use since the notification of the Compensatory Afforestation funds Management and Planning Authority (CAMPA) by the Ministry of Environment & Forests in April 2004. But only 28,086 hectares of non-forest lands had been received for compensatory afforestation, which was just 27% of the diverted forest lands. Further, compensatory afforestation had been carried out in a mere 7,281 hectares (i.e. 7% of the forest land handed over to non forest use).

The quantum of funds for compensatory afforestation had grown to Rs. 23,607.67 crore by the end of 2012. However, as per CAG the states / UTs had not deposited all monies collected towards Compensatory Afforestation Fund. 'The divergence in data of transfer of funds available with Ad-hoc CAMPA and collected from

28 Indian Council of Forestry Research and Education:'Mid Term Evaluation of the NAP Schemes implemented through FDAs', June 2008, Page No. v

29 Comptroller & Auditor General of India: 'Compensatory Afforestation in India', Report No. : 21 of 2013

States/UTs was Rs. 6,021.88 crore, which was 26.32% of the principal amount with Ad-hoc CAMPA.'

The utilization of the released CA funds was low. Out of Rs. 2,925.65 crore of the compensatory afforestation funds released by Ad-hoc CAMPA during the period 2009-12 for compensatory afforestation activities, only Rs. 1,775.84 crore (61%) were utilized by the State/ UTs. In 11 of the states studied, the above utilisation ranged between 0% and 50%. These included some states in NE India like Meghalaya (0% utilization), Arunachal Pradesh (9%) and Tripura (32%)

The above are some recorded cases of delays in fund releases and poor utilization of funds. Similar instances cannot be ruled out in the case of afforestation projects carried out in the states of the NE region.

Sharing of Benefits

Another drawback in afforestation schemes carried out with the peoples' participation is that they are not very aware about the sharing of benefits, which are governed by legally non-tenable documents. As per the guidelines issued by the Government of India in 1990 for Joint Forest Management (JFM)[30] and the follow up guidelines for strengthening the JFM programme in 2000[31], the sharing of benefits is not dealt with in detail. Any Memorandum of Understanding (MoU) signed between the Forest Department and the JFM Committees has no legal status and such MoU exists for a limited period only.

As the Mid Term evaluation of the NAP carried out in 2007-08 by the Indian Council of Forestry Research and Education had observed, 'The rights under MoUs are weighted in favour of SFDs (State Forest Departments). Moreover, the benefits envisaged under project are too distant on time horizon and implementation of the scheme is only (five years) to provide a meaningful and clear incentive for community investments and

---

30 Letter No. 6.21/89-PP dated: 1st June, 1990 issued by the Ministry of Environment & Forests
31 Letter No. No. 22-8/2000-JFM (FPD) dated February 21, 2000 from the Ministry of Environment & Forests

support.'[32] Further, the lack of awareness about benefits may deter participation by women in afforestation works.[33]

Further, as per the Recognition of Forest Rights Act[34], forest dwellers have the right to collect and dispose of minor forest produce. Hence, they have little incentive to join hands with the Forest Department now for the **extension of JFM in 'good' forest areas** (with crown cover of 40%) as envisaged by the Ministry in its follow up guidelines for strengthening the JFM programme in 2000. The said guidelines state that in such forests, the JFM activities would concentrate on NTFP management.

Proposed People Centred Model for Planning & Implementation

In view of the above mentioned shortcomings of the current afforestation projects, especially in the hill states of the North Eastern region; it is proposed to outline a people centred approach for afforestation in these areas. The objective is to develop an alternative paradigm for the afforestation in such hill areas, wherein the planning and implementation of works are led by local communities / individuals.

The proposed model may be viewed as an *additional* approach to 'institutionalize the people's participation' for 'managing environment, forests, wildlife and challenges due to Climate Change' as envisioned for the 12th Five Year Plan.[35] It can supplement the existing efforts of the Forest Departments and other stakeholders, including the Joint Forest Committees. While developing this model, the local ground realities have been kept in mind and there is an effort to optimize the utilization of public funds.

The basic outlines of the proposed approach are given below.

Land for Afforestation

In the hill areas, land is customarily held by the community, clan or by individuals. The afforestation works may be carried out in such lands. Such works may be

32 Indian Council of Forestry Research and Education:'Mid Term Evaluation of the NAP Schemes implemented through FDAs', June 2008, Page No. 38

33 Ibid, Page No. 51

34 Scheduled Tribes and Other Traditional Forest Dwellers (Recognition Of Forest Rights) Act, 2006 (No. 2 Of 2007)

35 Planning Commission: 'Twelfth Five Year Plan (2012–2017) Faster, More Inclusive and Sustainable Growth Volume I', Chapter 7, Page No. 202

encouraged through plantation of trees on degraded forests (scrub land) and open forests (having crown density of 40% or less). The aided natural regeneration of forests may be encouraged.

It may be noted that over two fifths of forest cover in the NE region consists of open forests (having 10% - 40% crown density) and nearly 45% of the cover consists of moderately dense forest (40-70% crown density). Further, protected forest areas (Reserved Forests and Protected Forests) constitute only 25% of the geographical area of the region. If one leaves aside Assam, unclassed forests account for nearly three fifths of the recorded forest area of the rest of the region. Hence, there is an ample scope for taking up afforestation works by individuals or communities in the hill areas.

Preference may be given to cases where the quantum of land available for afforestation works is 10 hectares (or more) in a compact block, but this should not be a constraining factor. This aspect may be debated and modified. However, the advantages of having compact blocks for afforestation are to be considered carefully.

Association of Community / Individuals

The community, on whose common land the afforestation work is proposed, may associate as a society or trust to carry out the afforestation works. In case of individually owned lands, the land owner(s) and persons related to them or otherwise chosen by them may suitably associate to carry out the afforestation works. Such association may take the form of societies, trusts or companies registered with the appropriate registering authority.

The above associations may be certified by the Forest Department after vetting by the Gram Sabha or Village level Institution formed under the District or Regional Council in order to avail of public funds.

Planning of Works & Choice of Species

The planning of the afforestation works may be left to the community or association of individuals. This should not be constrained by the Working Plans of the Forest Department, but the plans should be intimated to the Department for its records and for receiving its support in matters like technical advice and permits for felling and transit.

The community / individuals may decide the area to be planted, spacing of plants, wage rates, components of work, soil and moisture conservation works, treatment of problem area, sourcing of planting materials etc. based on their own judgement. In such matters, they may seek the technical guidance from the Forest Department, professionals or other sources.

However, if the planned works have to be publicly funded (even partially), then the above mentioned plans have to be approved by the Forest Department after being vetted by the Gram Sabha or Village level Institution formed under the District or Regional Council. In such cases, photographs of the proposed area with geographical coordinates may be required to be attached with the plans while the same are forwarded for approval.

The choice of species may be left to the community / individuals who may grow fast growing species, horticultural crops, fodder and fuel wood providing species etc. However, preference may be given to species which do not need permission from the Forest Department as per the applicable rules governing the felling of trees on non-forest lands. In most NE states, the felling of horticultural trees like mango, jack fruit, guava, jamun (*Syzygium cumini*) etc. and of home-grown bamboo are usually exempt from permission requirements.

Implementation of Works

The works may be implemented by the Association of Community / Individuals as per their own plans. They may engage labour if sufficient voluntary labour is not available locally. All labourers / volunteers may be paid at market rates or the minimum wage rate. The different works like Advance Work, Plantation and Annual Maintenance may be carried out as per the best practices in the area of forestry.

The planting materials used have to be certified as being 'disease free' in case the vegetative propagation route is used through methods like cutting, bud grafting, layering etc. This is necessary to prevent the spread of diseases that may defeat the purpose of undertaking the afforestation works.

In case the works are needed to be publicly funded (even partially), then the implementation of works shall be supervised by the Forest Department and the release of instalments of funds should be linked to the progress of works certified by the field officials of the Forest Department, apart from the reports of the concurrent evaluation undertaken by independent agencies (as described later in this section).

Funding of Works

The afforestation works under the proposed approach can be funded from a combination of the following sources:

- Own sources of the individuals / community (in form of cash, kind or labour);
- Bank loans for commercially viable projects against reduced security requirements;
- Public funds from the following (for certified associations with approved plans):
  - ✔ MG NREGS (Rural Employment Guarantee Scheme)
  - ✔ CAMPA (Compensatory Afforestation)
  - ✔ National Afforestation Programme / National Mission for a Green India
  - ✔ Integrated Watershed Management Programme
  - ✔ Other Government programmes (Central / State Governments);
- Grants by Corporate Bodies / Individuals / Trusts (in case of donations made to community afforestation carried out by certified associations, tax exemptions may be considered);
- Corporate Social Responsibility Funds;
- External Aid (in case of large projects); and
- Other sources – which may be emerge from brain storming sessions.

The basic aim of diversifying the funding sources and including own contributions (in kind or labour), is to encourage the individuals and communities of the region to look beyond the Government and to develop a spirit of self help and initiative at the village levels.

Concurrent Evaluation of Works (for Publicly Funded Projects only)

If the afforestation works involve the use of funds, then the progress of works may be concurrently evaluated by independent agencies to record aspects like the physical progress of works, fund utilization, quality aspects, problems faced and solutions adopted etc.

The agency carrying out the independent evaluation may be required to take photographs of the plantation areas with their geographical coordinates. These photographs may be reviewed against the photographs of the areas furnished along with the proposal to detect any possible misuse of public funds.

Sharing of Benefits

In case of self funded individual projects, the benefits will accrue to the individuals. For the community projects without public funding, the benefits will go to the community members as provided for under their rules / understanding. In case the individual / community avail of bank loans, the same has to be repaid with interest as per the bank's terms.

For projects funded by Corporate Social Responsibility Funds, grants or donations etc.; the conditions of the corporate body concerned or donor has to be followed along with the provision of the laws of the land.

If public funds are involved or external aid is availed of with Government guarantee, then a legally enforceable agreement may be drawn up by the parties regarding the sharing of the benefits. The agreement will incorporate the terms of the Government / external donor which have to be understood and accepted by the community beforehand.

Further, a limited quantum of the benefits like fuel wood, fodder, small timber, medicinal plants etc. may be kept aside for vulnerable members of the local community including women headed households, except for forests raised with bank loans.

Role of the State Forest Department

The Forest Department will play a facilitative role in the entire approach. It can render technical assistance for planning and implementation of the works. The Department can help the associations to obtain planting materials from its own sources or its registered suppliers. It can also assist the community / individual to obtain felling and transit permits, including in states through which the timber has to pass while reaching markets.

In case public funds are involved, the role of the Department will be greater including the certification of the associations, approval of plans, supervision of works and coordination with the independent agencies appointed for concurrent evaluation of the works, including review of their reports.

Conclusion

The above model for development of forests on community and individual lands has been proposed based on the ground situation in the hill states of the region and the limitations of the present afforestation measures of the state.

The proposed approach is open for extensive debate and changes as deemed necessary. As an outcome, all attempts must be made by the stakeholders in the region and their well wishers elsewhere to mainstream the model (after all necessary modifications have met with stakeholder acceptance) and to create the ground conditions for its adoption by the local communities, so that a people led afforestation movement can take root in the hill states of the region. This is necessary as the NE Region is still losing forest / tree cover, despite having nearly two thirds of its area under forest. Thereby, local communities are being adversely affected in many ways.

The adoption of the people centred approach will develop the confidence of communities and individuals to develop their living standards on their own initiative, thereby breaking the on-going dependence on government handouts. This may have several positive implications for the growth of the North Eastern region of the country.

4.4 Developing an ecotourism model for Meghalaya

By Prachi Agarwal (IIM Shillong) and Ujjawal Kumar (IIM Shillong)

Abstract

Tourism is known to be a resource intensive industry which has a huge impact on the resources of the surrounding areas particularly the flora and fauna hence the concept of ecotourism has been widely getting recognition and acceptance however there are a number of practical hurdles which make it difficult to implement the concept. This research paper attempts to understand the concept of ecotourism and examines the various ecotourism models which have been implemented in various countries. The paper analyses the models already being used and their impact and the possibility of adapting successful ecotourism models from other countries. This paper specifically attempts to study and explore the possibility of adapting ecotourism models which have been successful in other countries to the North Eastern region of the country (in Meghalaya).
Keywords: Ecotourism, North East India, sustainable tourism, ecotourism models of Australia and Kenya, tourism management

Introduction

Tourism is an industry which has been growing at a fast pace. Tourism is a resource intensive industry and uses economic, environmental, social and cultural resources. It has three types of impacts on the area: economic impact, environmental impact and socio-cultural impact. Ritchie (1984) has developed a framework which categorizes the impact of tourism against four dimensions: physical/ environmental, socio-cultural, psychological and administrative. Some other authors include motivational factors in this framework as well. In this paper, we are more concerned about the first two factors hence would restrict the discussion to them. Impact of tourism can be understood as 'the development of tourism infrastructure using natural and cultural resources, leading to depletion and degradation of the natural resources with other socio-cultural issues'. The economic impact is in terms of providing means of generating revenue and inflow of foreign currency in the country. The environmental/physical impact is both positive and negative. Positive impacts include renovation of historic monuments and aesthetic development of natural tourist spots while the negative impacts include dealing with generated tourist waste and the threats faced by the fauna and flora of environmentally sensitive area. Globally natural forest area have been used for the construction of tourist facilities which leads to destruction of the very reason of tourism. The socio-cultural impact include the benefits of acceptance of the culture and traditions of the natives, cross cultural interaction and availability of job opportunities for the local people. Tourism is an industry which develops to exploit and threaten the very reason of its existence and success. The dilemma for the tourism industry has always been to find the optimal balance between financial gain and minimizing resource exploitation. This has led to a new concept of sustainable tourism or ecotourism which balances the financial benefits with environmental benefits and results in a positive socio-cultural impact.

Ecotourism

In four out of five countries, tourism ranks as one of the top five export earners. The number of international tourist arrivals surpassed 1 billion for the first time in 2011 and is forecasted to reach 1.8 billion by 2030. With continuing growth in travel there is growing concern among consumers and travel professionals about responsible travel. The concept of eco-tourism is a result of this thinking.

The purpose of Ecotourism is to preserve ecosystems while simultaneously creating economic profit. It has been defined by the Eco-tourism society as "responsible travel to natural areas which conserves the environment and sustains the well-being of local people".

Various models of Ecotourism: Introduction

This paper tries to understand successful models of ecotourism and what are the underlying characteristics of such models that can be applied to other tourist destinations. Some of the successful ecotourism models are as follows-

A) Australian Eco-tourism model:

It has an accreditation system of rating tour operators and resorts on the basis of their "greenness".

It has recognized some 5800 locations as protected areas which have been specifically designed and internationally defined as areas dedicated to the protection of biodiversity in Australia.

A number of community based nature conservation programs have been initiated to protect and regenerate native vegetation, e.g. "One billion tree program", save the bush program etc.

Apart from conserving the environment, eco-tourism also aims at providing jobs and economic advancement to the aboriginal people of Australia. There are programs that involve the local people in natural and cultural resource management. These programs provide skills and training to work as guides, interpreters, cooks and office staff. Also it promotes unity amongst the community and feeling of ownership and responsibility towards conservation of their resources.

This model also advocates training indigenous people to protect and preserve official reserves and national parks by putting them in authority positions to promote the feeling of ownership amongst the natives.

B) Kenyan Eco-tourism model:

This model proposes creation of a conservancy and making it prosper to such an extent that it assists local communities to have access to employment, schools, healthcare and revenue generating wildlife schemes.

The second model is of a company called Abercrombie and Kent that donates part of its revenue to different wildlife parks and sanctuaries. Here the company's motive is profit. The park may use part of the money to employ local people but Abercrombie and Kent does not engage with the local people directly. Their most important way of impacting the nature is by making the tourists aware of the plight of the environment and how it's degrading quickly. This way the company helps in providing employment to the locals as well as creating awareness among the tourists about how their actions impact the environmental balance of the area. This is a multiple stakeholder benefit model where the company, locals and tourists have active roles to play which result in responsible tourism.

Various models of Ecotourism: Challenges

Problems with existing models of eco-tourism:

a) Leakage:

A study revealed that out of every dollar spent on tourism $ 0.40 went to buy imports for tourist demands, another $ 0.40 went to private hotels and other businesses and $ 0.20 went to host governments in the form of taxes. Very little of the money spent by tourists is actually left for conservation and invested back into the communities. Most of the so called eco-tourist models suffer from this leakage of funds. A truly eco-tourist model should ensure that the money spent is used to provide local employment. Indigenous products should be encouraged and sold.

b) Employment:

It has emerged as a sad truth that in most cases local people are employed on low paying service jobs such as potential maids, waiters and gardeners. In most of the cases, these jobs are favored to more sustainable jobs like fishing, farming, arts and craft. This arises from the fact that most of the locations witness huge inflow of tourists during the particular seasons. Although GDP and employment rates may show increase, these jobs do not empower the local people in the real sense. The government should pitch in and provide training to the local people so that they are ready for jobs requiring more skills and better remuneration. In addition to revenue generation for locals, the locals being aware of the history and environmental sensitivity of the tourist spot would ensure that the visiting tourists are also made aware of the same and made to understand about how important it is to support locals in protecting the flora and fauna of the site.

c) Indigenous cultures threatened:

It has been seen that local people are forced to adapt their culture to what the tourists want to experience. Influx of tourists impacts the culture, as these communities which had little outside connection start seeing people of different cultures in huge numbers. It has also been seen that local people have aversion towards such parks and sanctuaries because these are built on their farming lands and are inaccessible to them. This is a very sensitive issue and is a major cause of most of the cultural differences being observed in many tourist places. The development of urban entertainment facilities to satisfy tourist needs is many times not acceptable to the locals as it is in direct conflict with their cultural and social beliefs and practices.

d) Environmental impact:

This is the most important problem with eco-tourism. If a tourism destination becomes popular, it inevitably leads to its failure to maintain its uniqueness which attracted the tourists in the first place. The amount of infrastructure required to be built in order to accommodate the increasing number of tourists results in huge loss to the bio-diversity of the place. Local areas start getting polluted, more and more deforestation occurs to make way for hotels and business centers, improper management of the waste generated leads to degeneration of the local environment and many other problems.
The influx of more and more tourists is sure to have an impact but this can be reduced by proper management practices.

e) Model of working together:

It is said that with proper cooperation between the industry, governments, NGOs and local communities there will be successful implementation of eco-tourism. This view of working together is fundamentally wrong because the interests of all these groups are different. The power shifts more into the hands of the powerful institutions with financial backing. Rules get bent and are not followed to the spirit, ultimately compromising the efforts towards effective implementation. The model of working against each other is more in line with the aim of having effective policies that are applicable in the real sense and maintaining a balance.

Ecotourism model for Meghalaya

Based on the challenges and a study of the successful models across the world we propose a three-fold multiple stakeholder involvement eco-tourism model for Meghalaya as follows:
a)Community based model:

Meghalaya is the abode of India's hill communities. Dance, music and sports reflect their way of life. There are about twenty-four communities in the state amongst which fifteen are scheduled tribes that have migrated from other states. There are twelve non-tribal communities who have migrated for trading and business purposes. Amongst the many tribes the most important are Khasi, Jaintia and Garo. The hills are the lifeline of these communities and hence no tourism model can relegate them. The model that we propose gives the community major control and involvement in the eco-tourism project. The community can take the help of government or other agencies in implementing these projects but the major control over the revenue and benefits must lie with the community. Community leaders must be actively involved to understand their expectations from the government and tourists. They can then act as influencers in their community to create awareness among the locals for the need of tourism projects and increase their acceptance amongst the community. They can also help in identifying volunteers from the community for taking positions of authority to ensure that no harm comes to the natural resources.

b) Government should act as a support:

The government should help these communities in managing the resources by giving proper training for skill enhancement. It should also manage the other stakeholders in such a way that motives of all stakeholders go in sync. It should ensure that outside private players do not run away with the money and that most of the revenue generated is invested back for the preservation of the eco-system and the development of the local population. Since the government has a non-profit motive only it can be relied to do this job properly. The major challenge for government would be to gain the trust of the locals as most of these tribes have their own apprehensions about the motives of the government.

c) Sensitizing the tourists:

Uniqueness of the local culture should be advertised. One of the reasons for degradation of environmental resources is lack of knowledge about the local culture and the sensitivity of the natural resources of the area and the impact of tourist activities on the same. Tourist destinations should be positioned in the minds of the tourists as environmentally important for biodiversity so that they are sensitive to the requirements of the local population and respect their culture. Tourists must not only enjoy the beauty of the place but must also experience the unique culture of the locals and mingle with them giving due respect to their beliefs and traditions.

Conclusion

Ecotourism has been gaining wide recognition and acceptance due to the resource intensive nature of the tourism industry. Despite the benefits of ecotourism, there are a number of practical hurdles which make it difficult to implement the concept. Each area is unique in its mix of resources, social factors and economic needs hence a successful ecotourism model should not just ape practices from other models but study the adaptability of those practices in the given region, their impacts and their acceptability by various stakeholders. Meghalaya has highly unique cultural and environmental resources hence a community based model with the support of various stakeholders will be more successful. A combined effort by sensitizing the tourists, natives and active contribution by the government will result in financial gains with minimal harm to the natural resources of the area.

References:

a) http://www.unl.edu/plains/ecotourism-namibian-models.pdf
b) http://databank.nedfi.com/content/tourism-meghalaya
c) http://web.stanford.edu/class/e297c/trade_environment/photo/hmodels.html

Part 5: Renewable Energy

5.1 Renewable Energy – Blowing Right

By Dr J Cyril Kanmony and Vinodh K Natarajan

Introduction

Energy played a vital role for having a better life even in the primitive stage of history. In the early stages of human civilization human energy was the only source of energy. Human muscular power had provided the mechanical energy that was needed for day to day living. The invention of fire was an important happening in the progress of mankind as burning wood enabled cooking of food and heating of dwellings easy. Fire was also used for making and sharpening of bronze and iron tools which were used for hunting. At a later stage of human civilization, animal power was made use of for doing works that required more power than human power. The use of animal power for ploughing fields, drawing water and thrashing of food grains, helped to increase agricultural productivity. Thus even in the early stage of civilization human and animal energy helped to increase productivity and for improving the quality of human life.

It was in the beginning of the 12th century, in Northern England, the first step towards the development of modern sources of energy took place. This development occurred due to the discovery of the burning property of hard black rocks available in Northern England. It ultimately led to the excavation of vast coal deposits in England. A new era had started in the history of energy generation and coal became the major source of energy. During the first half of the 14th century coal began to be used for domestic heating in coal producing areas of Britain. The Industrial Revolution, which began in Britain in the 18th century helped in large-scale coal mining. During the Industrial Revolution coal provided the main source of primary energy for industry and to power steam engines used in transportation. International trade expanded exponentially when coal-fed steam engines were built for the railways and steamships. Thus industrializing countries in the 19th and early part of the 20th century started using coal for transportation and increasing trade (Kaldellis & Zafirakis, 2011)

The exploration of oil in the latter half of the 19th century and subsequently the invention of generator to produce electricity changed human history by providing humanity with such means, comforts and facilities of life that could not be dreamt of in the previous centuries. In the late 1950s the emergence of alternative energy sources such as oil, natural gas and nuclear power used for electricity generation revolutionized the entire range of energy production world-wide. Energy came to be regarded as an universal input and a fifth factor of production. Energy consumption becomes a major indicator of economic development and the development of a sustainable, long-term solution to meeting the world's energy needs has become an important issue in recent times.

It has been estimated that the demand for power or electrical energy will grow by nearly twice the rate at which the economy grows (Global Wind Energy Council, 2010). Current energy systems are failing to meet the needs of the world's poor. Worldwide, as of 2010, 2.6 billion people rely on traditional biomass for cooking and 1.6 billion people do not have access to electricity. The projected cumulative investment required between 2005 and 2030 to meet energy needs is almost US$ 20.1 trillion, but even if this investment undertaken, 1.4 billion people will still lack access to electricity in 2030 and 2.7 billion will still rely on traditional biomass for cooking and heating (UNIDO, 2010). Thus there is wide gap between supply of and demand for energy. Energy is also considered as an index of economic development and human progress.

Energy and Economic Development

One of the essential indicators of economic development and human progress during the era of post-industrial revolution is energy consumption. This is evident as, during post-industrial revolution most economic activities depended mainly on the effective utilisation of energy in fields of production and infrastructure development. Thus in the 1960s high positive relation between per capita income and per capita electricity consumption was observed. Countries that had abundant supply of energy have realised substantially higher economic growth. The table given below illustrates this relationship in selected countries.

TABLE 1.1
PER CAPITA NATIONAL INCOME AND PER CAPITA ELECTRICITY
CONSUMPTION IN SELECTED COUNTRIES (1966)

Country	Per capita National Income (current US$)	Per capita Electricity Consumption (kWh)
USA	3842	6345
Sweden	2732	6484
UK	1925	2703
Japan	986	2171
Taiwan	245	593
India	92	75

Source: Tyner Wallace (1978),
PCNI = Per Capita National Income, PCEC = Per Capita Electricity Consumption

During the last two and half decades, the scenario has changed to a certain extent. There are countries that required positive economic growth though there is negative per capita energy consumption. And so caution is required when one tries to establish one to one correspondence between per capita energy consumption and per capita income. However, the values of compound annual growth rate (CAGR) show that there is positive relationship between percentage change in per capita income and percentage change in per capita energy consumption. The CAGR for per capita national income (PCNI) was 9.31 between 1973 and 1991, when the per capita electricity consumption (PCEC) was 3.41, but decreased to 4.07 between 1991 and 2011 as PCEC decreased to 1.04. The table 1.2 shows the percentage change in per capita national income (PCNI) and per capita electricity consumption (PCEC) in selected developed countries.

TABLE 1.2
PERCENTAGE CHANGE IN PER CAPITA NATIONAL INCOME AND PER CAPITA
ELECTRICITY CONSUMPTION IN SELECTED DEVELOPED COUNTRIES FOR THE
PERIOD 1973 – 2011

Country	% Change 1973 to 1991		% Change 1991 to 2011	
	PCNI	PCEC	PCNI	PCEC
Norway	419	53	224	-3
Luxembourg	577	19	133	10
Switzerland	-	50	114	5
Sweden	309	82	94	-12
Australia	292	101	174	26
Netherlands	322	47	152	32
United States	236	42	107	9
Austria	509	75	126	32
Finland	523	106	96	26
Canada	243	56	129	2
Belgium	339	69	127	21
Singapore	691	219	259	65
Japan	691	64	59	17
Germany	389	41	100	8
France	349	101	104	15
CAGR*	9.37	3.41	4.07	1.04

Source: World Bank Database, 2013, * computed value, CAGR = Compounded
Annual Growth Rate

The table 1.3 shows the percentage change in per capita national income and per capita electricity consumption in selected developing countries. The CAGR shows, though energy consumption decreased from 6.09 during 1973–1991 to 5.44 during 1991-2011, the PCNI increased from 5.67 to 9.44. This indicates the decrease in the energy use intensity in all countries including developing countries.

TABLE 1.3
PERCENTAGE CHANGE IN PER CAPITA NATIONAL INCOME AND PER CAPITA
ELECTRICITY CONSUMPTION IN SELECTED DEVELOPING COUNTRIES FOR
THE PERIOD 1973 – 2011

Developing Countries	% Change 1973 to 1991		% Change 1991 to 2011	
	PCNI	PCEC	PCNI	PCEC
China	119	216	1314	501
Brazil	283	170	273	65
India	133	186	314	137
CAGR	5.67	6.09	9.44	5.44

Source: World Bank Database, 2013

This decline in the energy use intensity can be attributed to two reasons. Frist after the period of the 1973 oil shock, developed countries made huge investments in energy saving devices. Second developed countries tend to experience a decline in energy consumption after a phase of high economic development. This is because during the initial stages of economic growth infrastructure development and industrial development consume a great deal of energy. Once this stage is over, there develops consumer and service industries, most of which require comparatively less energy. Thus the constraints created in the wake of the oil crises prompted many countries to change their production and consumption pattern of energy. The same oil crisis also prompted many countries to make investment in renewable energy sources and invest in energy efficient technologies.

Hence when countries push for greater economic growth it increases energy consumption which creates huge supply shortage as well as increases energy-related carbon dioxide emissions (CO_2). It is expected that carbon dioxide emissions will increase by some 50 per cent between 2014 and 2030 unless major policy reforms and technologies are introduced to transform the way energy is produced and consumed. Developing countries will account for three quarters of the increase in carbon dioxide emissions between 2004 and 2030 unless major transformative policies and technologies are introduced in the next few years (U.S. Energy Information Administration, 2013). Thus the need arises for finding new and alternate sources of energy generation. There are a number of sources for generating energy. As non-renewable sources are depleting and creating environmental damages, in recent years, huge investments are being made in renewable energy sources, thus changing the dynamics of energy generation all over the globe.

Energy sources

Primary sources of energy are classified as non-exhaustible/renewable or exhaustible/non-renewable sources. Secondary sources are derived from primary sources. Energy from the ground that has limited supplies, either in the form of gas, liquid or solid, are called non-renewable resources. They cannot be replenished or made again in a short period of time. Energy that comes from a source that's constantly renewed, such as the solar and the wind, can be replenished naturally in a short period of time. Energy that is converted from primary sources are secondary sources of energy. Secondary sources of energy are used to store, move, and deliver energy in an easily usable form. Examples include electricity and hydrogen.

Moreover energy sources can also be classified based on the nature of their transaction as commercial and non-commercial sources. Coal, oil, natural gas and hydroelectric power constitute the main sources of commercial energy or electric power. The main non-commercial energy sources are firewood, cow-dung and vegetable wastes, together referred to as biomass energy (Indian Institute of Science, 2013).

Non-renewable energy sources

Two distinguishing features of non-renewable sources are; they get exhausted when used as an input in the production process and the rate of their utilisation far exceeds the rate at which they are formed. Oil (petroleum), natural gas, coal and uranium (nuclear) are examples of non-renewable energy sources. Oil, natural gas and coal are called "fossil fuels" because they have been formed from the organic remains of prehistoric plants and animals. Oil and gas form from organic material in microscopic marine organisms, whereas coal forms from the decayed remains of land plants. Tar (oil) sands and oil shale are less common forms of fossil fuels and are less widely used because extraction of oil from these deposits is more expensive than producing other forms of fossil fuels.

Fossil fuels are limited in reserves and are expected to get completely exhausted in the coming sixty years. This means that there is a pressing need to look at other sources of energy. The need is even more urgent as energy from non-renewable sources is produced and made usable through laborious and environmentally damaging processes. The transportation of fossil fuels from the place of extraction to the site for further processing adds to more environmental damages. Over-reliance on oil as a resource has created environmental dangers and has undermined the energy security of the entire world. This is evident as the world has witnessed many energy security crisis like oil crises of 1973, Gulf War of 1991 and Iraq War of 2003 and environmental dangers like acid rains and climate change.

Renewable energy sources

Renewable sources of energy are inexhaustible and usable as they exist. They are used where they are available thus reducing transportation costs. Electricity generation using renewable sources helps in reducing the emission of harmful gases. The use of renewable sources of energy reduces our reliance on oil, and thus safeguards national security. The renewable resources are hydro energy, solar energy, wind, and energy from wastes (such as biogas and agro-wastes). The whole system of renewable sources is pollution free and environment friendly. There is no adverse effect on global environment. On the other hand burning of fossil fuels such as coal, oil and gas emit greenhouse gases (GHGs) that are recognized as being responsible for climate change (International Energy Agency, 2002). It is this feature of renewable energy sources which has led to the need for investing in non-renewable sources. The renewable sources like oil, coal and, to a lesser extent, natural gas are responsible for emission of CO_2 (the main greenhouse gas), SOx and NOx. These gases cause acid rains and are responsible for climatic changes across the globe (Grimaud & Rouge, 2005).

The emissions caused in using non-renewable energy have increased. Global consumption of coal (responsible for about 40 % of total CO_2 emissions) grew in 2011 by 5 per cent, whereas global consumption of natural gas and oil products increased by only 2 per cent and 1 per cent, respectively (British Petroleum, 2012). Global emissions of carbon dioxide – the main cause of global warming – increased by 3 per cent in 2011, reaching an all-time high of 34 billion tonnes in 2011. The top six countries which emit CO_2 gas are China (29 %), the United States (16 %), the European Union (11 %), India (6 %) the Russian Federation (5 %), and Japan (4 %). From 2000 to 2011 an estimated total of 420 billion tonnes of CO_2 was emitted due to economic and human activities (including deforestation). India is the fourth largest CO_2 emitting country and in 2011 it emitted 2.0 billion tonnes of CO_2 (JRC/PBL European Commission, 2011). The recent emissions although high have been reduced to a great extent due to the use of renewable energy sources.

In 2011, globally about 0.8 billion tonnes of CO_2 emissions was avoided due to the use of renewable energy sources which otherwise would have been emitted if fossil-fuel were used for power generation. The total potentially avoided emissions in 2011 have been estimated at roughly 1.7 billion tonnes CO_2 when including the hydropower capacity (Olivier & Janssens-Maenhout, 2011). The reduction in pollution was made possible due to the increasing share of renewable energy sources excluding hydropower, such as solar and wind energy and biofuels in energy generation. Investments in renewable sources although still very small is increasing with accelerated speed. Globally, it took 12 years from 1992 to 2004 for investments in renewable energy to double its share from 0.5 per cent to 1 per cent (of the total sources used for energy generation). But by 2011 the share of renewable energy sources had increased to 2.1 per cent.

This shows that renewable energy sources are being looked as alternative energy sources for electricity generation and other productive uses. Nevertheless along with environmental benefits the cost of producing electricity from renewable sources must also be considered. The wide use of non-renewable energy sources is mainly due to the generation cost advantage it has over renewable sources. But for sustainable development it is very essential to overlook short term benefits and concentrate on long term energy security and environment sustainability.

Among renewable energy sources wind energy is an important energy source. Globally the share of wind energy is increasing. Thus a look at the wind energy and its development at the international level and national level is undertaken in sections below.

Wind energy

Wind devices were used thousands of years ago, with the vertical axis windmills found at the Persian-Afghan borders around 200 BC and the horizontal-axis windmills of the Netherlands and the Mediterranean following much later (1300-1875 AD) (Global Wind Energy Council, 2010). It was during the last two centuries when the technology of wind energy made its first actual progresses.

Early Development

The figure 1.1 shows the evolution of the wind systems in the USA during the 19th century. Between 1850 and 1970 over six million small machines were used for water pumping. The first large wind turbine with 12 kW rated power that was used to generate electricity was installed in 1888 at Cleveland, Ohio. During the late stages of World War I, use of 25 kW machines throughout Denmark was widespread (Dodge, 2006).

FIGURE 1.1
INSTALLATION OF WIND ENERGY FROM (1850) TO (1990)

Source: *Adapted from Meyer, 1995*

European countries continued the developments in wind energy after World War II. It was during the period between 1935 and 1970 countries like Denmark, France, Germany, and the UK showed that large-scale wind turbines could work. The development of large-scale wind turbines and generators was based on technology of airplane propellers and monoplane wings. After 1970, in Germany a series of advanced horizontal-axis designs were developed while in Denmark, the Gedser mill 200 kW three-bladed upwind rotor wind turbine (WT) operated successfully. (Meyer, 1995).

Post 1973 Oil Crisis Development

After the oil crisis of 1973, the United States Government invested heavily in research and development (R&D) of wind energy. Following this investment, in the years between 1973 and 1986, the commercial wind turbine market progressed from domestic and agricultural utility to interconnected wind farm applications. The led to the development of wind turbines with 50 kW to 600 kW rated power (Gipe, 1991) (de Carmoy, 1978). Throughout the 1980s and the 1990s, in northern Europe, windmills installations increased gradually. At the same time the US government provided huge incentives which led to the installation of 16,000 windmills with rated power/capacity ranging between 20 kW to 350 kW in California (Righter, 1996).
After 1990 Europe emerged as the leader in the wind energy market (Ackermann & Söder, 2002). Many European countries invested in wind energy due to the high cost of electricity generation through non-renewable sources and also due to the presence of excellent wind resources leading to the creation of a small but stable wind energy

market. Globally during the last two decades wind energy has gained prominence as governments have been looking for providing clean and sustainable energy.

Energy generation and consumption: the global outlook

The biggest challenge today for the global economy can be summed up in five words "More Energy, Less Carbon dioxide". The twin problems of depletion of non-renewable energy resources and environmental pollution pose a serious threat at the global level. Even though huge efforts are taken by developed countries to harness energy in an economical and environment friendly way, there are still difficulties in achieving this objective. A look at the current trends in energy supply and consumption at the global level will give a holistic view on the energy problem.

TABLE 1.7
TOTAL PRIMARY ENERGY PRODUCTION (In BILLION kWh)

Countries	1980	1990	2000	2008	2009	2010	% Change 1980 to 2010
World	84190	102142	116350	143079	142784	149099	77
China	5310	8318	11364	22959	24631	26485	399
United States	19683	20717	20900	21453	21284	21915	11
Russia			12217	15396	14776	15594	28
Saudi Arabia	6573	4665	6327	7374	6691	7250	10
Canada	3011	3928	5312	5573	5369	5378	79
Iran	1156	2247	3047	3914	4178	4279	270
Indonesia	1239	1554	2252	3349	3685	4038	226
Australia	951	1804	2830	3476	3629	3784	298
Brazil	557	1101	1864	2510	2615	2774	398
Norway	858	1700	3018	2967	2894	2768	222
Mexico	1677	2244	2747	2687	2524	2572	53
United Arab Emirates	1139	1615	1983	2382	2203	2239	97
Algeria	821	1393	1814	2161	2069	2087	154
Venezuela	1689	1848	2746	2225	2066	2052	21

Source: US Energy Information Administration International Energy Statistics, http://www.eia.gov/cfapps/ipdbproject/IEDIndex3.cfm

It can be inferred from the table 1.7 that developing countries have shown very high growth rate in energy production after 1980. Between 1980 and 2010, China and Brazil have seen a growth of 399 per cent and 398 per cent respectively in energy production.

However, developed countries like United States and Canada have registered a growth of only 21 per cent and 79 per cent respectively. From the table 1.7 it is observed that the total energy production of the world has grown by 77 per cent which indicates that energy requirements all over the globe are increasing.

TABLE 1.8
TOTAL PRIMARY ENERGY CONSUMPTION (In BILLION kWh)

Countries	1980	1990	2000	2008	2009	2010	% Change 1980 to 2010
World	82963	101385	117221	143767	142861	149591	80
China	5065	7618	11994	24889	27651	29558	484
United States	22874	24754	28953	29087	27706	28726	26
Russia	NA	NA	7659	8682	8113	8591	12
Japan	4453	5499	6567	6415	6064	6379	43
Africa	1991	2774	3527	4711	4666	4784	140
Canada	2870	3217	3898	3969	3837	3809	33
Brazil	1178	1686	2500	3029	3055	3311	181
France	2458	2674	3211	3309	3145	3230	31
Korea, South	515	1126	2296	2897	2922	3159	513
Iran	464	909	1471	2373	2650	2669	475
United Kingdom	2590	2716	2851	2721	2574	2612	1
Saudi Arabia	487	981	1422	2183	2117	2300	372
Italy	1792	1970	2221	2297	2154	2234	25

Source: US Energy Information Administration International Energy Statistics, http://www.eia.gov/cfapps/ipdbproject/IEDIndex3.cfm

The table 1.8 shows the total energy consumption of the top 13 countries excluding India for the year 2010. From the table 1.7 and 1.8 it is seen that while the world energy consumption has increased by 80 per cent, the world's primary energy generation has risen by only 77 per cent. In order to meet the increasing energy demand, countries have to increase energy generation. Table 1.8 shows that developing countries' energy consumption has increased more than developed countries. It is seen that while China's energy consumption has grown by 484 per cent from 1980 to 2010, the United States energy consumption has grown only by 26 per cent. Nevertheless, developed and developing countries have to increase energy generation to meet the rising demand. But increased demand needs to be met through renewable energy sources due to rise in cost and pollution caused by non-renewable sources of energy.

TABLE 1.9
TOTAL RENEWABLE ELECTRICITY NET GENERATION (In BILLION kWh)

Countries	1980	1990	2000	2008	2009	2010	% Change 1980 to 2010
World	1754	2279	2871	3730	3868	4167	138
China	58	125	223	597	639	771	1238
United States	285	361	361	393	430	440	55
Brazil	130	209	309	386	411	433	40
Canada	252	298	363	381	379	366	45
Russia	NA	NA	165	166	176	168	2
Norway	83	120	141	139	125	118	42
Japan	89	101	105	106	107	115	30
Africa	60	56	77	98	102	111	84
Germany	NA	NA	41	95	99	110	NA
Spain	30	26	36	63	74	98	231
Sweden	59	74	83	82	80	83	40
France	69	55	71	75	71	79	14
Italy	49	35	51	59	71	79	61

Source: US Energy Information Administration International Energy Statistics, http://www.eia.gov/cfapps/ipdbproject/IEDIndex3.cfm

From the table 1.9 it is clear that globally the renewable energy generation has been increasing. As of 2010, China leads in the production of energy from renewable sources with a total of 771 billion kWh. Globally the total generation of energy from non-renewable sources is 1,49,099 billion kWh, while from renewable sources it is 4167 billion kWh. This shows that energy generation from renewable sources is a mere 2.8 per cent of the total energy generation. Thus countries are facing a very difficult situation. On the one hand they have to increase the use of renewable sources of energy and on the other hand they have to meet the rising energy demand. Nonetheless it is very clear that on the renewable energy front both developing and developed countries are equally increasing their share.

TABLE 1.10
WIND ELECTRICITY NET GENERATION (In BILLION kWh)

Countries	1990	2000	2008	2009	2010	% Change 2000 to 2010
World	3.53	31.36	220.30	276.05	341.53	989
United States	2.789	5.59	55.36	73.89	94.65	1593
China	0.002	0.61	14.80	26.90	44.62	7215
Spain	0.014	4.72	32.95	38.12	44.17	836
Germany	NA	9.35	40.57	38.64	37.79	304
United Kingdom	0.009	0.94	7.10	9.30	10.18	983
France	0	0.07	5.69	7.91	9.97	14143
Canada	0	0.26	3.71	6.64	9.56	3577
Portugal	0.001	0.17	5.76	7.58	9.18	5300
Italy	0.002	0.56	4.86	6.54	9.13	1530
Denmark	0.61	4.24	6.93	6.72	7.81	84
Australia	0	0.06	3.09	3.81	4.80	7900
Netherlands	0.056	0.83	4.26	4.58	3.99	381
Japan	0	0.11	2.95	3.62	3.96	3500
Sweden	0.006	0.45	2.00	2.49	3.50	678
Turkey	0	0.03	0.85	1.50	2.92	9633

Source: US Energy Information Administration International Energy Statistics, http://www.eia.gov/cfapps/ipdbproject/IEDIndex3.cfm

The table 1.10 shows the countries having the highest quantity of electricity generation from wind. It is evident that during the last decade wind energy has grown globally by 989 per cent. In 2010 out of the total 4167 billion kWh of energy generated from renewable sources, energy from wind constitutes only 341.53 billion kWh (8.19 %). The use of wind energy for electricity generation is noteworthy as in 1990 the total units generated from wind was only 3.53 billion kWh. This shows that there has been a huge increase in investment in wind energy during the last two decades.

Energy generation and consumption: the indian scenario

The Indian economy has experienced unprecedented economic growth over the last decade. As of 2013, India is the ninth largest economy in the world, driven by a real GDP growth of 8.7 per cent in the last 5 years (7.5 % over the last 10 years). In 2010 itself, the real GDP growth of India was the 5th highest in the world. This high order of sustained economic growth is placing enormous demand on its energy resources. The demand and supply imbalance in energy is pervasive across all sources requiring serious efforts by Government of India to augment energy supplies as India faces severe energy supply constraints. India's energy demand continued to rise inspite of slowing global economy. Petroleum demand in the transport sector is expected to grow rapidly in the coming years with rapid expansion of vehicle ownership. Per capita Energy Consumption increased from 1,204.3 kWh in 1970-71 to 6419.53 kWh in 2011-12, at a compounded annual growth rate of 4.06 per cent. The energy intensity which shows the amount of energy consumed for generating one unit of Gross Domestic Product increased from 0.128 kWh in 1970-71 to 0.165 kWh in 1985-86 (at 1999-2000 prices), but it has again come down to 0.148 kWh (at 2004-05 prices) in 2011-12. The installed capacity of the power sector, as of March 2012, stands at 236.38 Gigawatt of which 211.48 (87.55 %) Gigawatt from non-renewable sources and 24.9 (12.45 %) Gigawatt was from renewable sources. The energy generated from thermal power plants constitute 66 per cent of the total installed capacity of 236 GW, hydroelectric about 19 per cent and 15 per cent being a combination of wind, small hydro-plants, biomass, waste-to-electricity plants, and nuclear energy (Ministry of Statistics and Programme Implementation, 2013).

The Government of India has taken steps to increase the generation of energy. It has signed the civil nuclear co-operation deal which would add capacity in the nuclear energy sector. New initiatives on gas based power plants are expected. Most importantly, new and renewable energy, including wind power, bio-mass and solar power are given importance even by the state governments. During the Eleventh Five Year Plan, nearly 55,000 MW of new generation capacity was created and 855 Terawatt hours of electricity was generated in 2011-2012. Yet there continued to be an overall energy deficit of 8.7 per cent and peak shortage of 9.0 per cent (Reserve Bank of India, 2013).

India faces a significant challenge in providing access to adequate, affordable and clean sources of energy especially electrical energy and cooking fuel to a large section of the population, most of who live in rural areas. India's domestic energy resource base is substantial, but still the country relies on imports for a considerable amount of its energy use, particularly crude petroleum. Resources currently allocated to energy supply are not sufficient for narrowing the gap between energy needs and energy availability. Indeed, this may widen as the economy moves to a higher growth trajectory. India's success in resolving energy bottlenecks therefore remains one of the key challenges in achieving the projected growth outcomes. Further, India's excessive reliance on imported crude oil makes it imperative to have an optimal energy mix that will allow it to achieve its long-run goal of sustainable development. Thus the government is looking for a transition to cleaner forms of energy in terms of access to electricity and other modern energy forms which would provide long term energy security as well as provide better health to society. By focussing on clean energy alternative like solar and wind and conservation and efficient utilization of energy resources the government is trying to narrow the gap between demand and supply of energy.

Installed Capacity and Capacity Utilisation of Energy

The state of preparedness of the country for generation of the energy it requires and efficiency of the technology used in the generation can be analysed by the indicators such as installed capacity and capacity utilization.

TABLE 1.11
TRENDS IN INSTALLED GENERATING CAPACITY OF ELECTRICITY IN INDIA FROM 1970-71 TO 2011-12
(In Mega Watt)

As on	Thermal	Hydro	Nuclear	Others*	Total
31.03.1971	7,906	6,383	420	1,562	16,271
31.03.1976	11,013	8,464	640	2,132	22,249
31.03.1981	17,563	11,791	860	3,101	33,315
31.03.1986	29,967	15,472	1,330	5,504	52,273
31.03.1991	45,768	18,753	1,565	8,613	74,699
31.03.1996	60,083	20,986	2,225	11,787	95,081
31.03.2001	73,613	25,153	2,860	16,157	1,17,783
31.03.2006	88,601	32,326	3,360	21,468	1,45,755
31.03.2007	93,775	34,654	3,900	22,335	1,54,664
31.03.2008	1,03,032	35,909	4,120	24,986	1,68,047
31.03.2009	1,06,968	36,878	4,120	26,980	1,74,946
31.03.2010	1,17,975	36,863	4,560	28,474	1,87,872
31.03.2011	1,31,279	37,567	4,780	32,900	2,06,526
31.3.2012	1,56,107	38,990	4,780	36,510	2,36,387
CAGR 1970-71 to 2011-12(%)	7.36	4.40	5.96	7.79	6.58

*includes renewable sources and self-generating and railways
Source: Central Electricity Authority, 2013

From the table 1.11 it is observed that the total installed capacity for electricity generation in the country has increased from 16,271 MW as on 31.03.1971 to 2,36,387 MW as on 31.03.2012, registering a compound annual growth rate of 6.58 per cent. At the end of March 2012, thermal power plants accounted for an overwhelming 66 per cent of the total installed capacity in the country, with an installed capacity of 1,56,107 MW. The share of Nuclear energy was only 2.02 per cent (4.78 MW). Hydro power plants come next with an installed capacity of 38,990 MW, accounting for 16.49 per cent of the total installed capacity. There has been an increase in generating capacity of 29,861 MW over the last one year, which is 14.46 per cent more than the capacity of the last year. As on 31.09.2013 installed capacities for thermal, hydro, nuclear are 155968.99 MW, 39788 MW and 4780 MW respectively.

TABLE 1.12

INSTALLED CAPACITY OF GRID INTERACTIVE RENEWABLE POWER AS ON 31.03.2011 AND 31.03.2012

Renewable Power	31.03.2011	% of Total	31.03.2012	% of Total	Growth Rate (2010-11 to 2011-12)
Biomass	2,665	13	3,135	13	24.75
Waste to Energy	72	0	89	0	
Wind Power	14156	57	17,353	70	
Small Hydro	3042.9	15	3,395	14	
Solar	35	0	941	4	
Total	19971	100	24914	100	

Source: Energy Statistics Report, 2013

The table 1.11 shows that the total installed capacity of grid interactive renewable power, which was 19,971.03 MW as on 31.03.2011, had gone up to 24,914.24 MW as on 31.03.2012 indicating growth of 24.75 per cent. As on 31.09.2013 the total installed capacity had gone up to 28184.35 MW. Out of the total installed capacity of renewable power as on 31-03-2012, wind power accounted for about 69.65 per cent, followed by small hydro power (13.63 %) and Biomass power (12.58 %). As on 31.03.2012, there were 1,352 windmill systems installed used for pumping water and 7,286 remote villages and 1,874 hamlets were electrified by wind energy. This shows the importance of renewable energy in providing electrification to rural areas. As on July 2013 India has an installed capacity of 19,000 Megawatts (MW) of wind energy. Renewable energy sources (excluding large Hydro) currently accounts for 12.32 per cent i.e. 27,541 MW of India's overall installed power capacity. Wind Energy holds the major portion of 70 per cent among renewable (excluding hydro) and continued as the largest supplier of clean energy. The average cost of unit/kWh as of September 2013 was Rs.3.78 (Central Electricity Authority, 2013).

The growth of renewable energy in India is enormous and wind energy proves to be the most effective solution to the problem of depleting fossil fuels, importing of coal, greenhouse gas emission, environmental pollution etc. Wind energy as a renewable, non-polluting and affordable source directly avoids dependency on fuel and transport, and can lead to green and clean electricity. The wind potential in India is currently estimated at 80 metre hub height, as much as 102 GW. This figure was adopted by the government as the official estimate. However, Lawrence Berkley National Laboratory has stated the potential as over 300 to 400 GW (C-WET, 2013). The high growth of wind power in the past ten years is attributable to a multiplicity of enabling factors, including the evolution of a conducive policy and regulatory framework. The good thing is that the transition to renewable sources of energy has begun, and this transition is being led by wind power.

Renewable energy sources also provide environmental benefits. Coal thermal power plants are not environment friendly as these plants generate huge amount of GHGs such as SO_2, NOx, COx, SPM, Fly and bottom ash, and metallic dust. Hence it poses a huge problem. It is estimated that 1 MW of power generation from coal thermal produces greenhouse gases consisting of 19 tonnes of CO_2, 136 kg of SO_2, 7 tonnes of fly ash and 60 kg of particulate matter per day, for an average plant load factor of 75% (Peribesh, 2010).

On the other hand the pollution saving from a WEG having an average output of 4,00,0.00 kWh per year has been estimated as: Sulphur - dioxide (SO2): 2 to 3.2 tonnes, Nitrogen oxide (NO): 1.2 to 2.4 tonnes, Carbon dioxide (CO2): 300 to 500 tonnes and Particulates: 150 to 280 kg (Olivier, Janssens-Maenhout, & Peters, 2013). For instance, in the case of Muppandal Wind Farm the total installed capacity of as of the year 2010 was 79,425 MW. The amount of emissions avoided by using windmills, installed at the Muppandal Wind Farm, to produce electricity instead of fossil fuels is calculated and presented in the table 6.50.

Table 1.13
Pollutants Avoided for the Year 2010 Due to Installation of Windmills

Pollutants	Amount of Emissions Avoided Per day (ton)
CO_2	1509075
SO_2	10802
Fly ash	555975
Particulate matter	4765.5
Total GHGs Avoided	2080617.3

Source: Calculations based on values provided in Peribesh S, 2010

It is observed from the table 1.13 the amount of greenhouse gas avoided per day is 20.81 lakh tonnes. The amount of CO_2 avoided is 15.09 lakh ton. The CO_2 is the most harmful pollutant among the greenhouse gases. Thus, it is clear that using windmills offers environmental benefit to the region. This shows that saving on the pollution front is enormous when wind energy is used as investments made in wind energy, avoid fuel cost and carbon cost throughout the 20 years of life of the windmills.

Also, investment in wind energy acts as a permanent shield against ever increasing power prices. The cost per kWh reduces over a period of time as against rising cost for conventional power projects. Wind power project has one of the fastest payback period, lowest gestation period; low operation and maintenance (O&M) costs and minimal investment in manpower.

Conclusion

In this chapter an overview of wind energy is undertaken. Also linkages between energy consumption and economic growth have been discussed. Evidences from the secondary data collected showed that there is a huge thrust for the development of wind power technology to cope up with the ever increasing demand for electricity. Globally wind energy is very important as it has grown by 989 per cent. World-wide in 2010, out of the total 4167 billion kWh of energy generated from renewable sources, energy from wind constitutes 341.53 billion kWh. In India of the total installed generation capacity of renewable power, installed capacity of wind energy was 69.65 per cent in 2012. As of 2013, Tamil Nadu has 6,987 MW installed capacity of wind energy.

Moreover, there is evidence of positive relationship between per capita national income and per capita electricity consumption among developed and developing countries like India, China and Brazil. However, in developed countries the greater availability of energy, technical progress, and the employment of higher quality fuels has allowed less energy to be used per unit output and has reduced the constraint that energy resources place on the output of the economy and economic growth. Nevertheless energy security still remains important for all countries.

Bibliography

Ackermann, T., & Söder, L. (2002). An overview of wind energy-status. *Renewable and Sustainable Energy Reviews, 6*(1), 67-127.

British Petroleum. (2012). *Sustainability Review*. London: British Petroleum.

Central Electricity Authority. (2013). *All India Installed Capacity-State Wise/Utility Wise*. New Delhi: Central Electricity Authority, Government of India.

C-WET. (2013). *Information*. Retrieved October 31, 2013, from Centre for Wind Energy Technology (C-WET): http://www.cwet.tn.nic.in/

de Carmoy, G. (1978). The USA faces the energy challenge. *Energy Policy, 6*(1), 36-52.

Dodge, D. (2006). *The illustrated history of wind power development. Littleton.* Colorado: U.S. Federal Wind Energy Program.

Gipe, P. (1991). Wind energy comes of age California and Denmark. *Energy Policy, 19,* 756-67.

Global Wind Energy Council. (2010). *Global Wind Energy Outlook*. Retrieved October 18, 2013, from Global Wind Energy Council: http://www.gwec.net/publications/global-wind-energy-outlook/3543-2/

Grimaud, A., & Rouge, L. (2005). Polluting non-renewable resources, innovation and growth: welfare and environmental policy. *Resource and Energy Economics, 27,* 109 - 129.

International Energy Agency. (2002). *World Energy Outlook*. Paris: International Energy Agency.
JRC/PBL European Commission. (2011). *Emission Database for Global Atmospheric Research (EDGAR)*. Joint Research Centre (JRC) and PBL Netherlands Environmental Assessment Agency.

Kaldellis, J. K., & Zafirakis, D. (2011). The wind energy (r) evolution: A short review of a long history. *Renewable Energy, 36*(7), 1887-1901.

Meyer, N. (1995). Danish wind power development. *Energy Sustain Development, 2,* 18-25.

Ministry of Statistics and Programme Implementation. (2013). *Energy Statistics*. New Delhi: Implementation, Ministry of Statistics and Programme.

Olivier, J. G., Janssens-Maenhout, G., & Peters, J. A. (2013). *Trends in global CO2 emissions: 2012* . Hague: PBL Netherlands Environmental Assessment Agency.

Olivier, J., & Janssens-Maenhout, G. (2011). *Part III: Greenhouse gas emissions: 1. Shares and trends in greenhouse gas emissions; 2. Sources and Methods; Total greenhouse gas emissions. In: 'CO2 emissions from fuel combustion,*. Paris: International Energy Agency (IEA).

Peribesh, S. (2010). *Biodiversity-Ecosystems Management and the Green Economy, Orissa,*. Bhubaneswar: State Pollution Control Board, Orissa.

Reserve Bank of India. (2013). *RBI Bulletin*. New Delhi: Reserve Bank of India.

Righter, R. W. (1996). Pioneering in wind energy: the California experience. *Renewable Energy, 9*, 781-784.

U.S. Energy Information Administration. (2013). *Annual Energy Outlook 2013 (AEO2013)*. Washington D C: U.S. Energy Information Administration (EIA).

UNIDO. (2010). *Energy, Development and Security: Energy issues in the current macroeconomic context*. Vienna: United Nations Industrial Development Organisation.

5.2 Renewable Energy and its Challenges: An Indian Perspective

By Mohit Gupta, Bikramjit Rattu, Jatin Sethi

Executive Summary

Indian Power sector is hugely dependent on coal as its primary energy source. Apart from coal, water, oil, gas, nuclear energy and renewable sources are also used for electricity generation, though the share of latter four is very less. India has the world's 5th largest electricity generation capacity and it is the 6th largest electricity consumer accounting for 3.4% of global energy consumption. The potential of India's renewable energy generation is about 3000 GW but only 29.8 GW which is less than 1% of the total potential has been tapped so far. Renewable energy share in total energy mix has risen from 7.8% in FY08 to 12.3% in FY13. Immense challenges on energy security are lying ahead for India. These include the urgency to immediately bridge the current gap in energy demand and supply and to ensure a secure energy future in the light of India's growing population and economy. As the prices of coal generated energy are increasing due to increasing reliance on imports, renewable energy promises not just a bridging solution to the present power crisis but also a permanent fix to India's ever increasing electricity requirements. The growth of renewable sector will boost the country's high economic growth aspiration and also benefit the millions of people in rural areas still waiting for electricity connections. In this research paper we will analyze the different central Government and state government policies to facilitate development of RE projects in the country. We will do a state wise analysis to demarcate the states having favorable conditions and policies for the growth of RE energy. Along with this we will study the challenges for the development of renewable energy sector in India, which can be predominantly classified as a) Institutional barriers b) Economic and Technological barriers and c) Market-related barriers.

1. Indian Power Sector

1.1 Overview

Power has been one of the major fuels which have been driving economic growth since time immemorial. Power has been unanimously recognized as one of prime inputs which have resulted in rapid economic growth. There is a strong two-way relationship between economic development and energy consumption. On one hand, growth of an economy, with its global competitiveness, hinges on the availability of cost-effective and environmentally benign energy sources, and on the other hand, the level of economic development has been observed to be reliant on the energy demand.

Figure 1 depict the relationship between year-on-year increase in generation of electricity and GDP growth rate . Note that one clearly follows the other in all years except for the most recent 2011-2012 when economic growth (growth in GDP) plummeted due to various other reasons (including but not limited to the effects of widespread problems in EU and high inflation at home).

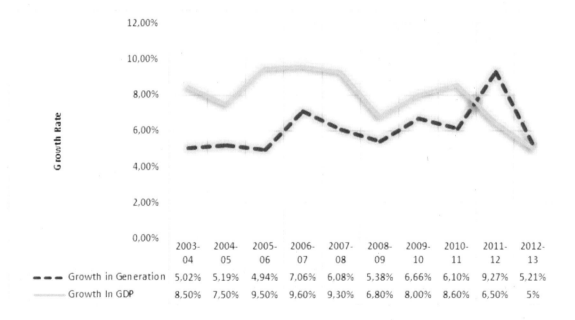

	2003-04	2004-05	2005-06	2006-07	2007-08	2008-09	2009-10	2010-11	2011-12	2012-13
▬ ▬ Growth in Generation	5,02%	5,19%	4,94%	7,06%	6,08%	5,38%	6,66%	6,10%	9,27%	5,21%
——— Growth In GDP	8,50%	7,50%	9,50%	9,60%	9,30%	6,80%	8,00%	8,60%	6,50%	5%

Figure 1: India growth in electricity generation and GDP growth rate - A clear relationship

1.2 Current Scenario

India has the fifth largest power generation portfolio worldwide. Coal and gas are the popular sources and account for 57% and 9 % share, respectively. The country has been rapidly adding capacity over the last few years, with total installed power capacity growing to 237.74 GW as of February 2014 from 98 GW in 1998. The country transitioned from being the world's seventh largest energy consumer in 2000 to the fourth largest one within a decade. Economic growth and increasing prosperity, coupled with factors such as growing rate of urbanization, rising per capita energy consumption and widening access to energy in the country, are likely to push energy demand further in the country.

2. Position of Renewable Sector in the Power Sector

Power Generation from renewable sources is on the rise in India, with the share of renewable energy in the country's total energy mix rising from 7.8% in FY08 to 12.3% in FY13. India has about 28.1 GW of installed renewable energy capacity as on 31 March 2013. Wind accounts for 68% of the capacity, with 19.1 GW of installed capacity, making India the world's fifth largest wind energy producer. Small hydro power (3.6 GW), bio energy (3.6 GW) and solar energy (1.7 GW) constitute the remaining capacity. In FY13, wind capacity additions fell to 1.7 GW from almost 3.2 GW in FY12 as a result of withdrawal of accelerated depreciation and Generation Based Incentive (GBI) benefit. Although the share of renewable energy in the generation mix has been rising over the years, India still has large untapped renewable energy potential.

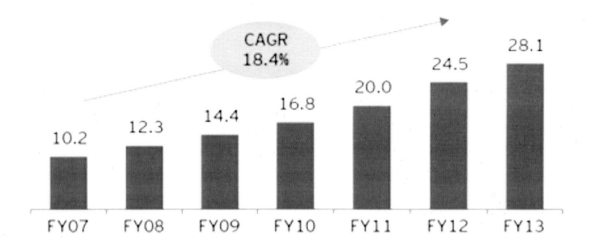

Figure 2: Growth of installed capacity of renewable energy in India (GW)
Source: MNRE

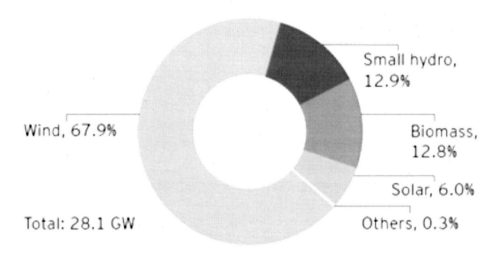

Figure 3: Installed capacity of renewable energy in India
Source: MNRE as on 31 March 2013

2.1 Investments

Investment in clean energy in India decreased 45% year on year to US$ 6.9 billion in 2012. The wind energy sector attracted US$ 3.4 billion, while the share of the solar energy sector was down 45% to US$ 2.32 billion.

Targets

The Government of India (GoI) has set a renewable energy capacity addition target of 29.8 GW for the twelfth FYP, taking the total renewable capacity to almost 55 GW by the end of FY17. This includes 15 GW from wind, 10 GW from solar, 2.7 GW from Biomass and 2.1 GW from small hydro. Investment in renewable energy is expected to almost quadruple to INR 3186 billion in the 12th FYP from INR 892 billion in the 11th FYP, implying average annual investments of nearly INR 640 billion.

To put things in perspective, planned renewable capacity additions during the 12th FYP are almost one third of planned conventional energy capacity addition during the same period. In FY13 targets were not met, as a result of decline in wind installations.

Table 1: Renewable energy actual installations and target

Renewable Technology	2010-11		2011-12		2012-13		2013-14	
	Target (MW)	Actual (MW)	Target (MW)	Actual (MW)	Target (MW)	Actual (MW)	Target (MW)	Actual (MW)
Wind Power	2000	2350	2400	3197	2500	1699	2500	512
Small Hydro	300	307	350	353	350	237	300	54
Bio Power	472	474	475	488	475	472	425	-
Solar Power	200	27	200	905	800	754	1100	75
Total	2972	3157	3425	4943	4125	3162	4325	640

Source: MNRE

2.2 Key Drivers of Renewable energy in India

(a) Energy Security Concerns:

India ranks fourth and sixth globally as the largest importer of oil, and of petroleum products and LNG, respectively. India's primary energy consumption between 2007 and 2011 increased at a CAGR of 5.8%, from 18.8 quadrillion (10^{15}) Btu to 23.6 quadrillion Btu. As a result of the increasing demand and stagnant domestic production, India now meets more than 70% of its oil demand through imports (increased from INR 4091 billion in FY10 to INR7264 billion in FY12).

Given the heightened competition for the procurement of fossil fuels, the prices of petroleum products have been increasing and have witnessed considerable volatility in recent years. The increased use of indigenous renewable resources is expected to reduce India's dependence on expensive imported fossil fuels.

(b) Government support

The government is playing an active role in promoting the adoption of renewable energy resources by encouraging private sector investment and mandating the use of renewable resources. It is offering various incentives, such as GBIs and tax benefits, to encourage the development and use of renewable energy sources.

(c) Climate Change

India is among the most vulnerable countries to the impact of climate change. In June 2008, India released a National Action Plan on Climate Change (NAPCC) comprising eight national missions. The plan aimed at promoting the understanding, adaptation and mitigation of climate change, energy efficiency and resource conservation. One of the missions, National Solar Mission, aims to promote the development and use of solar energy for power generation and other uses, with the ultimate objective of making solar energy complete with fossil based energy options.

(d) Increasing Cost competitiveness of Renewable energy technology

Renewable energy is becoming increasingly cost competitive compared to fossil fuel based generation. Renewable energy equipment prices have fallen dramatically due to technological innovation, increasing manufacturing scale and experience curve gains. This is particularly true of solar and wind technology where solar module prices have declines by almost 80% since 2008. Wind turbine prices have declined by more than 25% during the same period. Falling equipment prices have led to large scale deployment of these technologies in India and globally. India's installed solar capacity increased to 1686 MW at the end of FY13 from almost 20 MW in FY11.

(e) Distributed Electricity Demand

Renewable energy is a distributed and scalable resource, making it well suited to meet the need for power in remote areas, which lack grid and road infrastructure.

(f) Favorable Foreign Investment Policy

The government has created a liberal environment for foreign investment in renewable energy projects. In addition to allowing 100% foreign direct investment (FDI), the government is encouraging foreign investors to set up renewable energy based power generation projects on a build own operate basis in the country.

(g) Vast Untapped Potential

India has abundant untapped renewable energy resources. The country's large land mass receives one of the highest levels of solar irradiation in the world. It has an extensive coastline and high wind velocity in many areas. This provide ample opportunities for the establishment of land based renewable energy generation as well as for offshore wind farms. In addition the country's numerous rivers and waterways have strong potential to generate hydropower. India also has significant potential to produce energy from biomass derived from agricultural and forestry residues.

Table 2: Comparison of Estimated potential and installed capacity of different resources

Resource	Estimated Potential (GW)	Installed Capacity (GW)
Wind	102.8*	19.1
Small Hydro	19.7	3.6
Bio- Power**	22.5	3.6
Solar Power (billion GWh)	6	1.7

Source: MNRE, installed capacity as at end March 2013
*At 80 meter height, wind potential has yet to be validated with actual measurements
**includes biomass and bagasse cogeneration

3.0 State Wise Potential of Renewable Energy Sources

3.1 Small Hydropower

Small hydro power (SHP) accounted for a share of 13 percent in the total installed renewable capacity at end of March 2013 which is second largest after wind energy (68 per cent). Karnataka has the largest installed base of 964 MW, followed by Himachal Pradesh at 588 MW. The table below shows State-wise installed SHP capacities (end of 2012-13).

Table 3: State-wise installed SHP capacities (end of 2012-13)

States	No. of Plants	Capacity (in MW)
Karnataka	140	964
Himachal Pradesh	149	588
Maharashtra	51	300
Andhra Pradesh	67	219
Uttarakhand	99	175
Kerala	25	158
Punjab	46	155

MNRE has targeted capacity additions of 2,100 MW of SHP capacity in the Twelfth Five Year Plan. 6,474 potential sites have been identified for development of SHP plants with an aggregate capacity of 19,749 MW across different states of India.

Figure 4: Region-wise break up of identified potential SHP sites and capacity

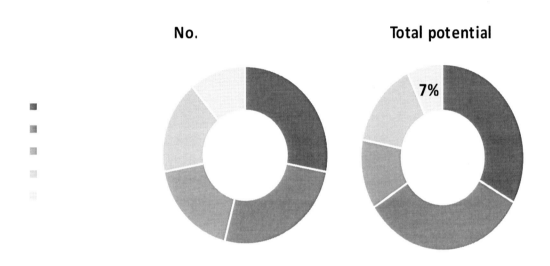

1,833 SHP sites with a potential capacity of 6,605 MW have been identified in northern India. Himachal Pradesh, with a SHP potential capacity of 2,398 MW, accounts for 36 per cent of the total potential capacity in this region. The southern region has a potential of 6,483 MW. Karnataka has the highest potential at 4,141 MW, which accounts for 64 per cent of the total potential capacity in this region. So, the major focus is in Himachal Pradesh in the north and Karnataka in the south.

3.2 Biomass Power

As on March 2013, the total installed capacity of biomass-based power has increased to

3,697 MW. Almost 562 MW of capacity has been added in 2012-13, of which nearly 475 MW was added by Maharashtra and Uttar Pradesh. Currently, chief sugar cane producing states- Uttar Pradesh and Maharashtra lead the market, with installed capacities of 782 MW and 767 MW respectively. The potential for power generation from biomass is nearly 17,500 MW (agro residue and plantations) while an additional 5,000 MW potential exists in bagasse-based co-generation.

Table 4: State wise installed biomass capacity in major states

States	Capacity (in MW)
Uttar Pradesh	777
Maharashtra	757
Tamil Nadu	539
Karnataka	491
Andhra Pradesh	381
Chhattisgarh	250

Table 5: State-wise potential capacity for bagasse-based power co-generation in India

State	Biomass Potential (MW)	Bagasse Potential (MW)	Total	% of Total Potential
Punjab	3172	300	3472	15
Maharashtra	1887	1250	3137	14
Uttar Pradesh	1617	1250	2867	13
Haryana	1333	350	1683	7
Karnataka	1131	450	1581	7
Gujarat	1221	350	1571	7
Tamil Nadu	1070	450	1520	7
Bihar	619	300	919	4
Andhra Pradesh	578	300	878	4
Others	4910	-	4910	22
Total	**17538**	**5000**	**22538**	**100**

Punjab has the maximum potential of power generation through biomass while leading sugarcane producing states like Uttar Pradesh and Maharashtra have the maximum potential for bagasse-based power generation. These 3 states account for 42 per cent of the total biomass and co-generation capacity in the country.

3.3 Wind Power

Considering major states, the current capacity utilization is just 14%. More than 75% of the total potential capacity lies in the states of Gujarat, Andhra Pradesh, Karnataka and Tamil Nadu. While Tamil Nadu has ultilized 36% of its potential capacity, this number is quite low in the states of Karnataka and Gujarat (under 10%), and in Andhra Pradesh it is just 2.3% (see Figure).

Table 6: State-wise Wind Power Capacity and Potential

Installed Capacity (MW)		Estimated Potential (MW)			Installed as % of Overall
State	Total Installed Capacity	@50m	@80m	Overall	
Andhra Pradesh	447.7	5394	14497	19891	2.3%
Gujarat	3174.9	10609	35071	45680	7.0%
Karnataka	2135.3	8591	13593	22184	9.6%
Kerala	35.1	790	837	1627	2.2%
Madhya Pradesh	386	920	2931	3851	10.0%
Maharashtra	3021.8	5439	5961	11400	26.5%
Rajasthan	2684.9	5005	5050	10055	26.7%
Tamil Nadu	7162.3	5374	14152	19526	36.7%
Total	19,048	42,122	92,092	1,34,214	14.2%

Figure 5: Total Installed Capacity of Wind Power as a percentage of Total Potential

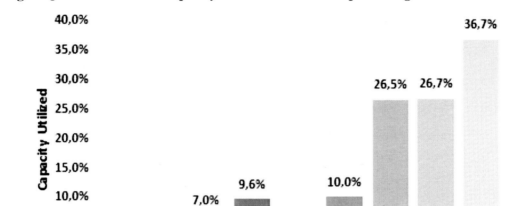

Capacity additions were led by states such as Maharashtra and Andhra Pradesh, which added 1.1 GW and 300 MW respectively (in 2013-14) driven by attractive preferential tariff. Moreover, the financial health of state distribution companies (discoms) is relatively better. On the other hand, capacity additions in Tamil Nadu continued to remain low due to inadequate evacuation infrastructure and significant payment delays from the discom. Inadequate evacuation infrastructure led to significant generation loss of 1.2 billion units over Jan-Dec 2013. Further, developers faced payment delays of over one year due to weak financial health of the state discom.

In Karnataka, while preferential tariffs are unattractive, capacity additions were steady due to additions from captive consumers on account of high industrial tariffs. In the near future, Maharashtra, Andhra Pradesh, Rajasthan and Madhya Pradesh are expected to lead capacity additions driven by favorable economics. In addition, relatively better financial health of discoms such as Maharashtra and Madhya Pradesh are also expected to support additions. This is also reflected in the upcoming projects which are at advanced stages of construction

Figure 6: State-wise Capacity Additions in 2013-14

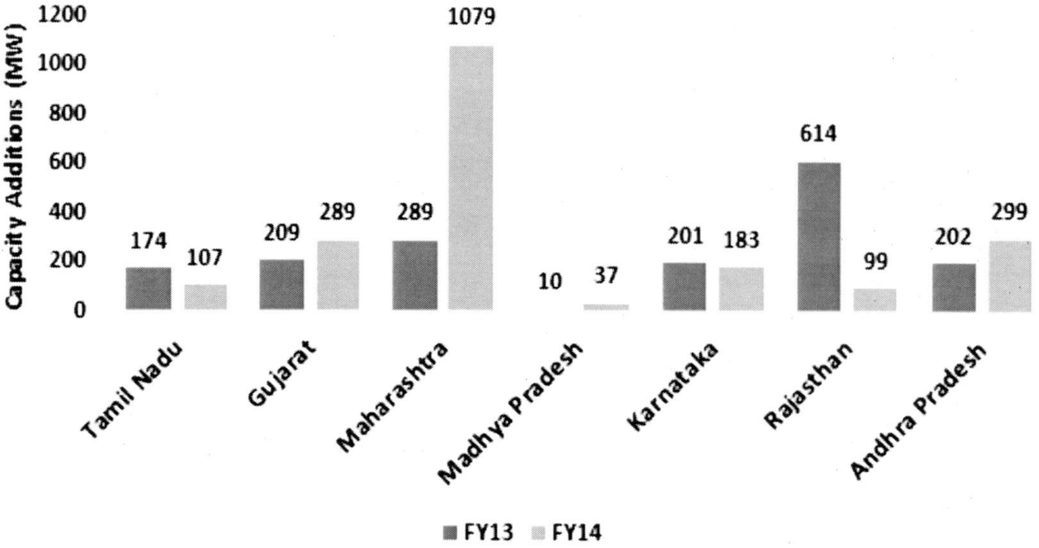

3.4 Solar Power

Solar power capacity has observed rapid growth over the last few years to reach 1,686 MW (as of March 2013). Gujarat and Rajasthan lead in terms of capacity commissioned, accounting for more than four-fifths of the total installed solar power capacity in the country.

Figure 7: State-wise split of Solar Power Projects

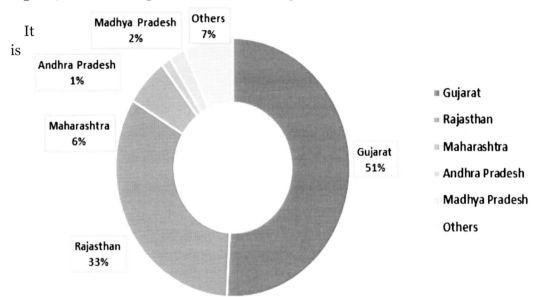

expected that 400 MW capacities will be added over the next 2 years under state solar policies despite PPAs signed for 750 MW. This is largely on account of aggressive bidding and poor payment security mechanism.

Aggressive bidding is seen under various state policies such as Tamil Nadu, Andhra Pradesh and Rajasthan. In states such as Uttar Pradesh (UP) and Punjab, bidding has been comparatively less aggressive as capacities were awarded based on reverse bidding. But, poor evacuation infrastructure in UP, high land prices in Punjab and possible delays in payments due to weak financials of both state discoms is expected to limit additions. Madhya Pradesh, on the other hand, is expected to witness healthy capacity additions given attractive tariffs, favourable policies such as banking through the year and long gestation period.

Moreover, states such as Gujarat, Orissa, Kerala and Andhra Pradesh have been encouraging rooftop projects over the last 18 months. Gujarat has installed grid connected rooftop projects in Gandhinagar (5 MW) and has such projects under implementation across five cities namely, Vadodara (5 MW), Mehsana (5 MW), Rajkot (6.5 MW), Surat (5 MW) and Bhavnagar (3.5 MW). Andhra Pradesh has introduced rooftop policy providing net metering facility to customers under which the consumer can utilize the solar energy generated for self-consumption and inject the excess power in the grid. The state government of Orissa has also approved a proposal for installation of solar panel on rooftops of all government establishments in Bhubaneshwar and Cuttack area.

The figure below shows the source-wise installed capacity of renewable energy. It can be seen that the major contribution is from wind energy. Then, solar energy is the next major contributor making its considerable share only recently. Now, the main area of focus is on solar energy and wind energy.

Figure 8: Source-wise installed capacity of renewable energy

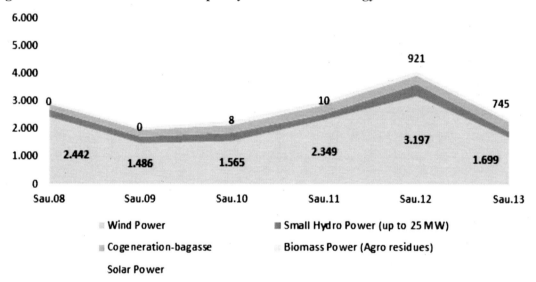

4. Government commitment for future of renewable energy (Policy Support for RE in India)

Government interventions remain the backbone of RE market development across the globe. A review of policies and regulatory frameworks across countries indicates that commercialization of RE technologies remains dependent on government support, be it in the form of fiscal support or other support like favorable access to the grid.

International experience is replete with successful examples of governments leveraging these instruments to scale up RE deployment. Some of the most successful examples are Germany (soft loans for residential solar photovoltaic systems and feed-in tariffs for wind and solar), Japan (net metering, grants for demonstration projects and subsidy for de-centralized residential solar photovoltaic systems), California, U.S. (production and investments tax credits, net metering, renewable portfolio standard for states, and feed-in tariffs for all RE technologies), Texas, U.S. (RE purchase targets) and Spain (high feed-in tariffs for solar).

Availability of suitable policy instruments provides the right incentives for the development of RE with the view of ensuring greater long term adoption and global cost competitiveness. India has been at the forefront of RE development due to its proactive policy and regulatory frameworks. India has successfully designed and launched a number of policy instruments which have enhanced the viability and bank ability of RE projects. The use of these instruments at the state and the central levels has allowed large scale deployment of RE and development of new, business models across the country. The key policy instruments for promotion of RE include: tax incentives, FiTs, subsidies, RECs, and GBI. However, India's experience with such instruments has not been without challenges: the design and implementation of these instruments has often been hampered by uncertainty on continuity and frequent revisions. This section of the report identifies some of these instruments, describes their design, use and the constraints which have been limiting their effectiveness.

4.1 Tax Incentives

4.1.1 Income Tax Exemption

All companies in India are required to pay taxes on their profits. At present, the corporate tax rate is 32.45 percent for income below INR 100 million (USD 1.6 million) and 33.99 percent for incomes above INR 100 million (USD 1.6 million). The GOI, under Section 80-IA of Income Tax Law Act, 1961 (IT Law), exempts all infrastructure assets (this includes RE generators) from income tax for a block of any 10 consecutive years out of the first fifteen years of operation.

4.1.2 Accelerated Depreciation

In order to promote RE, the GOI provides a higher depreciation rate (80 percent for plant and machinery) for non-wind RE projects vis-a-vis 7.84 percent for thermal power plants and 15 percent for other power equipment. An additional 20 percent depreciation is available for all manufacturing and production companies in the first year of operation. Thus, non-wind RE assets and wind assets can be depreciated 100 percent and 35 percent respectively in the first year.

The benefit was withdrawn in April 2012. This withdrawal negatively impacted the growth of wind capacity. For instance, during the FY 2012-13, only 1,700 MW of wind power capacity was added as compared to 3,164 MW in the previous financial year.

4.2 Feed-in Tariffs

One of the most successful policy instruments for promoting RE has been the FiTs. State governments across the country have been providing long term support to RE through FiTs, also known as preferential tariffs. Under the FiT framework, RE power is procured by Distribution Companies (DISCOMs) at the FiT specified by SERCs. FiTs, applicable over a period of 10 to 25 years, ensure predictable financial returns over the life of the project. The SERCs determine FiTs for each RE technology (separately) using a cost plus approach based on following factors:

• Achievable capacity utilization factors based on the availability of fuel/resource
• Operating costs (cost of fuel, O&M expenses, capital replacement)
• Capital expenditure (project cost)
• Share of debt and the cost of debt; and
• Expected return on equity.

4.3. Renewable Energy Purchase Obligations

RPOs stimulate demand for RE by providing a guaranteed market for RE power. RPOs in India have been mandated by the Electricity Act, 2003 and the National Tariff Policy, 2011. RPO targets are defined as a percentage of the total power consumed or distributed by the obligated entities, which include any of the following groups of entities:

1. Distribution companies
2. Captive power consumers
3. Open access consumers

These obligated entities can meet their RPO targets either by generating renewable power from captive sources; purchasing renewable power; and/or purchasing RECs. If obligated entities are unable to meet their RPO targets through either of the above mentioned means, they face a penalty for non-compliance equivalent to the forbearance price of RECs. The obligated entities need to meet their RPO targets before the end of each financial year.

However there is a lack of consistency in the methodology used for determining RPO targets for a state. As a result, the RPO targets set by the states vary substantially, ranging, from one percent in Tripura to 10.25 percent in Himachal Pradesh. RPO targets have been adopted by most states but met by the obligated entities in only a handful of states. Penalty enforcement has been hindered because state utilities have poor financial health. So far, none of these entities have been penalized for non-compliance also, a proper monitoring system for tracking achievement vis-a-vis the RPO target has not been established.

4.4 Renewable Energy Certificates (RECs)

The Central Electricity Regulatory Commission (CERC) has included the purchase of RECs as one of the ways of meeting the RPOs. The REC program aims to provide market based incentives for RE developers and distribute the marginal cost of RE deployment nationwide. The REC program has two objectives: to facilitate achievement of RPO targets for obligated entities not able to invest in RE; and to facilitate creation of RE capacities in regions with the least cost of generation and abundant RE resources.

CERC, through the REC framework, has bifurcated the electricity and renewable components of RE. Power generators can sell electricity and RECs to two distinct users. Projects availing REC benefits cannot take advantage of any of the preferential benefits (concessional wheeling charges, banking facility, electricity waiver or sale of power to DISCOM at FiTs). The projects availing RECs can sell power under open access to third party or group captive customers or sell power to distribution companies at the average pooled purchase cost (APPC).

Projects must also be connected to the grid in order to be eligible for RECs. One REC is equivalent to 1 MWh of renewable power generated, and is valid for a period of two years from the date of issuance. These certificates can be bought and sold through two designated exchanges, i.e., India Energy Exchange and Power Exchange of India. Only eligible generating entities are allowed to sell and purchase RECs. The RECs cannot be resold and, once traded, can only be used by the buyer for meeting its RPO target. CERC has established a trading range for solar and non-solar RECs by setting a floor price and a forbearance price. These prices are determined based on the difference between the marginal cost of generation from RE and conventional sources.

4.5 Subsidies

4.5.1 Grid-connected RE

MNRE and several state governments, support the development of grid-connected RE through the provision of subsidies. For example, for biomass based RE projects, MNRE provides a subsidy of up to INR 2.5 million per MW (USD 40,000 per MW) to special category states, and up to INR 2 million per MW (USD 32,000 per MW) in the rest of India . Some states, such as Bihar, also provide a capital subsidy equivalent to 60 percent of the total project cost for biomass-based RE projects.

4.5.2 Rural Electrification Programs

MNRE also provides subsidies to encourage rural electrification based on RE resources. However, most of these subsidies are restricted to state implementation agencies and not-for-profit organizations. The subsidies provided through these programs include:

• Decentralized Distributed Generation (DDG) scheme under Rajiv Gandhi Grameen Vidyutikaran Yojana, 2005 (RGGVY): The DDG scheme covers all un-electrified

villages and hamlets with little or no electricity access. The scheme promotes a Build Operate Maintain and Transfer (BOMT) model.
• Remote Village Electrification Model: This is MNRE's flagship scheme and was started almost a decade ago (2002-03). This scheme covers villages that are not covered under the RGGVY program and have been designated as being remote by GOI.
• Jawaharlal Nehru National Solar Mission (JNNSM): One of the key components of the JNNSM is the development of small and off-grid solar PV applications which include DDG-based power plants. Under this program, MNRE supports village electrification projects that use solar energy with capacities up to 250 kWp through capital subsidies. • Interest Subsidy for Off-grid Projects through IREDA: MNRE also provides subsidized debt at a five percent interest rate for off-grid solar applications through IREDA.

4.5.3 Commercial Off-grid Projects

Biomass Projects

MNRE provides capital subsidies for the industrial use of biomass for both combustion and gasification projects. For biomass combustion projects, the subsidy amount is the same as that provided to grid-connected projects.

For biomass gasification projects, MNRE provides subsidies for capacities up to 5 MW for both electrical and thermal applications. These subsidies are up to INR 1 million per 100 kW (USD 16,000 per 100 kW) for dual gas systems and INR 1.5 million per 100 kW (USD 24,000 per 100 kW) for 100 percent producer gas systems. An additional subsidy of 20 percent of the capital cost is available for special category states.
Solar Projects

Under JNNSM, MNRE provides capital subsidies for solar plants used for captive consumption (up to a capacity of 100 kWp). Up to 30 percent of the capital cost is provided as subsidy, with a cap of INR 30 per Wp (USD 0.48 per Wp) for projects without batteries and INR 63 per Wp (USD 1 per Wp) for projects with batteries.

4.6 Generation Based Incentives (GBI)

4.6.1 Wind Projects

In December 2009, MNRE introduced the GBI scheme for wind energy projects to facilitate the entry of large IPPs. This scheme was available only to those developers who did not avail themselves of accelerated depreciation benefits and sold power to the state distribution companies.

Under the GBI scheme, IREDA provided an incentive of INR 0.50 per kWh (U.S. cent 0.8 per kWh) of wind power fed into the grid, with a total project lifecycle cap of INR 6.25 million per MW (USD 0.1 million per MW) and an annual cap of INR 1.55 million per MW (USD 24,700 per MW). While the target was to develop 4,000 MW through GBI, the scheme was discontinued in March, 2012, even though only 2,247 MW of wind capacity had been installed under the scheme.

4.6.2 Solar Projects

GBIs are provided to state utilities for the solar projects developed under the JNNSM's Rooftop PV and Small Solar Power Generation Program (RPSSGP). About 100 MW of solar capacity was allotted under this scheme in 2010, of which 98 MW has been developed across 78 projects. Under RPSSGP, state utilities purchased electricity from generators at the benchmark tariff of INR 17.91 per kWh (USD 0.29 per kWh). Of this amount IREDA refunded them all but a reference tariff of INR 5.5 per kWh (U.S. cent 8.8 per kWh), which increases at three percent annually.

4.7 Including Off-Grid Re Projects in Priority Sector Lending

In its revised guidelines, the RBI has recently included loans made to off-grid RE applications as part of priority sector lending for banks. This new classification provides benefits to off-grid RE projects, as outlined below:

• The RBI mandates banks to have 40 percent of their exposure to priority sectors (as defined by the RBI), but banks often find it difficult to achieve this target. Thus, the recent inclusion of off-grid RE projects to this target will enable such projects to receive more attention from banks.

• Loans covered under banks' priority sector targets are provided at concessional rates, which are one to two percent lower than normal commercial lending rates.

4.8 Central and State wise policies for renewable energy

After looking at the potential states where different renewable projects can be started. The policies in the state and central government are important for the existence of projects. The central and state polices for the renewable energy has been looked into here.

Central policies for renewable sources of energy (SHP)

Vide letter no. 14(03)2014-SHP dated 2nd July 2014, the Administrative Approval for 2014-15 and for 12th plan's remaining period for Small Hydro Power Programme (up to 25 MW Capacity) has already been circulated. Under this programme Central Financial assistance is provided for the following:

  · Resource Assessment and Support for Identification of new sites
  · Setting up new SHP Projects in the private / co-operative / joint sector etc.
  · Setting up new SHP Projects in the Government sector
  · Renovation and Modernization of existing SHP projects in the Government sector
  · Development/up gradation of Water Mills (mechanical/electrical output) and setting up Micro Hydel Projects (up to 100 KW capacity)
  · Research & Development and Human Resource Development

Karnataka state policy Small Hydro Power Projects: keynotes

Department of Energy, Government of Karnataka has made the Karnataka Renewable Energy Policy 2009-14, for the promotion of the renewable energy in the state. For the environmental benefits and the energy security of the state this policy is made with an objective to harness green and clean renewable sources of energy in the state. A fund with the name Akshaya Shakthi Nidhi will be made to facilitate Renewable Energy project financing and Energy Conservation and Efficiency measures. Green Energy Cess of Rs 0.05 (five paise) per unit would be levied on the electricity supplied to commercial and industrial consumers. Annual generation of Rs. 55 crore is estimated from this. Out of which Rs 50 Crores will be set apart for Renewable Energy project financing. Following are the assistive initiatives taken by the Karnataka state government through the policy to promote the Small Hydro Projects:

- Investment of 2700 crore would occur to achieve the target of harnessing 600 MW of power through mini hydro projects
- The Mini Hydro Project proposals which doesn't dry up the stream or river due to the diversion of water will be considered for development.
- Statuary clearances will be facilitated through single window mechanism, to pace up the successful expeditious commissioning of the targeted hydro projects
- KREDL to identify potential for development on Public Private Participation/Build Operate Own and Transfer (BOOT) mode
- Considering the environmental issues Mini Hydro projects in the Western Ghats Districts/Forest areas will be restricted to maximum 5 MW and preferably Run of the River (ROR) projects
- PICO hydel projects less than 10 kW will be identified by KREDL in fast track mode and central financial assistance of 90% of the PICO hydel projects cost provided by MNRE to be passed on to eligible beneficiaries

Himachal Pradesh state policy Small Hydro Power Projects: keynotes

Himachal Pradesh Small Hydro Power Policy above 5MW came into force in 2006 and was amended in January 2010. The main features of the policy are as follows:

- The eligibility criteria to become a producer under this category is any Private Investor /Cooperative Society comprising of the bonafide Himachalis
- Up to 2 projects can be allotted to the independent power producers
- The developer has the freedom to dispose off merchant power, however the Government of HP and HP State Electricity Board have the authority to check/refuse power.
- This policy offers free power @ 12% for 12 years, 18% for next 18 years and thereafter 30%.
- The projects under this policy will be eligible for all incentives by MNRE and

the State Government. Also incentives would be given for early commissioning

Himachal Pradesh Small Hydro Power Policy up to 5MW came into force in 2006 and was amended in January 2010. The main features of the policy are as follows:

- For up to 2 MW projects the producer has to be from Himachal or a member of cooperative society comprising of, preference is given for Himachalis even till 5MW.
- For permanent structures acquisition of land will be done by the government of Himachal Pradesh and for other purposed it will be leased out by Government at approved rates
- After 40 years of operation the projects would be handed over to the government.
- Power generated will be sold to HP State Electricity Board preferentially and if the developer intends to sell the power to a third party he is free to do so at a higher cost.
- No water royalty up to 5 MW for 12 years, 12% for next 18 years and beyond at 18% for sale within the state.
- Upfront premium exempted for projects up to 2 MW, is given as incentive for the new projects.

4.8.2 Solar power

Central policy for the Solar power in India

Jawaharlal Nehru National Solar Mission (JNNSM) is formed to promote the use of solar energy for power generation and other application, and also the use of other renewable energy sources like wind and biomass along with solar power.
Following are the key Highlights of the JNNSM Program:
- In this program state electricity boards not burdened with power having high priced
- Payments are guaranteed by the public entities
- A target of 20GW of grid connected solar power is set and is to be achieved by 2020
- Lucrative tariffs are allocated to the first 184MW projects

269

- Promotion of local manufacturing is also taken care off
- Other benefits like Generation based incentives (GBI), 80% accelerated depreciation income tax benefits on renewable energy products including solar are also there in the program

State Policies

Till 2011-12, only Gujarat and Rajasthan had a state solar policy. In 2012-13, various states such as Andhra Pradesh, Tamil Nadu, Karnataka and Madhya Pradesh have also announced solar policies given the sharp fall in capital costs for solar modules.

Following are the state policies which have been developed by different states to promote the use of solar projects, the key points of the polices are also being mentioned:

Gujarat

The state introduced the solar policy in 2009 and it is operative till March 31, 2014. Some the salient features of the policy are as follows-
- A minimum capacity of 5 MW for both (thermal & PV) and a maximum capacity 500 MW will be allowed
- Solar PV projects shall commission within 12 months from the date of signing PPA.
- PPA shall remain operational for a period of 25 years
- Land acquisition will be the responsibility of the developer
- The power evacuation transmission infrastructure shall be laid by the state at the cost of the developer
- Exemption from the electricity duty.
- Wheeling charge of 2 per cent of the energy will be levied
- Cross subsidy surcharge should not be applicable for open access consumers
- Developer will have to furnish a bank guarantee of Rs. 5million per MW at the time of PPA signing.

Rajasthan

The policy have come into operation with effect from April 19, 2011. The state plans a capacity addition of important policy highlights are as follows:

- PPA shall remain operational for a period of 25 years
- A minimum capacity of 5 MW for both solar thermal and solar PV projects. Maximum capacity 10 MW will be allowed for solar PV projects and 50 MW for solar thermal project
- Solar projects shall commission within 12 months from the date of signing PPA.
- The power evacuation transmission infrastructure shall be laid by the state at the cost of the developer
- Captive users shall be exempted from payment of the electricity duty

4.8.3 Wind Energy

Central Policies

Following are the incentives provided by the Central government through the policies made in the wing energy sector:
- In the Union budget 2013-14, generation-based incentive (GBI) was reinstated for wind energy projects and an amount of Rs.8 billion had been allocated for this purpose. GBI is available at Rs 0.5 per unit for a maximum period of 10 years subject to a cap of Rs.10 million per MW.
- Ten-year income tax holiday under 80 IA of Income Tax Act
- Concessional customs import duty on specified parts and components
- Excise duty relief

Earlier, accelerated depreciation of 80 per cent on wind assets in the first year of installation was available, which has been withdrawn with effect from April 2012.

State Policies

Andhra Pradesh

Following are the key notes/incentives of the policies regarding the wind energy in state:
- Captive generation are exempted from the payment of Electricity Duty, given the condition that the total electricity generated shall be utilized by them

- Each Eligible developer may be allocated available Govt. land to generate/harness up to a max of 200 MW of wind power initially.
- Only after commissioning of 100 MW capacity Wind farms in 1st stage in the allocated Government land, the Government may allocate land for another 100 MW capacity Wind Farms. The application from the developers for Government land will be considered on a first-cum-first-served basis
- Total Wheeling and Transmission Charges Including the losses in kind @ 5% of Electricity delivered to the Grid

Gujarat

Following are the key notes of the policies in wind energy in the Gujarat state:
- Except in case of TPS, the electricity generated from the Wind Turbine Generators is exempted from Electricity duty
- Wind Turbine Generators for Captive use are exempted from the demand cut to the extent of 30% of installed capacity
- The Wind Turbine Generators may be set up on, GEDA land /revenue wasteland , or private land if available

5. Challenges and Barriers in Renewable Energy Development

Despite the cost reductions achieved over recent years, the largest barrier to greater renewable energy use is its high cost. Intermittent electricity generation characteristics from renewable resources like wind and solar, result in their low reliability in meeting power demand, especially during peak periods. These technologies need to be supported by effective back-up power supply options, which increases cost. There are additional issues related to grid connection and costs of transmission. Lack of full cost pricing when determining the cost of competing energy supplies also hinders the development of renewable energy since the cost of environmental impacts are usually not included in energy prices. Renewable energy development is impeded under conditions of electricity markets undergoing transition when high discount rates and competition on short-term electricity prices within a regulatory framework disadvantage projects with high capital costs but low running costs, such as renewable electricity systems. In addition to cost-related barriers, non-cost barriers also inhibit the greater use of renewable energy. This is particularly the case with the imperfect flow of information and the lack of integrated planning procedures and guidelines. The barriers for the penetration of renewable energy technologies are broadly classified as a) Economic and Technological barriers b) Market-related barriers and c) Institutional barriers

5.1 Economic and Technological

Investment costs: This relates to the current high levels of capital cost of renewable energy technologies based on new technologies, low volume production and current manufacturing practices.

Technology Maturity-level: Renewable energy technologies such as solar have not attained technological maturity and are still in the developmental stages.

Technology Standards and Reliability: For most of the renewable energy technologies, technical standards not very well established. Technologies such as Solar PV have low reliability with uneven technical quality.

Resource Availability: The scale of operation of wind and solar technologies is constrained by matching supply with load duration curve, leading to very low Plant Load Factors (PLFs) with a very high percentage of unused capacity.

Location of Supply Sources: Renewable energy sources such as small hydro are very often located in remote, dispersed and inaccessible areas that necessitate high investment requirements in T&D for power supply.

Demand/Supply Match: High potential of renewable energy supply sources exist in areas with low level of demand due to developmental and socio-economic patterns. This supply-demand mismatch coupled with the problems in transfer of power from such regions leads to a very large share of the potential remaining unexploited.

Fuel diversity for biomass: There is a large diversity in biomass fuel supply and devices are specifically designed to handle these. The lack of adherence to fuel specifications in the case of biomass gasifiers by the consumers leads to operational problems of the technologies.

Peak Coincidence Factors: Low peak coincidence factors for renewable energy technologies, especially for wind and solar, make them unreliable sources for power supply during the peak periods.

Grid Stability: Unstable electricity grids and their low reliability in operation create problems in power off-take from renewable.

Reactive power requirements: Wind energy penetration is restricted by high reactive power requirements for start-up of operations that necessitate drawing of power from the state grid.

Maintenance and Servicing Infrastructure: Inadequate servicing and maintenance of equipments along with low reliability in operations lead to very low customer confidence and hampers technology adoption.

5.2 Market-related

Market Reforms: There are possibilities that market reforms adversely affect the penetration of certain renewable energy technologies. The reforms measures leading to setting up of an electricity market with competitive and reliable power supply, better grid operations and extension of the supply networks, lower transmission and distribution losses, tariff rationalization and elimination of subsidies and grants may bring down the penetration of renewables.

Privatization: Increasing private participation as part of market reforms policies can increase the cost of capital and make the high initial investment in renewable energy technologies unattractive. Privatization is also likely to dampen interest in serving rural markets where renewables have a comparative advantage. Shareholders may require higher rates to justify investments in rural markets, which are inherently perceived to be more risky.

Discount rate and Payback period requirements: Investments in renewable energy technologies are not attractive under high discount rates and short payback period requirements. Under such conditions, generation options that have relatively lower capital costs, shorter gestation periods, high efficiency and availability are preferred-none of which fit into the characteristics of renewable energy technologies except to a certain extent for biomass based generation.

Wheeling Contracts: The intermittent generation characteristics of renewable energy technologies and their site-specific nature may place the renewable energy developers in an unfavorable position regarding structuring of contracts for power transmission as compared to non-renewable energy developers. Renewable energy developers may not have equal access to transmission capacity. Intermittent generators may be required to pay higher charges per kWh than their dispatchable competitors to transmit power, with transmission charges being based on the rated capacity of the generator or the actual generation during peak periods. The site-specific nature of the renewables may be a drawback under some transmission pricing schemes where the rates are based on the distance.

Fuel Market for Biomass: For biomass-based technologies, the barriers are unsustainable biomass supply and non-existence of a fuel market, unreliable supply of biomass and frequent price fluctuations. Coupled with this are the difficulties in setting up of a fuel transportation network due to the transportation difficulties of biomass.

Trade Practices: Restrictive trade practices and imposition of trade barriers obstructs the import of advanced technologies and adversely affects their competitiveness. For example, high import duties on PV modules result in much higher prices than the international level and leads to very high costs in the system.

Energy and Electricity Pricing: Distortions in the pricing of different energy forms and an irrational tariff structure for electricity do not provide incentives for investment in generation capacity.

Transaction Costs: Due to non-existence of market for renewable energy, high transaction costs are involved in commercialization of technologies.

Power Purchase Structure: With the power purchase agreement structured at utilities buying power at fixed rates from generators, there may not be sufficient incentives for power generation from renewable sources with fluctuating cost.

Risk Perception: High-risk perception in adoption of most renewable energy technologies arises due to uncertainties regarding technology performance and low level of information and awareness surrounding these technologies. This is especially valid for renewable energy technologies like solar with a low level of technological maturity

5.3 Institutional

Regulatory Forums and Processes: The increased accountability of public expenditure may hinder push for renewables through financial incentives like grants, subsidies, soft-loans, etc.

Non-incorporation of renewable energy issues in the regulatory policy and lack of awareness among regulators further restrict technology penetration. Renewable energy projects are also adversely affected by frequent and inconsistent regulatory proceedings across states.

Policy Regime: Unstable and non-uniform policy regime across states and between the center and the states with no clear policies for third party sale, wheeling, banking and buy-back of power lower investor confidence in renewable energy projects.

Private Participation: Lack of well-defined policies for private participation and delays in clearances and allotments for private sector projects hinders private participation in renewable energy projects.

Co-ordination Issues: In the existing institutional arrangements, lack of co-ordination between planning and implementing agencies delays and restricts the progress in renewable energy development.

Nature of Incentives: The government push policy for penetration of renewables, driven by fiscal and financial incentives, is unsustainable. This is seen especially in the case of wind energy where lowering and removal of incentives led to almost capacity stagnation.

Allocation of Incentives: Due to lack of clear policy guidelines, the incentives provided by the government are often misallocated.

Marketing Infrastructure: Lack of consumer service orientation in terms of technology features and sales and service requirements and barriers in setting up of marketing infrastructure with promotion campaigns, after-sales service infrastructure, quality control measures, etc. for most of the renewable energy technologies restrict their penetration.

Availability of Finance: There are barriers in obtaining finance for renewable sector projects as investors are not very familiar and they lack awareness of renewable technologies. Moreover the risk perception is very high for renewable sector projects.
Financial Networks: A limited network of Financial Institutions to provide micro-credit access in rural decentralized regions crucially restricts the penetration of renewable energy technologies. Institutions like the Industrial Development Bank of India (IDBI) do not have provisions to supply micro-credit to local bodies through a network of nationalized banks having a wide rural reach.

Project Structuring: Intermittent fuel supply for cogeneration projects requires supplementary fuels for continuous power supply. Quite often, the supplementary fuel may be a fossil fuel like coal, oil or gas. Under the existing institutional arrangements, such a project using a combination of fuels may not qualify for IREDA's requirements for a renewable energy project.

Business models: Lack of successful and replicable business models hinders renewable energy technology adoption. This stems from the fact that most of the renewable energy projects lack sustainable commercial arrangements among the various participants.

Infrastructure Availability: Non-availability of infrastructure such as land and transmission and distribution networks in potential sites of renewable energy supply leads to low exploitation of their potential. This is especially valid for wind energy projects.

Networking with Local Organizations: There is insufficient networking with local organizations for flow of credit with the result that most of the credit flows to the corporate sector whose primary motivation is taking advantage of the financial incentives. This has disabled renewable energy promotion at the local level.

Rural sector Delivery Mechanisms: The lack of appropriate initiatives for rural sector delivery mechanisms hinders providing energy services using renewable energy for decentralized and rural applications.

6. Conclusion

Immense challenges on energy security are lying ahead for India. These include the urgency to immediately bridge the current gap in energy demand and supply and ensuring a secure energy future in the light of India's growing population and economy. As the prices of coal generated energy are increasing due to increasing reliance on imports, renewable energy promises not just a bridging solution to the present power crisis but also a permanent fix to India's ever increasing electricity requirements. The growth of renewable sector will boost the country's high economic growth aspiration and also benefit the millions of people in rural areas still waiting for electricity connections.

With regards to solar energy greater economies of scale, better technology and progressively cheaper panels and modules are bringing down the prices of solar generated power. But still these costs are not as low as compared to coal, nuclear or natural gas. To excel in solar power it is imperative that India develops an indigenous industry for solar panels and equipment which will further reduce the prices.

With the future in sight it is necessary that the government have an ambitious, logical but stipulated national renewable energy target based on generation. The current target from the NAPCC which targets 15% generation from renewable energy by 2020, looks conservative if we see the way renewable energy is developing and the costs of major renewable technologies are reducing. Logically the current target under NAPCC should be revised and scaled up higher based on the rapid growth, high potential and economic viability of renewable energy. This will bring a major transformation in the country's job sector also. There is a need of a rationalized, realistic and differential RPO which would help in creating energy equity in the country. The existing RPO target set up by different SERCs only factor capacity addition forecasts based on the potential of various renewable energy technologies and ignores other important factors which influence it. Electricity demand of any state is highly influenced by its industrial and commercial activities which increases the demand, in turn increasing the purchasing capacity of the state, and in a spiraling effect leads to more expensive electricity. Therefore, the Government of India through CERC should frame guidelines on differential RPO targets for all states based on relevant criteria.

Assessment of current RPO mechanism suggests that electricity utilities of only seven states meet their RPO targets, while the majority of states fail to meet their renewable energy obligation. The major bottleneck that prevents state electricity utilities meeting their obligation is lack of a proper compliance mechanism. Since there is no uniform and stringent compliance mechanism in place, there is no pressure nor mandate on electricity utilities in the states to meet their RPO target. The Forum of Regulators (FOR), constituted under the Electricity Act, 2003, should also set up a mandatory and uniform RPO compliance code for all states which shall be adopted by SERCs across the country. The compliance code should have both penalty and reward elements.

The current RPO mechanism lacks uniformity in provisions for a longer trajectory for RPO targets in different states. Currently only few states have longer RPO trajectory. Longer trajectories of RPO's have an inherent advantage of reducing uncertainties for state utilities as plan for renewable energy supply and procurement can be made accordingly which will have a positive impact on the pricing and tariff for electricity from renewable energy sources. Therefore, the Government of India should set a timeframe under which all SERC's should set long term RPO frameworks which should include annual RPO targets for its electricity utilities and other obligated entities for a minimum period of 10 years up to end of the 13th FYP.

There is still lack of interstate transmission of renewable energy and lack of clarity on interstate generation and transmission which are acting as a major bottleneck for the growth of this sector. This restricts significant development of renewable energy infrastructures under inter-state generation and transmission scheme because renewable energy projects commissioned under state's renewable energy policy cannot enter into a long-term electricity agreement with other states. The Government of India through CERC should set guidelines that allow renewable energy developers from any state to undergo long-term power purchase agreements with other state power utilities in a similar manner as with conventional electricity power projects.

So the role of renewable energy sector is definitely going to gain a much important share in India's future energy needs. While many big projects are already underway, many major projects will also be coming in the future as the government of India understands the importance and value of renewable energy. It is expected that the momentum will pick up very shortly.

Bibliography

1. MNRE website. www.mnre.gov.in
2. MNRE annual report
3. India Energy Exchange website, http://www.iexindia.com/
4. CEA Website: http://www.cea.nic//
5. Energy Statistics released by Central Statistics Office, Ministry of Statistics and Program Implementation, Government of India
6. World Bank Databank
7. Energy Statistics released by Central Statistics Office, Ministry of Statistics and Program Implementation, Government of India
8. Crisil "Schemes for development of New and Renewable Energy ", PIB 12 August 2013
10. Twelfth Five Year Plan (2012-17), Planning Commission, Government of India, http://planningcommission.gov.in/plans/planrel/12thplan/pdf/vol_2.pdf
11. Load Generation Balance Report (2012-13), Central Electricity Authority, http://www.cea.nic.in/reports/yearly/lgbr_report.pdf
12. Indian Wind Energy Association, http://www.inwea.org/installedcapacity.htm
13. State Owned Electricity Distribution Companies: Some positives, though several concerns remain, ICRA, http://www.icra.in/Files/ticker/Power20Distribution20Note.pdf
14. Annual Report 2011-12, Power Finance Corporation, http://www.pfcindia.com/writereaddata/userfiles/file/Annual20reports/ann_rpt1112_27082012.pdf
15. India Solar Generation Facility by Asian Development Bank, http://www.adb.org/site/private-sector-financing/india-solar-generation-guarantee-facilityorig

Part 6: Social Justice

6.1 Green Concern of Indian Education System: Status and Prognosis

By Dr Seema Singh

Abstract

Environmental degradation has been considered as a bi-product of economic development. However, the continuous and ruthless plundering of the nature has very grim consequences. The United Nations (UN) has included environmental degradation in its list of top ten high-level threats faced by our planate till date. Now, the essential task of development is to design and implement policies and programmes which encourages the efficient use of resources and adopt technologies that lead to less environmental harm which is intricately linked with labour force skills. Green education or green issues need to be incorporated in the education system. In this background, the Chapter discusses growth and status of green education in India. It also discusses anticipated demand for manpower with green sensibility and skills so that, emerging gap between demand for and supply of manpower with right kind of skills may be assessed and suggests measures to fill the gap.

JEL classification- I-23, L-72, O-13; Q-01; Q-20; Q-42: Q- 55; Q-56

Key words: Natural Recourses, Environmental Degradation, Economic Development, Green Education

1. Introduction

Environment[1] is a vital input in any production process and as available in surplus, very often, it is substituted for other factor of production as capital. The traditional societies had developed methods through which they use to give time for regeneration[2]. However, with the industrialisation[3], the equilibrium in the environment[4] has disturbed and natural resources are not getting enough time to regenerate. The continuous and ruthless plundering has brought us on the edge[5]. The damage caused to the natural resources has grim consequences and one of them is climate change[6]. The United Nations (UN) has included environmental degradation in its list of top ten high-level threats faced by our planate till date. The achievement of sustained and equitable development remains the greatest challenge before humanity today. Countries including India[7], are incorporating sustainable development policies into their development agenda. The essential task of development is to design and implement policies and programmes which encourage the efficient use of resources and adopt technologies that lead to less environmental harm which is intricately linked with labour force skills. This is only possible when environmental issues are adequately identified, scientifically understood, appropriate technological solutions are applied for their mitigation and sustainable resource utilization methods, the green methods are inducted into the ways workers perform their trade, profession or occupation. A re-orientation of the education system is, hence, required to impart green education which will lead to a heighten sense of responsibility towards ecological sensitivity and development of eco-friendly technology. The benefits of 'demographic dividend'[8] can only be reaped by India, if strategies are developed and implemented to transform people into human capital with green sensitivity. The onus is on the Indian education system to prepare the youth with same. Some efforts have already been made in this direction throughout the world in general and India in particular. In this background, the Chapter discusses present status green education in India. First a brief history of growth of the green education has been discussed in the second section which is followed by state of green education in India in the third section. The fourth section high lights the employment potential of the green sector. The gap between demand and supply for green sector has been discussed in the fifth section. The Chapter end up with conclusion.

2. A brief history of green education

The history of education which is sensitive towards environmental issues reveals a close connection between changing concerns about the environment as well as its associated problems and the way in which such education is defined and promoted. The concept of green education was first discussed[9] by Rousseau as 'Nature chapter'[10] in the 18th Century in his book entitled, "Emile: or, Education". The nature chapter movement used fables and moral lessons to help students develop an appreciation for nature and embrace the natural world (Rousseau, 1762). Since then, the area of chapter has changed in nomenclature as well as its scope and approach many times and over the period, has become more aggressive and has focussed on more rigorous scientific training. Ultimately, it crystallised as the modern environment education movement. It gained significant momentum in the late 1960s. People, all over the world had seen the fall out of atomic bomb at Hiroshima and Nagasaki and were afraid of the ill effects from radiation, the chemical pesticides and the significant air pollution and waste. Their concern for the health of people and natural environment led to unifying phenomenon known as environmentalism. The first article about environment education as a new movement appeared in Phi Delta Kappan in 1969, authored by James A. Swan (Swan, 1969). However, the period of 1970s can be considered as more effective for initiating formal environmental education. USA passed the National Environmental Education Act in 1970 to incorporate formal environmental education into K-12 schools to make students aware of the environmental problems. The scientific bodies and international organizations were also working in their sphere for development and expansion of environmental education. The Stockholm Declaration[11], the Belgrade Charter[12], the Tiblisi Declaration[13] are some of the major international initiatives taken under the auspices of UN which discussed role of environmental education in preserving and improving the global environment and sought to provide the frame work and guidelines for environmental education. Other countries, first developed and then developing, gradually followed USA and incorporated environmental education in their school curriculum. Even the 1980s were also important decade during which public environmental concern continued to heighten, giving environmental education a stronger impetus in schools. This decade was also significant since environmental education's holistic philosophy began to take root. This was reflected in the broadening nature and scope of environmental education, marked by moves towards an inter-disciplinary dimension and from a more local to a global approach (Tilbury, 1993). In India, the National Policy on Education' 1986 made compulsory inclusion of environmental education at elementary level in India. During the same year, Malaysia and Indonesia also included compulsory teaching of environment science in their school curriculum (Tiwana & Jerath, 2003). Progressively, teaching of environmental science was extended up to Post Graduate and Ph.D. level as an independent stream of education as well as cross over stream as environmental economics, environmental accountancy etc. In the 1990s, mounting concern over environment and development problems has meant greater support for an educational approach, which not only considers immediate environmental improvement as an actual goal, but also addresses educating for 'sustainability' in the long term (Tilbury, 1995). However, during that period, flavour was more of awareness and scientific chapter which co-existed with usual activity going even though there was, time to time outcry from environmentalist and concerned citizen groups. In 1997, the Kyoto protocol[14] was signed which can be considered as a major mile stone in the process of the development of green education. If energy use remain unchecked, emission levels will keep on rising over time. Thus under the treaty, greenhouse gas emissions are capped with the objective of stabilizing CHG concentrations in the atmosphere at a level that would prevent dangerous anthropogenic interference with the climate system. One of the mechanisms under the Kyoto Protocol to achieve reduction of greenhouse gases is through trading of emission permits

(Sobti and Sharma, 2007) which has given rise of a market[15] for carbon credits[16]. Markets are used to allocate the emissions among the group of regulated sources. Thus, the number of companies needing to buy credits is expected to increase, and the rules of demand and supply will push up the market prices. Thus, carbon credits create a market for reducing greenhouse emissions by giving a monetary value to the cost of polluting the air (UN, 1997). It has given boost to the entrepreneur to be environment sensitive. Focus has turn towards development of eco-friendly processes and ultimately, eco-friendly technology. A resolution has been adopted to make the Special Climate Change Fund (SCCF) fully operational and asking the Global Environmental Facility (GEF) to evolve guidelines for priorities and procedures to finance the Special Climate Change Fund (SCCF). Two new climate funds for developing countries have been created. The Special Climate Change Fund (SCCF) will finance projects on adaptation of technology to prevent climate change and technology transfer. A collective commitment by developed countries to help developing countries reduce emissions, preserve forests, and adapt to climate change; and a goal of mobilizing $100 billion a year in public and private finance by 2020 to address developing county needs. The accord also calls for the establishment of a Copenhagen Green Climate Fund, a High Level Panel to examine ways of meeting the 2020 finance goal, a new Technology Mechanism, and a mechanism to channel incentives for reduced deforestation (Ghosh Roy and Ashtt, 2007) and hence forth, environmental education is sharing the space with green education which is the last and latest phase in its growth path. Showing concern towards environment has become monetarily rewarding also. Development, innovation and adoption of eco-friendly technology have taken shape of a highly rewarding business model. Engineering education institutions throughout the world and so as in India, they are taking keen interest to design new courses as well as blending existing courses with sufficient input of green technology. College of Engineering of Virgenia Tech University has started a graduation programme on green engineering (University Website, 2011). Some business schools have started MBA in Green Economy. Societies of professional engineers as well as corporate bodies are also taking initiatives to train professionals to comply with the environmental norms. International Organisation of standards (ISO) has designed and developed a whole series i.e. 1400[17] which is regarding environment management (ISO 1401, 2004). International Federation of Consulting Engineers (FIDIC, French acronym), Institute of Electrical and Electronics Engineer (IEEE)[18] are other international bodies for engineers which have developed standards and conduct workshops for making practicing engineers environmental sensitive. Corporate houses, as L'Oréal[19] is funding projects for development of eco-friendly technology.

3. State of green education in India

Increasing importance which is being given to green education in school and universities curricula throughout the world has already been discussed in the previous section. This section discusses the state of green education in India which for convenience of discussion, can be divided into two as informal and formal on basis of format and nature, though large part overlaps each other.

3.1. Informal Green Education

This is an area of chapter which is being imparted more in informal rather than formal way both within and outside universities. Schools and colleges have various programmes outside the class rooms, in which students are actively involved. Under National Service Scheme (NSS) which is a programme of Ministry of Youth Affairs and Sports, there are several programme for green education where students are activity involved (http://nss.nic.in). The University Grants Commission in its Country Wide Classroom (CWCR) Programme telecasts programme on environmental science every Saturday between 7.30-9.30, 13.30-1.30, 17.30-19.30 and 0.30-1.30. Further in order to encourage private documentary producers, educational institutions/ NGOs, for making films related to environmental issues and to provide them a platform to show their work to the concerned persons and general public. University Grants Commission (UGC) is organising Prakriti Festival (Films on Environment, Development and Human Rights) regularly in different parts of the country in collaboration with universities/ educational institutions located there. This Festival attracted a large number of filmmakers, Non Governmental Organisations (N.G.O.s), students, academia and administrators, development workers and media. These programmes ultimately increase awareness among masses about environmental conservation (Dubey, 2010). Several NGOs all over the country, are working on the issue of green education which ranges from the enhancing sensitivity towards conservation of electricity and water to protection of environment as initiatives taken by 'Taru Mitra'[20], an N.G.O. which sensitizes students of high schools and universities towards environmental issues. Others are working on development of equipment to conserve electricity or other natural resources.

3.2. Formal Green Education

There has been a long-history of environmental education component in our school curriculum. Even the Kothari Commission (1964-66) suggested that aim of teaching science in the primary school should be to develop proper understanding of the main facts, concepts of our surrounding and environment (GoI, 1964). However, aggressive thrust for environmental education at school level came with National Policy on

Education (NPE) in 1986 and National Action Plan (NAP), 1992 in which environmental issues, environmental concerns and the conservation were identified as core areas of the curriculum. Following the direction, many State School Examination Boards and Central Board of Secondary Examination (CBSE) emphasized the need to educate children about the environment. However, even then there was very little perceptible change in our approach to environment education transaction. National Council of Educational Research and Training (NCERT)'s National Curriculum Framework "NCF"-2000 and 2005 laid down enormous emphasis on environmental education to the extent of making it as important as other subjects. Again, there is debate on the issue that whether it should be taught in infused way or as a separate subject (NCERT, 2005). All stakeholders have agreed on the fact that the treatment of the subject need to be different at primary, secondary and higher secondary level. Along with natural environment, children should chapter aspects of their local environment which has been affected by human activity. For example, these may include farming, industry and sewage disposal, mining or quarrying. Wherever possible, this should be based on first-hand observation, but some of the significant activities related to environment were highlighted in the curriculum of the secondary school. The students need to have theoretical inputs and solution as well as an appreciation for these issue so that when they became citizen, they can use specific design and technology (Gopal and Anand, 2008). At graduation level, it is being taught both as a separate and as a cross over stream of chapter in most of the universities. However, TERI University which has made a name for itself in the rapidly growing field of sustainable development, has won praise from industry executives and academics for tackling some of the world's most pressing environmental problems, including poverty[21] and pollution. Many of TERI graduates have been snapped up by multinational companies like Suzlon Energy Limited, one of the world's leading players in harnessing wind energy, and Ernst & Young, an accounting firm. All students at TERI are required to take a broad range of courses in such subjects as Economics, Policy, Sociology and the hard sciences. But before graduation students are suppose to do internship with companies or government agencies, and tackle actual environmental projects. (Neelakantan, 2010). Hence, the programmes offered by TERI has component of green education.

As the pass outs of technical and vocational education (TVE) school entre into trades that have an immediate and direct impact to environment, UNESCO is more concerned to make them green sensitive and emphasis on infusion of environmental education courses in existing curriculum rather than specialised courses. Earlier, the compulsory foundation courses in the secondary vocational schools were having only five percent component of environmental education but has been revised in 2003 to 15 per cent. Pandit Sunderlal Sharma Central Institute for Vocational Education, Bhopal has developed several competency based vocational curricula and several text books and manual and conducts orientation programmes for teachers (Tiwana N.S. and Neelima Jerath, 2003). At graduate and post graduate level also, environmental engineering is being taught at a separate Chapter as well as a component in other branches of engineering. However, it is skewed towards post graduate level as there are more courses at post graduate level rather than degree and diploma. One of the reasons may be the nature of environmental issues which requires interdisciplinary approach and the post graduate students are better equip to infuse environmental issues with other subjects. However to make a strong foundation, engineering science is being taught as a compulsory subject of all branches in the first year at undergraduate level. Not only engineering colleges but the corporate sector is also taking keen interest in providing green training. The education and talent development division of HCL Info systems, has launched an IT training program for Green Computing, in partnership with Global Science and Technology Forum (GSTF). As part of the partnership, HCL with GSTF offers the introductory training programs across 130 cities in India (HCL, 2011).

4. Employment Potential of the Green Sector

India is one of the lowest green house gas (CHG) emitters in the world on the per capita basis. Its emission of CO_2 equivalent per capita is nearly one-fourth of the corresponding global average. However, India is highly vulnerable to climate change, and committed to participate in the discourse to minimize the risk. It will try to create green job to alleviate the risk of climate change. According to ILO (2008) report entitled, "Green Jobs: Towards decent work in a sustainable, low carbon world", green job reduces the environmental impact of the enterprises and economic sectors or involve jobs that conserve the environment. A green job is employment in any industry contributing to preserving or restoring environmental quality in that sector and allowing for sustainable development. Specifically, but not exclusively, this includes jobs that help to protect ecosystems and biodiversity; reduce energy, materials, and water consumption through high efficiency strategies; de-carbonize the economy; and minimize (or altogether avoid) generation of all forms of waste and pollution. A green job can be white or blue coloured in any sector; agriculture, manufacturing, research and development, administrative and service sector such as IT, finance, teaching and so on (ILO, 2008). As the concept is new and its technical boundaries are not clear to all, it is very difficult to calculate the number of jobs. However, different estimations are being made and at the same time, various inclusive definitions is being given. Studies on how transition to a sustainable, low-carbon economy might affect employment states that there is overall job gains compared to "business-as-usual" scenarios. The more detailed of these studies address not just changes in the total number of jobs, but also underlying job movements as well as the quality of jobs. The global market for environmental products and services is projected to double from US$1,370 billion per year at present to US$2,740 billion by 2020. Clean technologies are already the third largest sector for venture capital after information and biotechnology in the United States, while green venture capital in China has grown more than doubled as 19 per cent of total investment in recent years. In India it may create nine lakh jobs (Jarvis Andrew, Adarsh Varma and Justin Ram, 2011; Ians, 2008). In general, green jobs are expected to be created almost all sectors but most jobs will be created in recycling and waste management. These jobs may be classified into three:

- Performing an eco-friendly process which consumes less of one or more resources. It may or may not require technical skills to perform as e-banking requires less Chapter which ultimately, means less cutting of trees.
- R&D for innovation, adaptation and development of eco-friendly technology is another segment of green jobs. Green jobs in energy supply could be in R&D for enhancing efficiency of conventional sources as from coal to gas and renewable power sources including hydro, nuclear, solar, geo-thermal and wind. In the transport sector, more fuel-efficient vehicles, including hybrids and cleaner diesel vehicles. In agriculture, jobs range from improvement in crop to grazing land management to increase soil carbon storage. Better rice cultivation techniques, livestock and manure management to reduce methane emission. At present there are almost 3500 engineering institutions with intake capacity of about 1.5 million. Though at present, there is not sufficient R&D is being carried on in these engineering colleges but, there is growing awareness about significance of R&D among these institutions.
- Management of Eco-Friendly Technology

This will be largest segment in which there will be engineering job as construction, installation and monitoring of power plant industrial efficiency including plant efficiency and carbon sequestration. A rise in green buildings and energy efficiency will lead to increase in demand for architects, engineers, technicians, plumbers, construction workers. In recent years, Europe is following aggressive air pollution regulation. Low Emission Zones (LEZs) have been made in which vehicular access is allowed only to vehicle that emit low level of air pollutants. Using new administrative data sets from Germany, the Chapter discusses the spatial substitution effects in green versus dirty vehicles and concludes that LEZs decreases air pollution by around nine percent in urban traffic centres (Wolff, 2014). Again renewable energy is now being considered a most desirable source of fuel than the nuclear power due to the absence of risk and disaster. So, R&D may be done for replacing fossil fuel with renewable energy source and for enhancing efficiency in energy use. Measures are being taken to enhance such technologies (Shahrouz et.al., 2014). It means there is need of more R&D in automobile which emits low level of air pollutants if India wants to increase its export of automobile to European countries and ultimately, more Engineers and Scientists are required for automobile R&D. There will be non-engineering jobs also. Increasing environmental awareness and stricter implementation of legislation supporting the environment will ultimately, mean increased environmental litigation, lawyers and policy writers. Growth of global carbon market will mean an increase in carbon finance consultants, analysts, financiers, a carbon accountant, business risk analyst and more.

5. Gaps and suggested measures to fill them

Though there has been a long-history of Environmental education component in the Indian education system ranging from school curriculum to Ph.D. in Environmental science. Majority of the concept related to environment are found in the school text books of biology, chemistry, physics, geography and social science, pedagogy is devoid of inculcating sensitivity towards environment. It appears to be still inadequately expose the student to their 'habitat'. There is need of active learning from the natural and social world around them. The prescribed activities, generally, are simply taught as a set material to be memorised through teaching in the class room instead of being pursued by students on their own with an open mind. Activity- based projects are again carried out in a routine fashion, sometimes, with improper involvement of parents or even commercial agencies. In contrary, the course should prepare them to initiate and carry on practical initiative for solving environmental related problem and moving toward a life of perfect harmony with their social and natural environment (NCERT, 2005). However, no amount of preaching to the citizenry about the perils of a polluted environment, the dangers of irresponsible disposal of wastes or deforestation and the benefits to mankind of greening the environment will make people act to control environmental degradation unless they are imbued with a deep concern for the common good, a sense of responsibility for maintaining a balanced and healthy ecosystem and a strong drive to achieve harmony with nature. (UNESCO, 1990, p. 191) and the green education tries to incorporate these aspect which unfortunately, environmental education has not been able to do include. In higher education also, market demand and stricter implementation of environmental rules will sensitize students towards abiding by the environmental norms. A chapter conducted in 2011 among fifty engineers working in construction sector in the Delhi NCR revels that the clients have become so environmental conscious that they have to deliver to remain in the market (Singh, 2011). Many automobile brands are being promoted on the basis of their environmental efficiency. So, higher education need to be more connected to the real world situation and students may be asked to work in an environmental sensitive manner to a real world situation.

6. Conclusion

Environmental degradation has been considered as a bi-product of economic development. However, the continuous and ruthless plundering of nature has very grim consequences. The essential task of development is to design and implement policies and programmes which encourage the efficient use of resources and adopt technologies that lead to less environmental harm. It, ultimately, intricately linked with labour force skills. This is only possible when environmental issues are adequately identified, scientifically understood, appropriate technological solutions are applied for their mitigation and sustainable resource utilization methods, the green methods are inducted into the ways workers perform their trade, profession or occupation. So, it is important for the education system to inculcate those values among students. The history of green education revels that it has always remained sensitive to environmental issues but its nomenclature as well as the scope has changed many times and has become more aggressive and scientifically rigorous in training. During 70s and 80s, environmental education was brought into formal education system throughout its spectrum, as a separate Chapter or blended with some other Chapter throughout the educational system in India. However, signing of several treaties in which Koto Protocol has made development, innovation and adaptation of eco-friendly technology as highly rewarding business model.

The level of treatment must be different at different level of education. In school curricula, the students must chapter aspects of their natural environment and concentrate on the aspect of local environment which has been affected by human activity. For example, these may include farming, industry and sewage disposal, mining or quarrying. At university level, along with theory and practical of subjects, students should do internship with companies or government agencies to deal with actual environmental projects. Engineering institutions should give more emphasis on R&D. It will enhance demand for Indian products in the international market also. There will be non-engineering jobs also. Increasing environmental awareness and stricter implementation of legislation supporting the environment will ultimately, mean increased environmental litigation, lawyers and policy writers. Growth of global carbon market will mean an increase in carbon finance consultants, analysts, financiers, a carbon accountant, business risk analyst and more. So, the students and institutions need to be more sensitive to the need of global market also.

Notes:

1. Environment as land, water, minerals etc. are used in some way or other, in each production process.

2. As method of shifting cultivation, 'Jhum Cultivation' which is practiced in the hilly area of North Eastern part of India.

3. Large scale production through machine.

4. One of the reason may be over exploitation of natural resources. But there are several other factors such as geographical, celestial, astronomical, physical etc. which effect environment.

5. There is a range of environment within which only human being can survive.

6. Sudden change in seasonal pattern of environment in specific geography which has adversely affected all the living being of that region.

7. The constitution of India in Article 48A and 51(A)(G) has discussed about protection of environment. Article 48A declares the state shall endeavour to protect and improve the environment and to safe guard the forest and wild life of the country. Article 51(A)(G) says that every citizen shall have duty" to protect and improve the natural environment including forest, lakes, rivers and the wild life and to have compassion for living creatures". A number of legislation have been enacted for the protection and preservation of environment. Some of the important legislations are:

   · The water (Prevention and Control of Pollution) Act, 1974;
   · The Water (Prevention and Control of Pollution) Cess Act, 1977;
   · The Air (Prevention and Control of Pollution) Act, 1981;
   · The Environmental Protection Act, 1986;
   · Hazardous Wastes (Management and Handling) Rules, 1989;
   · Public Liability Insurance Act, 1991;National Environmental Appellate Authority Act, 1997 (Ghosh Roy and Ashtt, 2007)

8. Contrary to aging population of developed countries, large cohorts of young population are poised to add to the working-age population in India.

9. It has been discussed in Vedas (old Hindu scripture)also.

10. The nature chapter movement (alternatively, Nature chapter or nature-chapter) was a popular education movement in America in the late 19th and early 20th centuries. Nature chapter attempted to reconcile scientific investigation with spiritual, personal experiences gained from interaction with the natural world.

11. UN Conference on the Human Environment held in Stockholm, Sweden, in 1972, declared environmental education must be used as a tool to address global environmental problems. The United Nations Education Scientific and Cultural Organization (UNESCO) and United Nations Environment Program (UNEP) created three major declarations that have guided the course of environmental education. June 5–16, 1972 - The Declaration of the United Nations Conference on the Human Environment. The document was made up of 7 proclamations and 26 principles "to inspire and guide the peoples of the world in the preservation and enhancement of the human environment." (UNEP. 1972.

12. The October 13–22, 1975 - The Belgrade Charter was the outcome of the International Workshop on Environmental Education held in Belgrade, Yugoslavia. The Belgrade Charter was built upon the Stockholm Declaration and adds goals, objectives, and guiding principles of environmental education programs. It defines an audience for environmental education, which includes the general public (Barry, 1976).

13. The Tbilisi Declaration- October 14–26, 1977 - The Tbilisi Declaration "noted the unanimous accord in the important role of environmental education in the preservation and improvement of the world's environment, as well as in the sound and balanced development of the world's communities." The Tbilisi Declaration updated and clarified The Stockholm Declaration and The Belgrade Charter by including new goals, objectives, characteristics, and guiding principles of environmental education. Later that decade, in 1977, the Intergovernmental Conference on Environmental Education in Tbilisi, Georgia emphasized the role of Environmental Education in preserving and improving the global environment and sought to provide the framework and guidelines for environmental education. The Conference laid out the role, objectives, and characteristics of environmental education, and provided several goals and principles for environmental education (Tbilisi Declaration, 1977)

14. The Kyoto Protocol was adopted in Kyoto, Japan, on 11 December 1997 and entered into force on 16 February 2005. The detailed rules for the

implementation of the Protocol were adopted at COP 7 in Marrakesh in 2001, and are called the "Marrakesh Accords." The Kyoto Protocol is an international agreement linked to the United Nations Framework Convention on Climate Change. The major feature of the Kyoto Protocol is that it sets binding targets for 37 industrialized countries and the European community for reducing greenhouse gas (GHG) emissions .These amount to an average of five per cent against 1990 levels over the five-year period 2008-2012 (UN, 1997).

15. The Kyoto mechanisms are:

    · Emissions trading – known as "the carbon market"
    · Clean development mechanism (CDM)
    · Joint Implementation (JI)

16. One carbon credit=one metric tonnes of carbon dioxide or carbon dioxide equivalent gases.

17. An EMS meeting the requirements of ISO 14001:2004 is a management tool enabling an organization of any size or type to:

    · identify and control the **environmental impact** of its activities, products or services, and to
    · **improve** its environmental performance continually, and to
    · Implement a **systematic approach** to setting environmental objectives and targets, to achieving these and to demonstrating that they have been achieved. (ISO, 2004)

18. Institute of Electrical and Electronics Engineer (IEEE) is another international bodies for engineers which provides a wide range of quality publications and standards that make the exchange of technical knowledge and information possible among technology professionals. With an active portfolio of nearly 1300 standards, IEEE is a leading developer of industry standards in a broad range of technologies. The collaborative approach of leaders of 160 countries, IEEE is a leading consensus building organization that enables the creation and expansion of international markets and helps to protect health and safety (IEEE, 2014).

19. Reducing energy consumption and tackling the challenges of climate change. as L'Oréal has founded Nicolas Hulot Foundation for Nature and Mankind, a non-profit organisation dedicated to educating the public about protecting the

environment and the beauty of nature. It helps with the Foundation's scientific work, support 150 field projects in 10 countries every year, raise public awareness of the need to preserve natural resources, and support the Nicolas Hulot School for environmental education. To build awareness of environmental and climate change issues among its 11,000 employees in France, L'Oréal joined the 'Défi Pour la Terre' (Challenge for the Earth) programme. L'Oréal contributes to the Foundation's three operational programmes: Promoting nutrition and a healthy diet and Preserving and restoring biodiversity (L'Oreal, 2010).

20. Tarumitra: Effort of the Students to Save the Earth (Dr. Anita Horsey (Retd from the Deptt. of History, Sophia College, Bombay). **Started in 1988 in Patna, Bihar, Tarumitra has grown into the biggest students' movement in India campaigning exclusively for the environment of the Earth. The organization is operative in about 200 high schools and colleges of Bihar, Rajasthan, West Bengal, Andhra Pradesh, M.P and Tamilnadu. Presently the Tarumitra activities are co-ordinated by Fr. Robert Athickal S.J., a Jesuit and an educationalist.** It has over 2,00000 members in over 1000 high schools and colleges. *Tarumitra* has also had several full time volunteers from ***India*** and abroad. Tarumitra has helped to set up a plant to fabricate parabolic solar cookers along with the traditional solar panels to harness solar energy. The students set up parabolic Solar Cookers in a park in the centre of Patna to demonstrate non-conventional, clean forms of energy. Tarumitras cooked hot snacks on the solar cookers for interested passers-by. Presently the Bio-reserve produces most of its power from solar panels. A total of 3 KV power is produced and it powers most of the energy needs of the place. Six computers, most of the fans and lights, one air conditions for the lab and a surface pump is run with the above power (www. http://tarumitra.org).

21. The Women of the Chipko movement in the Himaliaya showed that the poor, in fact, crared about their environment. The women of Reni village in Chamoli district stopped loggers from cutting their forests.

Reference:

Barry Joseph (eds.) (1976), "Connect", UNESCO-UNEP Environmental Education News Letter, Vol-1, No.1. p-1

Dubey Amitosh (2010), "Role of UGC's Films in Environmental Awareness" University News, 48(23), pp. 07-10.

FIDIC (2014) http://www.fidic.org/ down loaded on 01.06.2014.

Ghosh Roy Jayanta and Rashmi Ashtt (2007), "Ongoing Changes on Panet Earth Caused by Global warming" University News, 45 (44), pp. 20-22.

Gopal G.V. and V.V. Anand (2008), "Environmental Education in School Curriculum: an overall perspective papwer presented at the International Conference on Issues in Public Policy and Sustainable Development" at the Indira Gandhi National Open University, New Delhi between March' 26-28.

Government of India (GoI) (1964), "Kothari Commission Report", http://www.scribd.com/doc/87669769/KOTHARI-COMMISSION-REPORT-A-PRESENTATION retrieved on 04.4.2014

HCL, (2011), "HCL to impart training in Green computing", http://articles.timesofindia.indiatimes.com/2011-06-02/education/29612672_1_rothin-bhattacharyya-hcl-infosystems-infosystems-**executive-vice-president** down loaded on 28th October'2011IEEE 2011, (2011).

Jarvis Andrew, Adarsh Varma and Justin Ram (2011), http://www.ilo.org/global/publications/books/forthcoming-publications/WCMS_153458/lang--en/index.htmAssessing Green Jobs Potential in Developing Countries: A Practitioner's Guide down loaded on 7/11/2011

Ians (2008), "Green economy can create nine lakh jobs in India", http://www.siliconindia.com/shownews/_Green_economy_can_create_nine_lakh_jobs_in_India-nid-47356-cid-3.html down loaded on 12/10/2011.

IEEE (2014), "Institute of Electrical and Electronics Engineers" http://www.ieee.org/index.html retrieved on 04.6.2014

ILO (2008), "**Green Jobs: Towards Decent work in a Sustainable, Low-Carbon World**" http://www.ilo.org/global/about-the-ilo/press-and-media-centre/news/WCMS_098481/lang--en/index.htm down loaded on 07/11/2011ISO1401 (2004), "International Organisation for Standardization", http://www.iso.org/iso/about.htm down loaded on 09.01.2014.

ISO (2004), "ISO14000 SERIES ENVIRONMENTAL MANAGEMENT SYSTEMS" http://www.iso14000-iso14001-environmental-management.com/ retrieved on 04/6/2014.

L'Oreal (2010), "Access to education and occupational integration" http://www.sustainabledevelopment.loreal.com/communities/access-to-education-and-occupational-integration.asp down loaded on 20/11/2010.

NCERT (2005), Enviornmental Education as Infused in NCERT Syllabus for class ! to X!! as per NCF 2005" *ncert.nic.in/book_publishing/environ_edu/eei.pdf down loarded on 12.10.2011.*

Neelakantan Sailaja (2009), "India Education: Going Green" http://www.globalpost.com/dispatch/india/091012/india-education-going-green?page=full Retrieved on 12.4.2014.

NSS (2014), " National Service Scheme", Ministry of Youth Affairs and Sports, http://nss.nic.in retrieved on 20/5/2014.

Rousseau Jean-Jacques (1762), "Emile, or Education," Barbara Foxley (Translator) JM Dent & Sons London & Toronto, retrieved from http://oll.libertyfund.org/titles/rousseau-emile-or-education on 22.05.2014

Shahrouz Abolhosseini, Almas Heshmati, Jörn Altmann (2014), "A **Review of Renewable Energy Supply and Energy Efficiency Technologies**", IZA Discussion Chapter 8145, http://ftp.iza.org/dp8145.pdf retrieved on 31/5/2014.

Singh Seema, (2011), "Is Education System in India Prepared to Groom for Green Job?", 53rd Annual Conference of the Indian Society of Labour Economics, ML Sukhadia University, December 17-19.

Sobti R.C. and V.L. Sharma (2007), "Are we Sensitized to the Impact of Global Warming: Some Thoughts" University News, 45 (44), pp. 12-19.

Swan James A. (1969), "Phi Delta Kappan" Volume 51 Issues 1-10, Phi Delta Kappa inc.,

Tarumitra, http://tarumitra.org/ retrieved on 13.4.2014

Tilbury, D. (1993) Environmental education: developing a model for initial teacher education, PhD thesis, University of Cambridge, ftp://charmian.sonoma.edu/pub/references/Env_Ed_Sustainability.pdf down loaded on 21/11/2011

Tbilisi Declaration (1977), Intergovernmental Conference on Environmental Education: October 14-26. https://www.google.co.in/?gfe_rd=cr&ei=XJeNU-7ACObV8gfP-4HoAg#q=13+the+tbilisi+declaration+unesco+1978 retrieved on 24.4.2014

Tilbury, Daniella, (1995), "Environmental Education for Sustainability: Defining the new focus of Environmental Education" Environmental Education Research; 1995, Vol. 1 Issue 2, pp. 195-197.

Tiwana, N. S.; Neelima Jerath, (2003), Integrating environment education in technical and vocational education in Asia: report of the workshop, 3rd to 5th September 2003, Chandigarh, India http://portal.unesco.org/education/en/file_download.php/f9dff494ba9889e5 b23e5bdc3e854c82Workshop+Integrated+Report.pdf retrieved on 03.03.2014

United Nations (1997), "**Kyoto Protocol to the United Nations Framework Convention on Climate Change**", https://unfccc.int/essential_background/kyoto_protocol/items/1678.php retrieved on 25.5.2014

UNEP(1972), "Declaration of the United Nations Conference on the Human Environment" http://www.unep.org/Documents.Multilingual/Default.asp?documentid=97&articleid=1503 retrieved on 29.4.2014

UNESCO (1990) Sourcebook in Environmental Education for Secondary School Teachers (Thailand, UNESCO).

UNESCO (2002), "Universal Declaration on Cultural Diversity", UNESCO, Paris.

Virgenia Tech University, (2011) University Website, https://www.vt.edu/ retrieved at 25/7/2011

Wolff Hendrik, (2014), **Keep Your Clunker in the Suburb: Low Emission Zones and Adoption of Green Vehicles,** IZA Discussion Chapters No, 8180, http://ftp.iza.org/dp8180.pdf retrieved on 28 May 2014.

6.2 Maternal Health in India

By Dr Katherine Kennet

Maternal health is an issue that strikes at the heart of every family; every minute of every day a woman dies of a child-birth related cause and the majority of these deaths are preventable. In a country with a birth rate as high as India's (the birth rate in 2010 is 21.34, calculated by births during a year per 1,000 persons in the population at midyear) it is no surprise that this is a key issue, in fact, a quarter of the world's reported maternal deaths are in India . What I find particularly interesting is how in India, a country currently booming economically, the maternal health remains so poor, in fact, the maternal mortality ratio for India was worse in 2005 (450) than in 2004 (440). In this essay I shall attempt to answer the question of why so many women are dying of these preventable diseases, what current strategies are in place to reduce the numbers and what the future holds for India's women.

Setting the epidemiological scene of India

India is a massive country with a population of 1140 million people, it is hardly surprising that there are huge variations in all areas of life, especially health, across the vastly different geographical areas. India is split into 28 states of which the northern states tend to have the worst health indicator figures. For example, the maternal mortality ratio for Rajasthan (in the north) is 445, where as the maternal mortality ratio for Tamil Nadu (a southern state) is 134. This huge variability is what makes India so interesting and is reflected across all areas of Indian life.

When looking at India as a whole it is hard to gauge its position on the global stage; on one hand it has large areas of devastating poverty and until very recently was considered a "third world" country, but in recent years it has undergone massive economic change, economic growth and development (India's GDP has gone from 5.5 in 1998 to 9.1 in 2007). When it comes to basic needs, not only does India have a long way to go to reach the standards of the West, it also has massive inequality between rural and urban areas. This urban to rural inequality is mirrored in many aspects of maternal health, with 75% of India's births occurring in rural areas it is clear to see that addressing the rural maternal health needs will go a long way in changing the maternal health profile of India.

India's Gross national income per capita is $2930. This is well below the global average of $10307 and a fraction of the UK's at $36240. This massive disparity is reflected in the countries' total expenditure on health per capita: $109 in India and $2784 in the UK. This enormous difference puts the challenges faced by India's government into perspective and I shall discus their policies to tackle maternal mortality later.

Kerala: an unusual state

As I have already said, there is a huge variety in health indicators across India, not just between rural and urban areas, but also between states. It would therefore be incomplete to talk about India's epidemiology without mentioning Kerala: Kerala is a costal state in the south west of India and it is an anomaly when it comes to all parts of life. Kerala has a rich history of trade dating back five thousand years and is governed by the Left Democratic Front, a part of the communist party of India (an Indian Marxist political party). Its health indicators are so different to the rest of the country it is hard to believe it is an Indian state: life expectancy in Kerala is 74 (and expected to grow further in the next 10 years to 77 years) which is well above the national value of 64, and significantly higher than its neighbouring states of Tamil Nadu and Karnataka, which are at 66.2 years and 65.3 years respectively. This trend is followed when it comes to maternal health: the maternal mortality ratio in Kerala is 95 compared to India's 254 .

It is no coincidence that in 2008 the percentage of women in Kerala giving birth in a medical facility was 99.4%, of which 99.3% were in rural areas and 99.9% in urban areas. This equality is what makes Kerala so successful when it comes to health indicators. These figures are not as surprising when you look at the proportion living below the poverty line; Kerala only has 12.72% in comparison to India's 26.10 and the state's female literacy rate of 87.8% (this is the highest in India and well above the national average of 53.7%).

Why is maternal mortality important and how is it measured?

Maternal mortality is considered to be such a significant global issue that it is the fifth millennium development to reduce maternal mortality by 75% between 1990 and 2015. A maternal death affects far more than the family involved (although this alone has massive implications with children who have lost their mothers being up to ten times more likely to die prematurely) there is also an economic loss to the country as a whole; According to the United Nations Population Fund (UNFPA) women's unpaid work on the farm and at home account for one-third of the world's GDP this loss has a massive impact on the country's wealth.

It is measured by maternal mortality ratio: Maternal mortality ratio is the maternal death per 100,000 live births in one year (where maternal death is defined the "death of a woman while pregnant or within 42 days of termination of pregnancy, irrespective of the duration and site of the pregnancy, from any cause related to or aggravated by the pregnancy or its management but not from accidental or incidental causes.") Unfortunately, good quality data on maternal mortality is not available as many women who die due to pregnancy or birth die at home in rural areas where their deaths are not recorded. This lack of reliable data alone is an obstacle in tackling maternal health in India.

Why is pregnancy so dangerous in India?

There is no question that women in India have a lower status than those in the west. There are many reasons for this and to cover them all would require another essay but the main factors are that in Indian society men are more revered and respected. Men are far more likely to have been to school and to have been to school for a longer period of time. There are a number of reasons for this; despite free schooling being a constitutional right in India it costs a family to send a daughter to school in the hours lost in housework (it is normal for the girls of the family to help around the house), also there is very little chance that an education will lead to a job, especially in the poorer and more rural areas where the employment for women tends to agricultural or domestic. Another key cultural factor keeping women at a lower status than men is the issue of marriage. Traditionally, when an Indian woman gets married she moves in with her in-laws and comes with a "dowry". This dowry was originally a wedding gift from the bride's family to her new family to help with the cost of the wedding and to act as insurance in case she was mistreated more recently though, and despite anti-dowry legislation being in place since 1961's dowry prohibition act its usual for the dowry to consists of goods and cash payments to the groom's family. If this dowry is not forthcoming or not considered enough the groom's family commonly torture and harass the bride, often escalating to murder. These "dowry killings" and both under reported and so commonplace in India, that Delhi's main prison has an entire "mother-in-law's block" for the perpetrators. In 2008 alone there were 195856 cases of crimes against women including 81344 cases of cruelty by husbands or relatives. This demonstrates the shocking inequality between the sexes in India and shows how at risk the female population of India, even before the added medical dangers of pregnancy and childbirth.

Another key factor linked strongly with poor maternal outcome is the age of the mother when delivering her first child. One chapter found that women under the age of 20 were at a two and a half higher risk of death. This is particularly significant when you consider that in India the cultural norm is for women to get married at a young age (in Rajasthan, one of the northern states, where two thirds of all maternal deaths occur, the average age for a woman to marry is 16.05 years) and subsequently have their first child young (in Rajasthan the average for a first time mother is 17).

Then of course there is the birth itself. Often said to be one of the most high risk times in a woman's life, pregnancy is intrinsically full of potential threats to the mother's health, but if so much of the danger is biological, why are so many more women dying in India than other areas of the world? In answering this question we must look at where these deaths are happening: the majority of maternal death occurs out of the hospital or health-centre environment and the main causes are postpartum haemorrhage (around a fourth of maternal deaths in India), puerperal sepsis, eclampsia, severe anaemia and obstructed labour. Most of these causes are preventable with the correct medical resources and assistance both antenatal and during the birth itself. With such a large proportion of the population living in rural areas there is no underestimating the part physical access to maternal health care plays in preventing maternal death: if a woman develops problems during labour and the nearest hospital is two days walk away, her chances of survival are going to be significantly lower than a woman living in a city, moments from a health centre . There is also an issue of women not using the maternal health facilities that they have access too; the wealthier and more educated a woman in India is, the more likely she is to use maternal health facilities. This demonstrates that the bulk of India's maternal mortality is in the poorer sectors of society.

What are the Indian government doing to address the problem of maternal health?

One of the Governments recent initiatives was the Janani Surakash Yojana (which translates as safe motherhood scheme) known as JSY, is a conditional cash transfer scheme to incentivise women of low socioeconomic status to give birth in a health facility. (The idea being that fewer births outside medical facilities would lead to a lower maternal mortality rate). The scheme targeted the women most at risk of death from maternal causes by offering bigger cash incentives (up to 1400 rupees, which equates to $31.1) in rural areas and in high risk states. The scheme is implemented by community-level health workers who also aim to give all pregnant women at least three antenatal care visits. This scheme is the biggest of its kind in the world and provides cash to 9.5 million of the 26 million pregnant women in India this year. In a recent analysis of the schemes effectiveness researchers found that the more socially disadvantaged castes were far more likely to participate in the scheme. They also found that women with more years in education (up to 12 years) were far more likely to participate than those with fewer years of education, or those with no education at all.

Other findings included that although distance from a health facility did have a slight impact (i.e. the further the distance to travel, the fewer women attended), a far more significant relationship was found in the age of the mother: the younger the mother, the more likely she was to participate. These findings clearly show that the government's initiatives are having an impact, but is it enough? India clearly has issues regarding its large rural population, with one of the key problems being women living too far from the health centres. There has been much thought to address this by training up members of the community to act as health workers in rural areas. This prevents the potentially fatal delay between health issues occurring and getting to a health professional.

One chapter I looked into assessed the effects of women's groups in two of India's poorest and most rural areas: Jharkhand and Orissa. 40% of their combined population lives below the poverty line, an estimated 63% of the women who live here are illiterate and the female life expectancy is 60 years. The maternal mortality ratio in both these states is well above the country's average of 254 at 371 in Jharkhand and 358 in Orissa. The women's groups here met monthly and were lead by a local woman who was given 7 days residential training and supported through fortnightly meetings with district coordinators. Each of these local women ran many meetings a month in different rural locations to reach as many people as possible.

The groups gave information about safe delivery practices and care seeking behaviour through discussion of case studies, picture-card games, role play and story-telling. The outcomes of this chapter were striking with large reductions in not just maternal mortality but also neonatal mortality and moderate depression in new mothers. The latter was thought to be due to the support network created by these groups. Women's groups cannot replace trained medical care but I believe they certainly have a key role in maternal health in rural areas, providing simple information on topics such as hygiene and creating invaluable support networks at extremely low financial cost. There is no doubt over the cost effectiveness of training members of the community to run women's groups.

Conclusion

While writing this essay I have been shocked time and time again by the staggeringly large numbers of women affected by poor maternal health in India. This alone should be reason enough for India's government to prioritise maternal health in the years to come, and continue investing in schemes such as JSY and women's groups. I hope I have demonstrated that this is an important and complex issue, with key cultural issues right at its core, but, as the state of Kerala shows, pregnancy in India doesn't have to equate to life threatening danger. I believe that women's health is so intricately linked with their education, wealth and their position in society that to make strides in decreasing maternal mortality all these issues must be addressed. This may sound like a tall order but ultimately, there can be no justification for preventable and unnecessary deaths and I dearly hope India's government keeps that in mind.

References and supporting tables are available on request.

6.3 Gandhian Green Paradigm: A new vision for sustainable development

By Indira Dutta

Introduction

"We do not inherit the earth from our ancestors. We borrow it from our children." says Chief Seattle. In this modern age keeping this view in our mind we have to preserve and protect earth at any cost. In the journey of development, at present we are passing through a phase with dynamic change in science and technology. The race for materialism has plundered natural resources unethically. The whole globe has gained in terms of economic development but has failed in terms of sustainable development. At this critical juncture Gandhian Green Paradigm has shown a candle of hope to move towards sustainable development. The environment movement mushroomed in India right from the time of Gandhi but yet Gandhi was known as a symbol of peace, truth and non violence, freedom, justice, equality human right and harmony. He was a champion crusader of environmental preservation and protection of Mother Nature and he argued that the first and foremost question before humanity was to preserve, protect and ensure the stability of planetary system. Today the obsession with growth has pushed the limits before the carrying capacity of the planet. We have designed an economic system that is dependent on endless growth but this endless growth is unhealthy and unsustainable. So the need of the hour is that we have to rethink, reorient and restructure the global process. We all depend on biosphere for our survival but we all consume resources of Earth in such a way that we will leave little for the future generation. Today in the 21st century we need Gandhian prescription to build a future that is more prosperous, more just and more secure.

The real importance of Gandhi as an environmentalist lies not just in his vision and his understanding of the man-nature relationship but he categorically warned the world of the devastating consequences of the dynamic rush for development which ignores nature. He stated "A civilization built on renewable resources such as products of forestry and agriculture, is by fact alone superior to one built on non renewable resources, such as coal, oil etc. This is because former can last, while the latter cannot last."Gandhi also wrote in his famous book Harijan "true economics never militates against the highest ethical standards just as all true ethics to be worth its name must be at the same time be also a good economics, An economics just inculcates mammon worship and enables the strong to amass wealth at the expense of the weak is a false and dismal science. It spells death."

Truth and Non violence

Gandhi's two cardinal principles truth and nonviolence both were also green in nature He wrote "Nature has enough to satisfy everyone's needs, but not to satisfy everybody's greed."His truth has got a deeper meaning. It implies self realization. When a man self realizes himself he will not do anything wrong. He will give justice to everything including nature. His philosophy of truth is based on one single message of (advaita) non duality. His principle of non violence speaks that if you want to control violence then there should be fast on mind, body and soul. When we control all three we remain happy and do everything which is morally right. He said "Happiness is when what you think, what you say and what you do are in harmony."With it we could move towards sustainable development. Long back Einstein wrote on Gandhi "A leader of his people, unsupported by outward authority: a politician where rests upon craft nor the mastery of technical devices, but simply on convincing power his personality; a victorious fighter who always scorned the use of force; a man of wisdom and humility, armed with resolve and inflexible consistency, who had devoted all his strength to the uplifting of the people and the betterment of their lot, a man who has confronted the brutality of Europe with the dignity of a simple human being, and at all times risen superior. Generations to come, it may be, will scarcely believe that such a one as this is even flesh and blood walked on this earth."

Gandhi sought to return to golden age where people are one with natural surroundings. He wrote "It is a tragedy of the people that millions of people have ceased to use their hands as hands. Nature has bestowed upon us this great gift which is our hands. If the craze for machinery methods continues, it is likely that a time will come when we shall be so incapacitated and weak that we shall begin to curse ourselves for having forgotten."He was against personal and corporate profit. He was of the opinion that a locally based economy enhances community spirit. It takes care of themselves, their lands, animals, forestry and adds all the natural resources for the benefit of the present and future generations. What world thinks today Gandhi thought long back? The paradigm of sustainable development has its roots in Gandhian thinking.

Gandhi stressed on social transformation through rural reconstruction. He defined ideal village as follows "It will have cottages with sufficient light and ventilation, built of a material obtainable within a radius of five miles of it. The cottage will have courtyards enabling households to plant vegetables for domestic use and to house their cattle. The village lanes and streets will be free from all avoidable dust. It will have wells according to its needs and accessible to all. It will have houses of worship for all, also a common meeting place, a village common grazing its cattle, a cooperative dairy, primary and secondary schools in which vocational education will be a central fact, and it will have panchayats (village council) for settling disputes. It will produce its own grain, own vegetables and fruits and its own khadi (home spun cotton). This is roughly my idea of a model village. Here we get a glimpse of clean and hygienic environment.

We notice that 20th century is the most violent century in the human history. The violence is not only war but also in production, consumption and at the same time for controlling and commanding the natural resources. Today all of us are facing a common problem that how to come out of this growth trajectory which abates violence and promote excessive exploitation of natural resources. When natural resources are misused and abused repeatedly then sustainable development will remain a far cry. At this critical juncture Gandhian prescription is the only remedy to solve this threatening problem of mass destruction. The earth is one but the world is not. Treating nature as a resource to be plundered, food as a commodity and agriculture as an industry is degrading the earth. To bring the world together we have to follow Gandhian ethics i.e. Truth is the highest law and Non violence is the highest duty and then only we could fight out the new imperialism which is based on consumerism and militarism.

Trusteeship

Gandhi's view of trusteeship was green in nature. Trusteeship means that the surplus wealth needs to be kept in trust for common good and welfare of all. Everything we do must be economically viable as well as ethical so that we could bring a sustainable livelihood for all. Today the whole globe is marching towards economic collapse and we badly need the trusteeship philosophy of Gandhi. Trusteeship will bring sustainable consumption and sustainable production. It will utilize natural resource in a sustainable way because you are trustee and you need to take care of it. It ensures human dignity and equitable distribution of wealth and finally it provides a means of transformation of the present consumerist society into an egalitarian one.

Swaraj, Swadeshi and Sarvodaya

Swaraj of Gandhi basically means self rule. It does not mean only decolonization but it means creative regeneration of the nation. He mainly stressed on village regeneration based on larger principle of justice, love and hope. Swaraj is not a political concept but it is also an economic and environment concept. Gandhi believed in community development and guided the workers to engage in more systematic way with economic and environmental issues at the local level to achieve goals of sustainable communities and social justice.

Swadeshi (Home Economy) has taught that the spirit and soul of India rests in the village communities."The true India is to be found not in its few cities but in its villages. If villages will perish, India will perish too" Swadeshi is a programme for long term survival. Gandhi dreamt a decentralized homogenous hand crafted mode of production. In his words, "Not mass production but production by the masses". Swadeshi is a way to comprehensive peace, peace with oneself, peace between people and peace with nature. Swadeshi provides an answer to the destructive effects of globalization. Gandhi's Swadeshi was nothing but the Economy of Permanence.

Sarvodaya means upliftment of all as well as welfare of all. It is an ideal, a vision and a movement in Gandhian philosophy which explains the care and upliftment of humanity especially of the last and the least in the society. In fact he borrowed it from Ruskin "Unto the Last" i.e. greatest good for greatest number. It gives a message to bring a just and equitable society in the economic system. With sarvodaya the livelihood of the poor people will be protected and thus the property of commons will be protected.

Impact of Gandhian Philosophy on Foreign Thinkers
Arne Naess

Naess came under the influence of ethics of non violence of Mahatma Gandhi and Gandhian influence on ecosphy "T". The key concept of Naess ecosphy is self realization. Self reliance is the ultimate norm of his eco-philosophical system. He has said that "Call me Gandhi by all means. Gandhi is one of the people who has influenced me the most."Deep ecologically is intrinsically committed to the proposition that it is not possible to alter man's relationship to nature without altering man's relationship to man and relationship to self. Deep ecology recognizes the intrinsic worth of non-human world."Gandhi's Utopia is one of the few that shows ecological balance and today his rejection of the western world's material abundance and waste is accepted by the progressives of the ecological movement (Naess, 1974).The village romanticism of Gandhi has been considered as central to his environmental philosophy.

E.F. Schumacher

Schumacher identified Gandhi as the people's economist. He summed up Gandhian prescription for the salvation of India. He mentioned five pillars of Gandhian economic thinking where we find the glimpse of green economy. These pillars are 1. Non violent, 2. Simple, 3. Small, 4. Capital, 5. Rural based (Self- Reliant and Employment Oriented). Referring to his book "Small is Beautiful" Schumacher said when Gandhi said "Not mass production but production for masses" or when he talked about "decentralized rural based self reliant economy "or when he demanded "production and consumption must be reunited "all put forward one clear cut message that Gandhi long back cared for environment. Voicing his debt to the economic thought of Mahatma, Schumacher noted "A way of life that ever more rapidly depletes the power to sustain it and piles up even more insoluble problem for each succeeding generation can only be called violent......In short, man's urgent task is to discover a non violent way in his economic as well as his political life.......Non violence must permeate the whole of man's activities, if mankind is to be secure against a war of annihilation........Present day economics, while claiming to be ethically neutral, in fact propagates a philosophy of unlimited expansion without any regard to the true and genuine needs of man which are limited."He has also mentioned "Ever bigger machines, entailing ever bigger concentration of economic power and exerting ever greater violence against the environment do not represent progress: they are a denial of wisdom. Wisdom demands a new orientation of science and technology towards the organic, the gentle, and the non violent, the elegant and beautiful". The 21st century is obsessed with gigantism. We live under the illusion that big is big and big is powerful but the reality is that small is big economically, ecologically and politically.

Petra Kelly

Petra Kelly has drawn non violent inspiration from Gandhi and thought for a non violent world. According to her non violence speaks to power. She has explained "To my mind, the purpose of politics and political is to stand for the weak, for those who have no lobby or other means of exerting influence." Thus she speaks on a global scale for impoverished indigenous people and women as well as for trees, plants, animals and all the offspring of Mother Earth."She has noted economically favoured North as contrasted with the impoverished South. Amidst unprecedented threat human survival she has called for an unprecedented non violent cooperative action and creation of global culture of ecological responsibility. To all she cries out "Save the Planet". She has strongly declared that "An ecological society is a true society" Gandhi envisioned a society for strong villages, each one politically autonomous and economically self reliant. She took the inspiration from Gandhi and opined that we must work towards transforming all of our societies if we want to reach a non violent world order.

Gandhi's Impact on environmental movement in India

The environmental movements like Chipko Movement, Narmada Bachao Andolan (Save Narmada Movement) and Silent Valley Movement are the living examples of Gandhian Environmentalism. The key agenda of Chipko Movement was to carry forward the vision of Gandhi's dream of new society where neither man nor nature is exploited and destroyed. In fact, all these movements were based on conflict resolution techniques based on non violence and self sacrifice.

In 1970's a non violent movement known as Chipko Movement was a landmark event aimed at protection and conservation of the trees and forests from being destroyed. The word Chipko means "to stick" or "to embrace". On March 26, 1974 a group of female peasants in Reni village in Chamoli district, Uttarakhand, India acted together to prevent the cutting of trees and reclaim their traditional forest right. When Forest Department announced the auction of 2500 trees in the Reni Forest then Gaura Devi organized the women of that village to protect the trees from felling and forced the Government to investigate. Two years later Government placed a ban on all trees felling in the area. During Chipko Movement Sunderlal Bahuguna a noted activist coined a Chipko slogan "Ecology is a permanent economy". He said that the solution of present day problems lie in the reestablishment of harmonious relationship between man and nature. The Chipko Movement was completely non violent in nature.

Silent Valley Movement was a social movement aimed at the protection of Silent Valley, An evergreen tropical forest at Pallakad district of Kerala. It was started in 1973 to save the silent Valley Reserve Forest from being flooded by a hydroelectric project. After the announcement of dam construction the valley became the focal point of "Save Silent Valley". This undisturbed forest is home to many endemic and endangered species but it is the lion-tailed masque that has come to symbolize the Silent Valley in Kerala's Pallakad district. In Kerala ecological Marxist resorts to Gandhian way to fight environmental injustice. Kerala Sastra Sahitya Parishad (KSSP) and a renowned People's Science Movement (PSM) published their reports on ecological, economic and social impacts of the hydroelectric project Several committees have been appointed among which Dr M.S. Swaminathan Committee and MGK Menon Committee strongly opposed the project and finally the then Prime Minister Indira Gandhi advised the state to abandon the project and finally she announced Silent Valley as a National Park.

The Narmada Bachao Andolan (Save Narmada Movement) led by Medha Patkar is another example of significant satyagraha to building the dam on the Narmada river which could lead to drowning many villages. The Narmada Projects are the epitome of unsustainable development. According to Narmada Bachoa Andolan, the dams force the displacement of about a million people and affect many more, largely poor peasants and the tribals. The dam has caused huge ecological damage which mainly includes private habitats of rare species. Medha Patkar advanced the Gandhian argument that the struggle for the decentralization of power, with local people having the right to decide how their resources should be utilized. Like Medha Patkar, Baba Amte also fought for Narmada Bachao Andolan (Save Narmada Movement). Most of his life he devoted to the care and rehabilitation of leprosy patients at Anandwan but he left Anadawan with the words "I am leaving to live along the Narmada……Narmada will linger on the lips of the nation as a symbol of struggles against social injustice".

Effect of Great Thinkers on Gandhi

Gandhi as an environmentalism has been inspired by great thinkers like Confucius, Socrates, Tolstoy, Ruskin and Thoreau. Confucius, the great Chinese Philosopher always believed in harmonious combination of mind, body and soul. He believed in non violent way of life. According to him teaching of morals is the real education, and when a person is morally right he will not do anything to harm man and nature. Socrates, the Greek thinker was a soldier of truth. He said "One should never do wrong in return, nor mistreat any man; no matter how one has been mistreated by him ".He has shown the path of non violence and has taught what is virtue? What is justice? What is truth? Gandhi had great admiration for Tolstoy. In Crimean War he gave up his wealth and lived like a peasant. He was fascinated by Ruskin's" Unto the last". His Sarvodaya (upliftment of all) and Antodaya (Upliftment of the last) both are the living examples of Ruskin's contribution to Gandhi. Ruskin once said "If economic justice can provide the means of abundance for all, the final question to be answered concerns the human relationship with nature. In a remarkable setting he describes the beauty of nature in terms of human contribution-not the sublime extreme of heat and mountain but the temperate regions that are loveliest in habitation."John Ruskin was critical of industrialization and cherished pre industrial order. Henry David Thoreau whose essay on civil disobedience had influenced Gandhi believed that nature could exist without humans, a prospect that fascinated and frightened him, which eventually promoted him to focus on the relation between human being and environment (Moolakkattu, 2010).

Conclusion

Gandhi has left this world the year in 1948 but he has become immortal for his novel thinking in many directions. In his philosophy we get a clear glimpse of green Gandhi. In the 21st century when the world is facing a dark future due to environmental damage Gandhian prescription could save us all from this dooms day. Today we are in a moral dilemma that whether to grow fast or to slow down the growth. The growth of corporate culture has brought imperialism in new form. The nuclear proliferation and the threat of international terrorism both have added fuel to the fire. Globalisation, privatization, liberalization together have brought poverty, inequality and disparity. At this critical juncture we badly need this new Green Paradigm to save the humanity in 21st century. Martin Luther King Jr long back said "If humanity is to progress Gandhi is inescapable. He lived, thought and acted, inspired by the vision of humanity evolving towards a world of peace and harmony."This paradigm has provided a new vision for all to live sustainably and share Nature's resources equitably. It has preached people to live in harmony and peace and has taught us that instead of speedy economic growth we need growth in human being. For that we should respect nature and strongly believe in the philosophy of truth and non violence. Gandhi once said that "Non-violence is the greatest force at the disposal of mankind. It is mightier than the mightiest weapon of mass destruction devised by the ingenuity of man". Today we all are facing a biggest threat of destruction of planet earth on which the life depends. This paradigm will provide a new world order which is fit for today. Sam Pitroda rightly said that "Gandhi did not belong to an era, or an age. He belongs to the humanity for eternity." It is true that Gandhi has illumined the world and has given peace to innumerable hearts not only for present generation but also for the future generation too. What the world is thinking today Gandhi dreamt it long back.

References:

Louis Fisher- Gandhi- His life and Message for the World. Penguin, Group, USA 1982.

Mark. A. Lutz- Economics for the common good Routledge, London, 1998

Ajit K. Dasgupta- Gandhi's Economic Thought, Routledge, 1996

Bruce Nixon- All Rise-How Gandhi's thinking can help us in the 21st century Challenge, Chapter Schumacher Institute for Sustainable System, April 2007, No.3

Dayanidhi Parida- Challenges of 21st century and Gandhian Alternatives- Orissa Review, October 2009

Khoshoo T.N, Moolakattu, J.S- Gandhi and the Environment, Analyzing Gandhi's Environmental Thought, Tehri Press, New Delhi, 2009

Sanjay Kumar- Perspective on Gandhian Thought, Sonali Publication, 2012

Jai Narayan Sharma- Alternative Economics: Economic Thought of Mahatma Gandhi, Deep and Deep, 2012

Anil Dutta Mishra- Understanding Gandhi speeches and Writing: That Reveal his Mind, Methods and Mittion, Concept Publisher, 2012

Ramachandra Guha- Mahatma Gandhi and Environmental Movement in India, In Environmental Movement in India , Aren Kalland and Gerard Persoon (eds), Nordic Institute of Asian Studies & Routledge, 1998, pp-67

Bhikhu Parekh- Gandhi's Political Philosophy: Critical Examination, Macmillan London 1989, pp-72

E.F Schumacher- Small is Beautiful: A chapter of Economic as if people Mattered, Vintage Books, 2011, pp. 18

Arae Naess: Self Realization: An Ecological Approach to being in the World, In Thinking Like a Mountain: Towards a Council of All Being, Jone seed and Joanaa Maey (eds), Philadelphia: Society Publishers, 1988

Sasikala A.S- Environmental Thoughts of Gandhi for a Green Future, http://www.mkgandhi.org/articles/green_future.htm,   Accessed   on- 14/04/2014

Vandana Shiva and Jayonto Bandopadhyay- "Chipko in India's Civilization Response to the Forest Crisis", In India's Environment: Myth and Reality, Dehra Dun: Natraj, 2007, pp. 21

John S. Moolakkattu, Gandhi as a Human Ecologist, *Journal of Human Ecology*, 29 (3), 2010, pp-151-158

Photo: Odeta Grabauskaitė

Photos: Indira Dutta

Part 7: Green Economics: Aims and Features

7.1 Ten Key Values of Green Economics

By Miriam Kennet, Jeffrey Turk, Ben Armstrong–Haworth & Michelle S. Gale de Oliveira

The ten key values of Green Economics have been defined as follows:
1. Green economics aims to provision for the needs of all people everywhere, other species, nature, the planet and its systems, all as beneficiaries of economics transactions, not as throw away inputs.
2. This is all underpinned by social and environmental justice, tolerance, no prejudice and creating quality of life for everyone including future generations and all the current generations, including older and younger people.
3. Ensuring and respecting other species and their rights. Ending the current mass extinction of species. Ensuring biodiversity.
4. Non violence and inclusion of all people everywhere, including people with special needs and special abilities. Ensuring all nations have equal access to power and resources. Local people having control over their own destiny and resources. Increasing life expectancy, human welfare and per capita GDP in the least developed countries.
5. Ensuring gender equity in all activities. Educating, respecting, empowering women and minorities.
6. Ending current high mass consumption and overshoot of the planet's resources and returning to live within the comfortable bounds of nature in the climatic conditions under which humans built their civilisation. Choosing lifestyle changes over techno-fixes and eco-technology. Lowering our own carbon usage and living lightly on the earth. Changing how economics is done: from being an abstract mathematical exercise to embracing realism and the real world we all live in and share and in which we are all concerned stakeholders.
7. Valuing and respecting all people equally.

8. Poverty prevention. Climate change and instability prevention, adaptation, mitigation. Protecting the most vulnerable from risk. Ensuring the future of small island states.

9. Quickly reducing carbon per capita globally to 2 tonnes in the next 5 years and zero soon after. Limiting and reversing climate change. Moving to renewable energy sources.

10. Building a future-proofed economics to solve the current economic uncertainty and downturn which is suitable for the 21st century. Creating and nurturing an economy based on sharing, rather than greed and profit. Completely reshaping and reforming current economics to do all the above.

7.2 Green Economics:
Its Recent Development and Background

By Miriam Kennet and Michelle S. Gale de Oliveira

1. Introduction

a) Increasing interest in Green Economics and the Green Economy

Ban Ki Moon General Secretary of the United Nations, said that "We are living in an age of Global Transformation, an Age of Green Economics."

There has been a dramatic increase in interest in environmental and green economics and the transformation towards Green Jobs and a Green Economy.

Partly in response to concerns about unprecedented and rapidly accelerating anthropogenic climate change there are worries that "the very survival of the human species is at risk." We are also living in the 6th ever mass extinction of other species that the earth has ever experienced, (IUCN) with many mammals, fish and birds under threat. A growing population predicted at 9 billion, means the poor are more directly dependent than ever directly on the ecosystem, and geo political instability is becoming more common. Inequalities between people, within and between nations, and between present and future generations as well as social and environmental injustices are now significantly affecting the world economy. The bundle of natural capital resources, (forests, productive seas, agricultural land, healthy soil, air and water, food resources, rainforests) we can leave to future generations may actually be smaller than those of today. Climate change and sea level rise mean that current and future generations may inherit a world in which there will be less land available for cultivation or habitation, as well as depletion of forests, bleaching of coral reefs, protective mangrove swamps and other resources of all kinds including viable fish stocks or productive oceans. Massive dead zones are appearing in the sea and increasing desertification and soil erosion and declining forests and whole Ecosystems services are declining and the economy will be under threat.

b) People and institutions are looking for alternative solutions and innovation in economics

The current economic crisis has exposed deficiencies of mainstream economic concepts and the creation of new ones. These include for example by Paul Krugman in the USA and Stiglitz and Sen and Green National Accounting from President Sarkozy in France and McGlade at the European Environment Agency and more fundamental changes in economic thinking. Ecological economics (Daly) introduces absolute limits on "more is better than less." The mainstream regarded ecology related decision-making as having infinite natural boundaries, and simply aggregated human behaviour and "optimal" solutions from it. If the air or sea is so polluted that they can't sustain life, or the soil removed, or we have passed certain thresh holds or tipping points from which the natural systems can't recover, green economists propose doing different things, rather than substitution of one raw material with another. Standard neo-liberal economics models are insufficient for today's issues and are in urgent need of not only a major overhaul and has become "unfit for purpose," but also need replacing.

c) The broadening of scope and the arrival of "Inclusion" in economics

According to traditional market explanations *the invisible hand*" (Adam Smith) mechanism ensures that everyone benefits from the investment and activities of homo economicus or "rational economic man" and his spending preferences and choices. In spite of arising from selfish aims, they are presumed to benefit the whole of society. Most people on the planet are not white western educated wealthy men and cannot choose how to earn a living or how or become wealthy. So the absolute hegemony of markets is being fundamentally questioned in all its aspects: from the need to separate investment from savings banking, to its ability to solve climate change and its ability to solve the problem of poverty for which absolute as well as relative evels continue to rise. Similarly the role of "homo economicus" in the collapse of for example Icelandic banks, has led to laws to increasing the number of women at the helm or are brought into corporate board rooms and   to correct long standing imbalances of power, representation and wealth between men and women.

d) Mainstream economics solutions have reached a crossroads

Human economic development has always relied on technological advancement to address challenges in the past. So the switch from fossil fuels to biofuels to allow for the continuation of current transport modes, as business as usual, was a logical step which was fully embraced by large companies and large trading blocks such as the European Union. However, this competition over land uses and pushed up the price of fuel, caused a scarcity of land for dwellings, and food   riots all over the world, creating more poverty and land price spikes. This increasing investment and speculation culminated in the bursting of the   "bubble economy" and a complete collapse of land prices in several countries leading to a serious economic downturn. It has ended the economic period called the "Great Moderation" and we are now in a period called "The Great Contraction."

e) Vulnerability of the economy to Global environmental change: the example of Italy

In common with many other places today, the OECD has warned that the economy of Italy in common with several other countries is particularly vulnerable to the economics effects of global environmental change. There are changes in the climate, leading to health effects of encroaching tropical vegetation, "Alien Species" invasion, malaria and dengue fever reappearing. The warming world is causing sea level rise and affecting specific environments such as the city of Venice and its lagoon and many other coastal towns and in other countries whole small island states may disappear.

The increase in temperature is causing micro climate environments, leading to more warming in certain Alpine Regions, upsetting watersheds and the available Hydroelectric Power which drive the economy and industry. In particular the warming has led to melting of the glaciers, leading to the re-emergence of "Oetzee the Ice Man" for the first time in 5000 years. These changes are affectng tourism as the mountain tops are no longer snow covered. The rich agricultural traditions such as wine, apples and meat may be damaged in South Tyrol. Slope instability, caused by changes in water courses and other global environmental changes, has meant more train derailments in mountain areas too such as occurred this year in Bolzano. A transformation in the role of the car has led to large scale shut downs of car factories in the south and bans on using cars on certain days in larger Italian cities. Agriculture has to cope with advancing climate change and in general species moving northwards in the northern hemisphere according to some studies by up to an observed 5 metres per year. Plankton in the sea are moving significantly northwards affected by increasing acidification in the sea. In Italy tourism, a significant part of the economy, is threatened by the encroachment of a warmer tropical world, replacing it as a reliable and comfortable Mediterranean attraction and as a ski and winter walking holiday destination. The rapidly expanding Green Economy is particularly useful in offering the hope of Green Jobs and the crefation of 1000s of new ones to create a more sustainable economy.

f) Mainstreaming Environmental and Green Economics

The climate and biodiversity crisis solutions evolve into a blueprint for leading the world in the Green Economy . Solving the complex mesh of social and environmental justice is included in all aspects of Green Economics thinking, as are the costs and effects of climate change on the world economy. For example, the Stern Review of the Economics of Climate Change (2007) showed that spending up to 1% of GDP (recently corrected to 2%) would actually be a cheaper option than allowing runaway climate change to persist. The TEEB Report in 2010 by Sukhdev has done similar work in highlighting the even higher costs of biodiversity loss as we are now causing the 6th ever mass species extinction. For example, bee colonies are disappearing due to microwave disturbance to their navigation systems from mobile phones, and the cost of hand pollination (already happening in China) of crops would be catastrophic in the west. Einstein said that once the bees disappear humans will only have another 4 years to survive on the planet. Green Economics is an interdisciplinary science; on the one hand it is concerned with the theory and practical management of Global Environmental Change in all its aspects and on the other with the development Economics providing provisioning, sharing and distribution of the wealth of nature and human and naturally occurring resources. It is a developing progressive holistic approach which cannot be explained by simplistic, typically linear mathematics and fixed preferences of individuals. It extends beyond ecological issues to wider considerations of ideology, history of thought, evolution of society, the level of objectivity and the time specificity of solutions in a social science environment to be taken into account. These provide a much stronger basis to criticize and replace current reductionist mainstream economics. It embraces a wider set of values, including but not exclusively ecological values.

2. The arrival of Green Economics

a) Green Economics Strategies for addressing current crises

The Green Economy Initiative of the United Nations (2008) describes the crises as "Fs", Food, Fuel and Finance" and advocates a more growthist solution and the Lisbon 2020 Agenda also suggests Smart, Green, Growth is possible and desirable. A Green Economics perspective instead regards the crisis as a mixture of the current economics downturn, a crisis of poverty, climate change and biodiversity loss and proposes a composite set of solutions. These consist of a mixture of market instruments, such as carbon trading under the Kyoto Protocol, regulation, carbon quotas or even rationing of carbon use,as well as technological innovations and green developments. It advocates, most of all, a change in public attitudes and reduction in unnecessary consumption of the earth's resources and individual carbon footprints and for *life style changes*. A progressive holistic approach extends beyond ecological issues to wider considerations of ideology, history of thought, evolution of society, the level of objectivity and the time specificity of solutions. The European Greens propose that the economy must adapt to what the natural environment can tolerate, aiming for ecological sustainability, equity and social justice as well as self-reliance of local and regional economies, encouraging a true sense of community, based on democracy, transparency, gender equality and the right of all people to express themselves and participate fully in decision-making.

b) Environmental Economics

Environmental economics aims to factor in the costs of activities and impacts external, to a particular economics transaction. Market failure, its central concept, means that markets fail to allocate resources efficiently and this occurs when the market does not allocate scarce resources to generate the greatest social welfare. The best and most famous example is that of climate change in the Stern review. Biodiversity loss is also as serious, if not even more costly. The previous discipline of Environmental Economics has quite a main stream framework and does not specifically change activities or prevent impacts and only aims to simply find out how much things cost. Although useful information, it will not change what is done. It so omits the point that other options are available, or reassessing what is actually required. Similarly surveys are used to establish "Willingness To Pay," for its existence of a species, or its conservation or to visit a natural amenity for an environmental benefit popularised by David Pearce are often used for example in deciding on the fate of a natural amenity such as whether to conserve a species. The Stern Review proposes introducing a price for carbon, REDDS -debt for nature swaps and Carbon Storage and Sequestration and Discounting the future.

Common Property Rights are another concern first identified in this context by Coase and Hardin. When it is too costly to exclude people from accessing a contested environmental resource, market allocation is likely to be inefficient. Hardin's (1968) The Tragedy of the Commons popularized the challenges involved in non-exclusion and common property. "commons" refers to the environmental asset itself. Hardin theorizes that in the absence of restrictions, users of an open-access resource will use it more than if they had to pay for it and had exclusive rights and thus will often cause environmental degradation. Ostrom (1990) won the Nobel Prize this year for work on how people using real common property resources do establish self-governing rules to reduce this risk.

c) Ecological Economics

Ecological economics moves towards the primary role of energy and the laws of thermodynamics and energy flows and democratic decision making as subsets of the natural environment in its discourse. Ecological economics includes the chapter of the flows of energy, and materials and material flows and ecosystem services that enter and exit the economic system. For the first time we have a change to the core concepts and a move towards the human economy as a subset of the natural world. Ecological Economics now is being used in global institutions. Use and non use value for measuring costs of Ecosystems services degradation are being used for example by the United Nations.

320

d)   The Renaissance of Economics; the Green Economy rediscovers the roots of economics

Green Economics works in what it terms the four pillars of scope or activity, namely-1. Political and policy making, 2. academia especially science and economics, 3. business and 4. civil society including NGOs and most recently adding in a fifth, the general public and consumers. Everyone and everything on the planet is acknowedged to have economics or provisioning requirements to achieve desired optimal conditions. Green Economics describes itself as "Reclaiming Economics, for all people everywhere, nature, other species, the planet and its systems. " As a result even the volcanic activity which cost European Economies dearly this year, was able to be incorporated. For example it has been discovered that allowing the glaciers and ice caps to melt will increase seismic activity. The earth has a self regulatory mechanism, Gaia Theory by James Lovelock which controls the temperature at 14 degrees centigrade. Too much warming and the volcanoes erupt cooling down the planet. Too much cooling and the ice sheets form pressing down the magma and preventing earth quakes!

Green Economics a participatory approach is a development which   includes natural science data and works with it, as many of its teams are physicists and natural scientists who also have economics qualifications, so it is able to weld both natural and social science together. It is at core multi- disciplinary, and inter – disciplinary and pluralist and its decisions are based on the twin imperatives of human and natural science futures. It fully accepts that we all inhabit the earth anddethere is no economy outside of it. It reflects the current knowledge about the complexity of reality. It is characterised by a holistic perspective, the involvement of nature, and is very inclusive. It has evolved from a complete and fundamental philosophical renaissance of the origins of economics from the Greek Word oikia- meaning household or estate management, now evolved to   meaning the *earth*. The "oikonomia" -of Xenophon is now the economics and provisioning for the needs of all people everywhere, nature other species, the planet and its systems and also of the "Good life" of Aristotle.

3. The Cultural, Institutional, Academic Umbrella and Positioning of the Green Economy and its Chronology

a) The Transformation of Economics Disciplines and Schools of Thought

Under the Heterodox Economics Umbrella, are found   alternative,   holistic interdisciplinary,pluralistic set of methodologies and contributions. Pigou (1920) working on external effects and Coase examining the role of property rights. The USA and the UK struggle to decide who is liable for BP 's huge oil spill in American waters. The debate is evolving into a robust economics school or discipline and widening the scope of an alternative economic framework further, into Environmental economics by authors such as Hartwick and Solow, Ciracy Wantrup, Daly, Tietenberg, Markandya,

Pearce, Boulding, Jacob, Hillman, Ekins, Chichilnisky) and Ecological Economics (Soderbaum, Daly, Martinez- Alier).

Green Economics is influencing the economic debate and transforming existing policies and decision-making. 'Green' and Writers include Kennet, Heinemann, Hillman, Ekins, Reardon, Porrit, Gale de Oliveira, Dobson, Anderson, Barry, Reardon, Rao and Turk and Jociute..

A rapidly growing branch of economics, Green Economics is spreading into policy development in governments for example the Korean Government and also in Global Institutions such as the United Nations and the International Labour Organisations and the OECD. Each of these has a Green Economy Initiative or a Green Jobs Programme. Green Economics is being taught in Universities around the world and is also featured by the Dow Jones and Wall Street. The Green Economics Institute was founded in 2003 and its academic journal, *The International Journal of Green Economics* founded in 2005. Its background is in the "Green movement " hence a strong policy orientation combined with Economics Heterodoxy, as well as Environmental Science and Global Environmental Change and Management. The discipline builds on enlightenment ideas of reason and rights, post-modern ideas of different and power struggles and elites, and Malthusian limits to growth and the search for sustainability, and on eco-feminism. The Enlightenment brought a major impact on modern understandings of economics and the role of humanity in the natural world. However it tended to look for logic and reason rather than wisdom in nature, as Bacon explains : "The human mind which overcomes superstition is to hold sway over a disenchanted nature. What men want to learn from nature is how to use it in order to wholly dominate it and other men. That is the only aim." The backlash against 10 000 years of the domestication of animals, plants and women and the colonies is in full swing within Green Economics. So it is the acknowledgement that the quest for domination is over.

Green Economics argues that nature has its own intrinsic and existence value and extends this value to all life forms, (*Deep Ecology* by Arnae Naess) and thus seeks toreform economics to "provision for all people everywhere, all other species, the biosphere, systems, and planet." It is sometimes part of a broader ideology, sometimes part of Buddhist economics (Welford, Guenter Wagner 2006) advocating de-centralist, non materialist, and co-operative values and the concept of "enoughness" or sufficiency is important, as well as leaving enough resources for future generations. One key development was the book "Silent Spring" by Rachel Carson which exposed the effects of DDT and the practices of the chemical industry and the relationship between the economy, industry , the environment and our over all well being.

b) Sustainable Development Economics

Another important key development was the Sustainable Development Economics, developed by Professor Graciela Chichilnisky, and our Common Future which addressed this area of futurity In 1987. the United Nations World Commission on Environment and Development (UNCED) issued the Brundtland Report, defining sustainable development as meeting "the needs of the present without compromising the ability of the future to meet its needs." Sustainable Development economics gives equal weight to economics, environment and social aspects.

c) Green Economics as Practice

The Green Economy has been called the Economics of Sharing the earth and its economy amongst ourselves but also with other species and systems of the planet in addition but not exclusively also to ensure it remains hospitable for us and our way of life. It is also the economics of doing and is intensely practical. For example this means that there is much focus on green supply chains and Green Economics & procurement with the aim of creating social and environmental justice. It also advocates greener transport methods and slower local smaller scale production, even with slow travel and more train travel, slow food and degrowth to keep withing the earth's Carrying Capacity. It advocates *"Reduce, Reuse, Recycle, Repair, Restore, Relax, Recover"*

Green IT

The role of IT, once hailed as the ultimate saviour, is now regarded as a significant cause of climate change and so there is a move to decouple the big monopolies such as Microsoft and move towards more community owned human style, open source IT – and to limiting the carbon usage of server farms, saving carbon by virtualisation, using recylced and also recycling materials and managing and limiting the power usage much more.

Environmental and social dumping and checking for green and transparent supply chains

Large outsourcing of environmental and social standards to where they can't be seen (called dumping) is coming to an end. Equity, social and environmental justice are acknowledged as providing attractive competitive advantage in a modern economy.

Green Jobs

Increasing numbers of jobs are being created in this vast and innovative transformation- this green economy. The Green Jobs Initiative of the United Nations and the International Labour Organisation and the International Federation of Trades Union describes a green job as *"work in agricultural, manufacturing, research and development (R&D), administrative, and service activities that contribute(s) substantially to preserving or restoring environmental quality. Specifically, but not exclusively, this includes jobs that help to protect ecosystems and biodiversity; reduce energy, materials, and water consumption through high efficiency strategies; de-carbonize the economy; and minimize or altogether avoid generation of all forms of waste and pollution."* A Green Economics perspective of a Green Job is anything that is sustainable and contributes to social and environmental justice.

4. Instruments and Tools in Green and Environmental Economics

a) Geo engineering and Green Technologies

The use of technological solutions (also called Eco technology or Geo engineering or Technical Fixes). These include, solar radiation management, iron fertilisation of the sea, stratospheric aerosols, sucking carbon using giant artificial tree scrubbers, albedo management, air capture, urban albedo and algal-based CO_2 capture schemes, Carbon Storage, Sequestration or Capture. There is increasing concern with the idea that "Unintended Consequences" could occur if for example we seed the clouds as the Chinese Government has done this year to create rain or we use Sulphur Aerosol Particles to mimic the action of volcanoes in cooling the global climate. The "Precautionary Principle" is a major feature of a green economy which advises against trying untested technology. This would for example be used to prevent the kind of the oil spill or engineering at great depth without a clear strategy for clean up by BP. The change to green technologies involves the use of Rare Earth Materials, which are nearly all mined in China. Significantly this year, China ceased exporting them in order to supply its own home market and so made the production of green technologies more expensive and more difficult. "Local Production for Local Needs" will mean that the private car will be slowly replaced by modern and attractive lower carbon public transport, including car clubs, car-sharing, more cycling, and train travel. Governments introduced a green Car Scrapage scheme to encourage purchases of new cars. Greener alternatives such as slow travel are taking off, and train-travel is once again fashionable. Slow travel, slow cities, and the Italian idea of slow food are gaining in popularity. Lower carbon economies are now actively being created, to combat the current average of 10 tonnes carbon equivalent usage in Europe, 25 tonnes in the USA, 5 in China, and 1 in Africa. Policies include "Contraction and Convergence" firstly to limit each person's carbon to 2 tonnes of carbon equivalent per year, secondly to equalise global economies. Additionally, the acceleration of melting permafrost and the release of catastrophic amounts of methane would set in motion rapid climate change and sea level rise. Mainstream fossil fuel dependence has unacceptable costs, including pollution damage to fisheries and geopolitical struggles over supply chains from Russia to the Middle East. Fossil fuels are being replaced by microgeneration, Renewables and SMART grids, (linking areas of high wind to areas of high solar availability) more self sufficiency. Local and micro generation of energy is possible with Feed in Tariffs introduced in Germany and the UK.

b) Changes in attitudes to energy production and use: Lower carbon economies

British Petrol (BP)'s Deepwater Horizon oil drilling leak in the USA is an example of how the role of oil and fossil fuels in the economy is starting to be acknowledged as a limiting factor and is being questioned. Roughly 10 per cent of UK pension funds are linked up with BP and so the cancellation of the dividend from BP has deeply affected the UK economy but the oil spill has affected the economy of the US ruining for example fisheries but also coastal tourism and wildlife. The cost of oil is also a feature of the much criticised Iraq war too which reduced public acceptability of the costs of our current life style and how the idea of freedom, liberty and nonviolence fits with the idea of safe energy supplies from hostile, undemocratic or unstable regimes. Additionally there have been concerns about the effect of CO_2 use on climate and the acceptance that the 20th century economy was characterised by mass-production and economies of scale, ending the century with huge outsourced supply chains in human conditions for workers.

c) Carbon trading and market solutions Climate crisis : Kyoto Protocol and the Copenhagen Conference COP15

The Kyoto Protocol, (a market-based attempt to trade carbon to solve climate change), held its regular Conference of the Parties Conference in Copenhagen COP15 in December 2009. It received unprecedented interest, and over 40 000 people and most of the world's Heads of State flocked there. Small island states would disappear unless climate change is stabilised at an agreed at 1.5 degrees of warming. Other more powerful countries decided to ask for costs of stabilisation of the climate at 2 degrees of warming. The huge response led to an actual failure of the Conference as the organisers UNFCC were completely overwhelmed with the level of interest people showed in limiting climate change. Lord Stern said that "Climate Change was the biggest market failure the world had ever seen." Although he continues to remain within the market mechanisms promoting ever more growth as a solution, green economics tries to solve the climate problems by looking beyond only market mechanisms. Main stream Economics methods have to some extent relied on Cost Benefit Analysis and Discounting The Future but in a world where future resources may be depleted, and a weaker economy we should be doing the reverse. What is needed is to do different things differently.

d) Environmental Taxes and Regulations

An external effect was defined by Arrow as a "a situation in which a private economy lacks sufficient incentives to create a potential market in some good, and the nonexistence of this market results in the loss of efficiency." Externalities are examples of Market Failures in which the unfettered market does not lead to an efficient outcome, such as the costs of clean up of an oil spill, or the raising of the climate by fossil fuel use, or wastes collected and treated and can include energy products, transport equipment and transport services, as well as measured or estimated emissions to air and water, ozone depleting substances, certain non-point sources of water pollution, waste management and noise, in addition to the management of water, land, soil, forests, biodiversity, wildlife and fish stocks and on unleaded petrol and the fuels efficiency and climate change impacts of vehicles, the CO_2 emissions per km.

e) Regulations

The current economic crisis was caused in part by deregulation of the banking system which had separated casino banking or speculation in investment banking from that of the savings of the small investor. Regulation is a cornerstone of a green economy. Some of which include: REACH Directive on Hazardous Chemicals and the WEEE Directive on recycling of components for electronic equipment when purchasing electrical or electronic equipment, batteries and accumulators.

f) The Green New Deal – Keynsian Investment

Very popular with UNEP and with the Greens and with governments, implemented by the UN and by the Korean Government and many others using a Keynsian stimulus package to pump money into the economy and targeting it towards green innovations and sustainable projects. The age of stimulus projects is now over as the big clean up starts and frugality and living within our contemporary means is the order of the day.

5. The Broader Background of the Green Economy – Changes in Focus in Economics Today

a) The Limits to Growth

There is an increasing realization that we may have reached what has been termed the "limits to growth." We are brushing up against the finite limits to the earth's adaptability and its "carrying capacity" in the face of our human and continual onslaught on sustainable the climatic conditions, and use of resource assets have "overshot" beneficial levels. A green economics perspective argues that empowered and educated female citizens decrease population size faster while increasing a country's GDP. Some even suggest that overall "equity is the price of survival."

b) Prosperity without Growth

Currently gaining popularity, Prosperity Without Growth dialogues are spreading around Europe, and a fashionable Degrowth Movement has originated in France, promotes the kind of Steady State Economy envisaged by John Stuart Mill. Rather than being seen as a failed attempt at growth, Growth by Design is gaining in interest, if not in acceptance. This is partly a result of growth actually stalling in many Western

Countries and the realisation that growth above 2 tonnes of carbon equivalent per person is no longer a good long term proposition. The European Environment Agency and many other institutions are working on this and other aspects of Green Accounting and Indicators. In particular important benchmarks are progress towards the Millennium Development Goals, and the Millennium Ecosystems Services Assessment Goals, The GRI for measuring Corporate Social Responsibility, (O' Carrol) the GINI Co- efficient index,The HDI Human Development Index, the Happiness Index from the State of Bhutan and many other sustainability and social indicators as well as measurements of unemployment, trade deficit and sovereign debt. Since WW2 there has been an economics policy of encouraging high mass consumption but this has begun to be questioned. Conspicuous consumption is going out of fashion and we are moving into an age of more austerity and rebalancing. Commodity prices are fluctuating and there is a global economic downturn, large sovereign debt and rising unemployment all over Europe. Many countries and national institutions are exploring a green economy as the one ray of hope in this rather bleak landscape. The European Commission believes that this green technology will drive competitive advantage, and encourages green venture capital and Smart, Inclusive, Green, Growth as part of the Lisbon Agenda.

Conclusion

The Transformation into the Age of Green Economics is a very exciting period of economics innovation, offering choices of strategies from right across the spectrum. Much has happened in terms both of the evolution of Green Economics, Green Jobs and a much more effective economics system. It has spread as an important driver from Korea to the EU and as an important aspect of decision making such as in the successor to the deep sea oil spill. Environmental, ecological and green economics are all playing their part in this process as we move towards the development of an economics for the 21st century- an Age of global transformation- An age of the widely predicted 4th Industrial revolution, decarbonising our economies and working to enhance the future not to discount it! *A previous version of this chapter was first published in Encyclopedia Trecanni (in Italian), in 2010.*

References and supporting tables are available on request.

7.3 The Greening of Global Finance:

Re-Conceptualizing, Reforming and Reclaiming Finance for Resilience, Survivability and Sustainability in the 21st and 22nd Centuries

By Professor Maria Alejandra Madi and Miriam Kennet

Introduction

Finance, central banks and treasuries

During the last thirty years, most governments around the world have supported the long-run process of financial expansion that turned out to be characterized as the "financialization" of the capitalist economy (Foster, 2009). In this historical scenario, monopoly-finance capital became increasingly dependent on bubbles that, both in credit and capital markets, proved to be global sources of endogenous financial fragility. Financial and currency crises have also revealed that monetary and supervisory authorities have not coped with the complexity of the global, profit-seeking, innovative and speculative portfolios of investors and banks. Central banks, in a context of financial liberalization, have not faced these financial disturbances easily. Indeed, the credit squeeze, volatility in the valuation of assets, the menace of recession, the shift of investors toward liquid and safe assets, among other factors, have put unprecedented pressure on central banks and treasuries.

Central banks´ actions are no longer independent from private and public pressures. There are social and political tensions inherent in the current crisis: the impacts on livelihood conditions, the loss of social cohesion and the subordination of society to the bailouts of the financial systems are leading to social unrest, protests and attempted revolution! The increasing growth of sovereign-debts imposes the adoption of government austerity programs that mainly rely on taxpayers. As a result, the social tensions that have emerged within the markets have been shifted to the political sphere and are challenging the role of money as a public good.

Finance and Western societies

The failure of such speculation is then paid for not by investors but by the public. For ordinary people this is a disaster. They, who frequently have no shares, or savings, nor insurance against such eventualities, found suddenly that the quality of their lives, sometimes their entire lives or careers, has been deeply affected. For example, young people, when they first enter the job market, if they fail to find a job, or can't afford to pay the "investment bundle price" for their education, then their potential economic and career trajectory is severely restricted. This system in the West is causing the baby boomers, who had saved up enough money for a comfortable retirement, to spend all of it and more on their children's education. Education has traditionally been regarded as the state's cost to create a viable and competitive future workforce. Failing to provide this state service will undermine the very power of that state in the future because western countries will not be able to ensure a vibrant and viable work force now and in the future.

This issue is the single most important factor we are seeing in the flip from the hegemony of the West, especially Europe, to the hegemony of the East. The East invests very heavily in its children's and young people's education and future. Instead, the West spends its public money effectively repaying investors, banks and large corporations and institutions which have lost money in the global casino. Rather than for education, the public purse is now used to pay instead for wars designed to bolster large energy multinationals, the arms industry and private construction industry companies.

Against this background, large companies now engage their workers in what has been termed a "neo-feudal" relationship with those workers. This process, and the issuing of zero hours contracts, strips out the social advances and gains of the 19th and 20th century, turning back the clock by outsourcing and dumping any of the human, environmental and social rights of workers or even resources. Workers are now reduced to seeking temporary or insecure employment, even at the highest levels. We know of one such flexi security contract even at the international labour organization itself.

The twentieth century western assumptions of the moral right of workers to be looked after and to have security has been removed. This is occurring at the same time as the twentieth century western assumption of the moral right of young people to have their education paid for by the state has been removed and finally the twentieth century assumption of the moral right of citizens to have healthcare paid for by the state is being eroded.

329

Air and water are basic "commons resources" and a Nobel prize was given to Elenor Olstrom for her work theorising the commons. The Thatcherite liberalization of banking and state assets, such as telecoms and airlines, has now led to the financialisation of almost every public service imaginable, leading to a substantial reduction in the scope of activities of many states.

Attempts to theorise public ownership of these " commons" assets is unfortunately too late and they have nearly all been sold off, out of reach of citizens, and into permanent contracts. Almost all these assets are now owned by large corporations and traded. Even water, is traded as " an asset bundle" between huge contemporary superpowers with absolutely no moral or psychological connection or care for the vital contents of those bundles, even if they contain the water of millions of people who need to drink it. This astonishing situation is not only happening in poor developing countries but it is happening even in the West, in the main stream hitherto wealthy country, for example in the UK, the land of Queen Victoria and at the Heart of the former Empire. The descendants of her empire have voluntarily sold off their right to even own any of their own drinking water. This right, and the sale, has not gone to the citizen owners of that water but simply to the private large corporations, with no particular requirement to keep it safe and pure. Instead they have sold it on, and their Directors and some shareholders pocketed the enormous but one time profits.

This robbing of ordinary citizens of all their basic assets turns back the gains made against the so called "robber barrons" since about the 1300s, and replaces a country's wealth back into the hands of a small elite, who are then able to profit and speculate further to make huge amounts of money. Men, who are already hugely wealthy and powerful, make even more profits with common goods. The literature terms this process as "neo imperialism" when it was observed in the developing world. It was never discussed as a phenomena going on in England itself. If we take an historical perspective, this kind of process marks a huge regression of the social gains made over 800 years!

In addition to this lack of commitment on the part of contemporary Western states to social goals, the belief in autonomous monetary management has collapsed under the 2008 global financial crisis. Since the 1980s, the so called New Consensus Macroeconomic (Arestis, 2009), founded on the belief in the potential of the self-regulated markets to promote economic growth, turned out to favor financial accumulation and social exclusion. In this scenario, central banks and treasuries have lost the space and the will to maneouvre to promote financial stability and inclusive growth. Finance is not just related to management techniques, procedures or product phenomena but involves institutions, behaviours and policies. In a monetary economy, according to Keynes (1936), money, as the institution that is the foundation of the exchange system, is a link between the present and the future. The existence of a monetary economy of production is founded on credit relations, organized markets of financial assets, speculation and uncertainty. There is a set of interrelated balance sheets and cash flows among income-producing companies, households and banks. As Keynes highlighted, the tensions between money as a public good, issued by central banks, and money as a private good, created by banks, is inherent in the capitalist institutional set up. As a result of these tensions, trust is crucial in finance. Indeed, the foundations of trust are conventional, that is to say, socially and historically built. However, risk is inherent to finance, as Bagehot warned in his classical book *Lombard Street*:

"The peculiar essence of our banking system is an unprecedented trust between man and man: and when that trust is much weakened by hidden causes, a small accident may greatly hurt it, and a great accident for a moment may almost destroy it." (Bagehot, 1873, Chapter VI)

Finance, banks and the business cycle

Finance fosters the capital accumulation process that develops through time and involves credit contracts. Taking a Keynesian perspective, Hyman Minsky (1991) argued that finance could be apprehended in a changing historical framework where arise tensions between regulation and the strategies of innovative profit-seeking banks. Financial innovations impact upon banks' assets, liabilities, and capital. As a result, they could provoke sudden changes in market dynamics and financial stability. Indeed, in a context of uncertainty and speculation, the tensions between money as a public and as a private good, overwhelms central banks' actions, as we are seeing in the current bail-outs.

Considering the non-neutral role of finance through the business cycle, post-Keynesian economics emphasizes that financial instability relies on endogenous-driven fluctuations of credit and money supply. Minsky (1986) developed a financial instability hypothesis which states that financial crises happened to be recurrent in the capitalist economy after financial deregulation. In his own words, "*..it is finance that acts as the, sometimes dampening, sometimes amplifying, governor of investment. As a result finance sets the pace of investment*" (Minsky 1975:130). From his perspective, in a monetary economy, credit relations, speculation and uncertainty decisively affect the investment path, leading to endogenous credit crunches. In other words, growing investment puts pressure on the demand for funding – a function of bankers' expectation of future incomes. Increased investment and consumption leads to higher profit rates and present value of capital assets. Credit booms intensify while liquidity preference declines and, as a result, the resulting portfolios turn out to be extremely vulnerable to changes in interest rates, asset prices, credit strategies and monetary policies. When profits decline, as they inevitably do, credit and external sources of funding generally become restricted.

If we look at the current global economic downturn in terms of the lessons learned from Minsky, we can observe that the most important characteristics of this crisis arose from the activities of the financial sector. The recent American financial crisis, for example, has revealed how banks encouraged speculative and Ponzi portfolios, which were dependent not only on the future price of housing and securitized assets but also on the renewal of households' lending operations.

As Bagehot (1873) clearly said: *banks trade money*. In the current financial scenario, the interconnections between credit and capital markets foster the growth of banks' and institutional investors' assets. The other side of the "coin" shows higher corporate leverage and household debt. As a result, all of society has been subordinated to the trading of private money.

Finance and business models

In a Green Economics approach to finance, it is especially important to understand this current global challenge. The process of financial deregulation has been added to by new investment and consumption patterns, while government social and infrastructure spending has become increasingly restricted by policy rules based on surplus targets. Indeed, changes in the distribution of income, wealth and power have affected labor and working conditions. Consumers have expanded their spending as a result of banking policies implemented by governments under the auspices of the World Bank. Additionally, corporate decision making has been increasingly subordinated to speculative financial commitments (Minsky, 1975). A financial conception of investment has increased in the context where financial innovations aimed to achieve fast growth with lower capital requirements and could be used by managers to favor short-term financial performance (Fligstein, 2001). Managers and owners of firms have privileged short-term financial performance and shareholder value. Changes in corporate ownership, through waves of mergers and acquisitions, have created new business models where companies turn out to be simply bundles of assets and liabilities to be traded. Hence the services companies provide even for health, education, care in old age, energy, heating, lighting, our food, our farming, our grain, our basic needs and, our water- the very "staff" of life, have all been turned into bundles of assets and liabilities to be traded, without a care for the terrible dangers that this poses to survivability, sustainability or resilience of " civilization" or us as human beings or our welfare. The staple crops of grain and rice have been patented and are "owned" by large agribusiness and should these companies fail then we might well fail as a species!

Hence, current corporate governance has come to have the privilege of mobility, liquidity and short-term profits based on high levels of debt. Along with these new business strategies, new perspectives on social reproduction have been driven by short-term profits and competition. Mergers and acquisitions have subordinated ownership changes, financial restructuring and company efficiency. In truth, working conditions have been constantly reorganized and reconfigured by finance. Finance has fostered systemic contradictions and tensions in both social and political spheres (Chesnais, 1996).

Finance, patterns of consumption and the planet

The only way investors can obtain a profit from this set up, is to require ever increasing growth from companies and in share values. They also require that this happens in the short term, in fact the very short term, usually within companies, month by month or at least year by year growth figures as almost the sole measure of success. To achieve this, sales must be created by people consuming ever faster and ever more goods, even if they don't want them. This never ending consumption has been stimulated artificially by credit and the very successful advertising industry. Even the term "Green Consumption" is a misnomer. To be "Green," we need to actually reduce the overall level of consumption and the overall level of impacts on the environment. For example, designing "green aeroplanes" might make us feel virtuous but the most green thing to do is to abandon our short term holiday flight and get on the train, bicycle, coach, or walk, or rather holiday nearer home. Reduction in mileage is probably the greenest option!

But we as a species and particularly our Western "civilization" have evolved in a very specific set of climatic, planetary cycles and conditions in the last interglacial, and no one knows if we can cope with significant future changes. Nor indeed do we know if our agriculture and our economy can cope with a catastrophic loss of underpinning conditions and resources.

Further in a world of finite resources, and severe environmental challenges, actually we need people to slow down and to stop devastating the resources of the planet, to stop consuming the resources of the planet, and to stop thereby consuming the planet

Most governments and countries have begun to create a "green economy plan" and are exploring what they can do within the margins of constantly declining and depleting natural assets, as the economy comes under more pressure.

"Green Economics" aims to recommend ways of moving forward to manage a much lower rate of consumption and ways to increase natural, social and environmental assets (sometimes called natural, social and environmental capital). (At the same time, it argues for the empowerment and education of women as the best way to decrease the gross number of people).

Finance and Green Economics

The understanding of these challenges requires an alternative methodological approach. Indeed, a Green Economics approach to finance looks beyond the dynamics of the financial markets in order to take into account a "long-term, earth-wide and holistic context" where equity and inclusiveness could be understood within a multidisciplinary range of knowledge (Kennet and Heinemann, 2006).

The collapse of the Glass Steagall Act was the legal vector by which many of these changes were enabled, the little old lady's life time investment was protected from the ravages of disembodied speculative "casino style" investment by large institutions and corporations, as regulations ensured that the two processes were entirely separate in different institutions. Morally the state was perceived to be the champion of that little old lady's savings. The casino banking was regarded as risky and therefore was kept entirely separate. It was known that the lady's savings would be possibly invested carefully in the casino banking but that her broker would protect and advise her should she ever want to speculate, but equally she could choose never to touch the casino.

Today, after the repeal of the Glass Steagal Act, the banks are all speculating and the entity in which she puts her life's savings is the exact same entity which risks its entire portfolio and which often has no gearing at all, no underlying assets and is heavily in debt itself. Unfortunately this applies today, also not just to banks, but to many Western Sovereign Economies as well putting the entire system at serious risk.

Most of the Western Sovereign economies are technically bankrupt with the worst debt of the lot being the Japanese state and the UK, Portugal, Spain and Ireland not far behind. During this period, of the West's Great Contraction, whilst sovereign debt was growing to catastrophic proportions, a parallel process has been taking place in which countries with large sovereign wealth funds, almost entirely in many cases built on oil exploitation, have learnt how to invest those funds for the benefit generally of their national treasuries. Generally, however, such countries do not have a democratic sharing of assets (with the exception of Norway & Singapore). Hence, we have the global economy being driven by huge sovereign wealth investments and cash rich decision making and power with no democratic accountability.

In China, the State is the owner of many "private" firms and uses its immense wealth to invest around the world and buy up assets from cash strapped countries. This is rapidly changing the global financial landscape as its main aim is to invest its large amounts of capital, as its GDP expands rapidly. This means that its finance is no longer related to the assets it buys and so leads to more disembodied investment, which will ultimately deplete those assets.

Also much of the USA economy currently owes to Chinese investment so the balance of political power has shifted. The USA has to heed what its paymaster's wishes and cannot in some circumstances afford to contradict China. This was firstly illustrated in the well-known case of Rio Tinto's workers being imprisoned in China after a price negotiation didn't go China's way, and she chose to simply lock them up. The USA attempted to get these foreign nationals out of the Chinese prison but for, the first time, China showed its muscle and the USA had no leverage and had to give up.

The second time China flexed its muscles, was at the COP 15 Kyoto Climate Summit in Copenhagen (2008) where China overtly for the first time stopped any result happening and claimed to be able to implement a green economy without any treaty. The reason turned out to be that China owns most of the world's rare earth metals and so it realised it could afford to hang on to them and to profit from their exploitation themselves. China began to understand that having huge amounts of the world's cash in its reserves means it could start to do what it liked!

If *finance* is about repaying debt, and the closure of a financial obligation, the word meaning to *finish,* then, today's financial arrangements could almost be seen as the opposite, the opening, the beginning of "feudal serfdom" and the inability to pay off debts. If we think for example of student loans in the UK, a young person goes to University and begins to take out loans of the size of a mortgage. In the past a mortgage was only allowed if a person had a job large enough for them to have reasonable chance of paying it off in time to realise the asset and to be able gain from it- for example owning a house for say 40 years of their life time.

Today a student loan is given so the young person can pay for the full cost of their education, even though there is no possibility that they would earn a single penny for many years and they have no guarantee of any job at all at the end of the period. Thus, citizens grow up with huge debts hanging over them, for their entire adult life and no chance of paying these debts off. This is a contemporary form of "slavery" and since sometimes the parents pay it off- it can be seen to have all the hallmarks of "intergenerational slavery and serfdom" that characterised feudal times in the middle ages or the period of slave and bondage trading of the early modern period. There is a danger that these debts will be passed down to successive generations too.

Indeed it is often contended that the depletion of environmental and biodiversity resources in the 20th century has left a world with fewer concrete environmental assets or benevolent conditions for us as a species or for future generations to meet their needs.

A Finance fit for the 21st and 22nd Centuries: Reconceptualising Finance A Renaissance in Finance.

In order to do well in the 21st and 22nd centuries, the West and developed economies, equally with developing economies, need to consider themselves economically free and unfettered from fear and bondage, with full rights to self-determination and workers. Furthermore, citizens need to be financially secure and to able to plan an economic life time without fear of debt or slavery and with an increasing, not a depleting set of natural, economic and social assets. This would allow populations to flourish and to innovate at a time of increasing global environmental instability, in the face of which we need people to be fully able to perform and to be able to use the full range of human ingenuity to find solutions.

It's not good enough that those how already have plenty of wealth can get their hands on even more whilst the rest of the population go hungry or in fear. The whole population must share – "green economics is about the economics of sharing, caring and supporting each other" (Kennet, 2012). No one and no organisation, no large corporate can claim to be "green" if they simply remove a bit of carbon from their lorries but squander, deplete and remove natural assets and resources or services from ordinary citizens, this is not "green" but it's robbery and it's cynical "misleading window dressing" and it needs to be exposed as such. "Green" means social and environmental justice as well as caring, sharing and supporting each other" and these concepts are indivisible. One part does not exist without the other. If one part of this equation is missing, then it can't be designated as "green". The single most important factor in this respect is the education and empowerment of women (MDG Millenium Development Goals) which will lead to a reduction in the human population. This will, in turn, lead to a reduction in all human impacts on the earth leading to more environmental and social justice as we stated in the *New Scientist* (Kennet, 2009).

The term "*Finance*" comes from the word to finish or repay, it is vital we enable most of the world to have access to finance, when it needs it and for citizens to be able to afford to meet their basic needs and to assert their common ownership of natural, social and human resources. The word "*company* " does not come from profit, greed or shares but rather from "*breaking bread with someone else,*" it denotes a human and social scale of activity. A very far cry from where we are today. The word *"economy"* comes not from the city or men trading in shares, but rather it means from the management of the *"household"* from the Greek *"oikia"* meaning simply *" house."* Our global home today is the earth. *Let us reclaim these terms and make them work for us as citizens again.*

This Chapter is designed to reclaim finance and to have a renaissance in our financial life in the 21st and 22nd centuries, where all people can flourish and do well and where we can share in the restocking of our planet with natural assets instead of depleting them. A world where we are continuing to cause planetary and environmental chaos and instability in its systems.

As current global finance has subordinated social reproduction, the main question is, as Minsky (1986) warned, *Who will Benefit?*. The global crisis that erupted in 2008 showed that current global finance, as an historical set of institutions, products, procedures, behaviours and policies have made potentially more likely, the risk of collapse of the financial system. This situation has deep negative consequences for the real economy and society.

In order to support sustainable development, it is time to rethink global finance, as well as creating an effective policy agenda for global and corporate governance, prudential regulation and supervision of systemic risk which are so very urgently needed. This Chapter brings these ideas to a wider readership and starts off moves in that direction. We urge all our readers to get involved and to press for a changes in our economic and financial life to achieve some of these ideas.

References

- Arestis, P. (2009), *Fiscal Policy within the New Consensus Macroeconomics Framework*, Cambridge Centre for Economic and Public Policy, CCEPP WP06-09, University of Cambridge.

- Bagehot, W. (1873), *Lombard Street: A Description of the Money Market*, reprinted by Project Gutenberg. Available at http://www.gutenberg.org/catalog/world/readfile?fk_files=2332161 [28/06/2013].

- Chesnais, F. (1996), *La mondialisation financière: genèse, coût et enjeux*, Paris: Syros.

- Fligstein, N. (2001), *The architecture of markets,* New Jersey: Princeton

University Press.

• Kennet, M. and Heinemann, V. (2006), "Green Economics: setting the scene", _Int. J. of Green Economics, vol. 1, 1/2, pp. 68 – 102._

• Kennet, M. (2009) The New Scientist. " The folly of Growth"

• Hedvig Berg, T., Seeberg, A., and Kennet, M., (2012) Green Economics Methodology. An Introduction. The Green Economics Institute.

• Keynes, J.M. (1936), _The General Theory of Employment, Interest and Money_, London: Macmillan.
• Minsky, H.P. (1975), _Can "It" Happen Again?_, Armonk: M.E. Sharpe.

• Minsky, H.P. (1986), _Stabilizing an Unstable Economy_, New Haven: Yale University Press.

• Minsky, H.P. (1991), "Financial crises: systemic or idiosyncratic", _Levy Economics Institute of Bard College Working Chapter_, No. 51.

Photo: Miriam Kennet in Bangalore, India, 1981

Photo: Oxford University 2013 with Indira Dutta

Photo: Dr Natalie West Kharkongor

**Photo Odeta Grabauskaitè: Indira Dutta lecturing about Ghandi at Oxford
University**